HOTSPOTS

REVISITED

SERIES PRODUCER
CEMEX BOOKS ON NATURE
PATRICIO ROBLES GIL

RUSSELL A. MITTERMEIER
PATRICIO ROBLES GIL
MICHAEL HOFFMANN
JOHN PILGRIM
THOMAS BROOKS
CRISTINA GOETTSCH MITTERMEIER
JOHN LAMOREUX
GUSTAVO A.B. DA FONSECA

PREFACE
PETER A. SELIGMANN

FOREWORD
HARRISON FORD

CEMEX
2004

In recent years, thanks to the efforts made by CEMEX and other organizations that share with us the commitment to promote biodiversity protection, it has been possible to define new, innovative environmental strategies and policies for curbing the deterioration of *hotspots*, Earth's most endangered terrestrial ecoregions.

The *hotspots* concept was developed in 1988 by British ecologist Norman Myers; since then, it has been supported by organizations such as Conservation International. The dissemination and impact of this concept were widened in 1999, with the presentation of our book *Hotspots. Earth's Biologically Richest and Most Endangered Terrestrial Ecoregions*, the second volume in a series of works published jointly with Conservation International and Agrupación Sierra Madre.

The scientific information gathered to date has made it possible to identify new areas of great ecological importance to be included within the hotspots classification, as well as to obtain relevant data on zones that had originally formed part of this category. Thus, we have been able to make progress in what definitely should be considered a global priority: the conservation of biotic resources. In the diversity of lifeforms we find the very possibility of maintaining the wide range of alternatives for achieving sustainable development.

Convinced that the goal of ensuring a living planet requires a foresighted strategy along with collective, coordinated efforts, at CEMEX we are very proud to work once again with Conservation International and Agrupación Sierra Madre, presenting this new book, *Hotspots Revisited*.

On the pages of this volume, you will find clearly stated the ways and spaces in which we should focus our attention and resources in order to achieve the survival of the greatest possible number of species and ecosystems. Included among the new terrestrial ecoregions considered as hotspots is the Sierra Madre Oriental and Occidental of Mexico. Located there is El Carmen, a project of wide scope that CEMEX has promoted for five years now for the purpose of having a direct bearing on its conservation.

We hope that the enhancement of the *hotspots* concept and the strategies proposed in this new book will contribute towards thinking on a world scale and acting on a local one so as to successfully meet the challenge posed by biodiversity conservation.

As a worldwide enterprise fully committed to promoting sustainable development, at CEMEX we are confident that the resources devoted today to this goal will entail the best possible investment for ensuring the permanence of biodiversity on our planet.

CEMEX

The Garden of Eden was green, lush, and rich in wildlife, and a sanctuary where humankind and nature lived in harmony. Sadly, this image is no longer a reality for those unique places which harbor the majority of life on Earth. We share our world with at least five million species of animals and plants, and perhaps as many as 30 million. This biodiversity is our most precious resource —our living heritage. All cultures revere this diversity in one way or another, through music, art, literature or tourism. All religions charge humanity with caring for life on Earth. Biodiversity is what distinguishes our planet from the rest of the universe; indeed, it defines us. Biodiversity is unique and irreplaceable.

Around the world, however, greed and poverty conspire to extinguish this variety of life. Overconsumption is the most grievous of these insults. Our world's forests and other natural habitats are being decimated to feed the lust of the so-called "developed" world for timber, minerals, exotic pets, luxury foods. Meanwhile, unjust distribution of wealth forces billions of people in the "developing" world to depend on exploiting the remaining scraps of nature. They hunt the last wildlife and clear the last habitats for marginal agriculture. As the world becomes more tightly interconnected, the threat of invasive species becomes ever more potent. Such exotics are the death knell for those species that have evolved without such predators or competitors. Cataclysmic global warming looms on the horizon.

Neither the places where species live nor the threats that we impose on them are uniform around the planet. Those places holding the greatest concentrations of biodiversity also face some of the most intense pressures. More than half of the world's plant species and more than a third of Earth's mammals, birds, reptiles, and amphibians are found in just 2.3% of its land surface. Most of these areas are tropical, like the Atlantic Forest, the Caribbean, Madagascar, Sundaland, the Philippines, and the Tropical Andes. They are called the *biodiversity hotspots*. No matter how successful conservation activities are elsewhere on the planet, unless threats are reduced in these soon, we will lose at least half of Earth's diversity of life.

These biodiversity hotspots hold some of the highest human population densities on the planet and some of its poorest people. Their poverty is a direct result of the destruction of forests, erosion of soils, pollution of rivers, and overharvesting of wildlife. Some environmental destruction is fatal. For example, deforestation often causes disastrous flooding, but also the emergence of infectious diseases. Most of the world's bloodiest wars are unleashed in the hotspots, too, often driven by resource conflicts. Somalia, Afghanistan, Palestine, northern Iraq, Timor, Haiti: all lie in hotspots harboring exceptional numbers of plant species found nowhere else.

Thoughtless exploitation of the Earth's plenty has destroyed the Garden of Eden. Human actions have exterminated the harmony of nature and depleted the gifts of clean water, productive soils, clean air, and the abundance of life-forms required for people to lead healthy lives.

The challenge which Conservation International has accepted is to work in these hotspots to prevent irreversible loss of biodiversity and to eradicate absolute poverty. Fortunately, many of the solutions to these two problems coincide. The highest priority is maintenance of the remaining natural vegetation cover in the hotspots. This provides habitat for biodiversity and ecosystem services like clean water for people. In the longer term, it will be necessary to restore the natural habitats across much of the hotspots. Meanwhile, reduction to sustainable levels of the harvesting of natural food, fiber, and fuel will be essential if these resources are to persist.

Of course, these solutions will not come for free. Protection, restoration, and sustainable use of the natural ecosystems of the hotspots will impose short-term costs on those least able to afford them. They will only be possible, therefore, with a dramatic increase of resources flowing from the "developed" countries to the hotspots of the "developing" world. But these resources are far from unaffordable for the former. Over the next 10 years, an investment of $100 billion is needed in these priority hotspots. By comparison, the war in Iraq 2003-2004 has so far cost the United States $168 billion in military spending alone.

Among the most important ways to meet this challenge is through partnerships at many different levels, including the private sector. In this regard, we are particularly pleased with our long-term relationship with CEMEX. Their efforts to reduce their industry's environmental footprint and their support for biodiversity conservation in Mexico have demonstrated their commitment and leadership, and their support for this outstanding series of books, now in its twelfth year, has had a major impact around the world.

The hotspots concept was first developed in 1988 by the ecologist Norman Myers. Now, 16 years later, and after several revisions and updated analyses, it has emerged as the dominant paradigm for global conservation strategy. As we enter this new millennium, the time has come for the world to recognize that the geography and solutions of global poverty align closely with those of the biodiversity hotspots. Only by tackling these two agendas together will we truly be able to end poverty and conserve life on Earth.

PETER A. SELIGMANN
Chairman of the Board and CEO
Conservation International

"I'm not a biologist, nor an expert on global strategies to safeguard threatened species and vanishing habitats. But I am deeply concerned about the future of our planet," Harrison Ford tells us in the Foreword of this book.

This concern is shared by many of us who fight for the permanence of life on Earth and are united in a search for solutions. Yet usually we comprise a concert of voices that does not manage to be heard due to the tremendous complexity of the world in which we live. Thus, we need a single voice, such as that of Harrison Ford, so that we may be heard.

Among the different priorities set on an international level, the conservation movement is like the "new kid in the neighborhood," whose popularity is growing, but who is far from gaining the attention he needs. This movement has to compete for resources allocated to needs deemed to be the most pressing for humankind: food, health, education, religion.

Nevertheless, nature has always been closely linked to traditional human preoccupations. Nature, or rediscovering it, now defines many religions in the world, and has constituted a major theme for our artistic and cultural expressions. Lastly, no one can question the fact that meeting our basic needs in terms of health and food depends on whether or not our natural environment remains sound.

This book provides us with a clear strategy for conserving biodiversity, and indicates a line of action to be followed, but society as a whole is who utilizes natural resources and who can promote and achieve a change in the way these are consumed. And society is also the one to determine the need for maintaining the diversity of life on this planet and the extraordinary variety of opportunities it affords. If we want biodiversity conservation to be adopted as one of the most important social priorities, we must organize and carry out an intense campaign to "sell it" as an attractive, extremely essential product.

The *hotspots* concept was presented in another title of the collection we have been producing for CEMEX. In the proposal we are making today, that concept has been strengthened thanks to an updating of information on the former *hotspots* and data on new areas that have been defined as such, which altogether more than justify the publication of this volume. However, there is another reason which, in my opinion, is also very important: the rules of the market.

As a conservation movement, we have forgotten that we live in a consumers' society and that any product we wish to introduce onto the market should be handled according to certain rules. Moreover, we must continually redesign the product we are selling —in this case, the new priority ecoregions of the world— to keep our public interested and thus gain greater penetration and have a better market position.

For this reason, one of the problems we confronted in producing this book has turned into an obstacle keeping us from really being effective in communicational terms. The scientific bases defining this conservation strategy are novel, compelling, and foresighted, but that is not enough to make them reach decision-makers. Every decision calls for the support of a majority of society, sometimes running against the economic interests of minority groups that could be affected.

The need to transform the natural world into a product that society demands leads us to another matter. *Biodiversity includes all plant and animal species*, not necessarily only those that are known or even charismatic. Nature as people are familiar with it, that which seems most appealing to us, is but a minimal fraction of biological diversity. Countless books and magazines have filled our eyes with images of beautiful flagship species —some of which have even become icons for conservation campaigns—, while the great majority of species, among them endemic ones, are virtually unknown.

When producing this book, we found ourselves faced with the huge problem of a lack of images for many species and regions that have not been photographed by professionals because they are not appealing enough for most publications. In that sense, we are inspired by the work of Cristina Mittermeier, one of the compilers of this book, in getting together a group of photographers that will open up new perspectives for communicating the most pressing priorities for nature conservation.

For their part, scientific institutions should incorporate the concept of marketing in their structure; in fact, communication departments of conservation organizations will have to become true "advertising agencies." That is the only way our product, the natural world, will benefit from an attractive, novel form of promotion that may successfully compete in the aggressive world of sales.

They say that money makes the world go round. Today we have the opportunity to define our future and, by taking strategic advantage of marketing and advertising, we may decide what course we wish our planet to take in the future.

PATRICIO ROBLES GIL
President
Agrupación Sierra Madre and
Unidos para la Conservación

FOREWORD

Five years ago, I was asked by my colleagues at Conservation International to write the Foreword for *Hotspots*, an ambitious assessment of our planet's at-risk biodiversity. Although I have had the honor and privilege to serve on CI's board of directors for the past 12 years, I was reluctant to accept the assignment. I'm not a biologist, nor an expert on global strategies to safeguard threatened species and vanishing habitats. But I am deeply concerned about the future of our planet.

It is clear that any effort to address these complicated issues would demand the most complete and scrupulous scientific understanding. As part of the initial analysis, all of the world's major terrestrial environments had been inventoried, with 25 emerging as having exceptional endemism, being severely threatened, and in need of immediate conservation attention. Some of these regions were regarded as obvious priorities right from the start. Others came as surprises as the data was analyzed.

The original *Hotspots* had a remarkable effect. *BBC Wildlife Magazine*, in celebration of its 40th anniversary, declared *Hotspots* one of the Top 40 Wildlife Classics published during the last four decades. Shortly after publication of *Hotspots*, the World Bank, the Global Environmental Facility (GEF), the MacArthur Foundation, and the Government of Japan joined with Conservation International to create the Critical Ecosystem Partnership Fund (CEPF), and to date have committed $125 million specifically for conserving the world's hotspots. Meanwhile, a growing number of institutions continue to incorporate the results into their programs. Perhaps just as importantly, the hotspots analysis has spawned serious debates about where today's precious conservation dollars should be spent to achieve the greatest future impact. The study focused squarely on one issue —preserving biodiversity— and then systematically measured, assessed, and assigned priorities. One could argue that it would be better to focus on global issues of birth control, poverty, disease, unsustainable energy use or atmospheric pollution. Undoubtedly, these are clearly critical in the long term to the quality of life on Earth. But in the race to prevent the extinction of the greatest portion of Earth's living heritage, nothing advances our understanding and guides our strategies as well as the hotspots model.

That's why this updated analysis is so important and why it has quickly become another essential element in the conservationist's tool chest. The experts have added several new regions to an already substantial list of global priorities. These new hotspots range from the Pine-Oak Forests of Mexico and the southwestern U.S. to the Horn of Africa, from the Himalaya to Japan. Some of these regions, like those of the Solomons and Vanuatu that form the new East Melanesian Islands Hotspot, didn't make the original hotspot list because their habitats were still largely intact. They weren't considered threatened at the time. Yet in the blink of an eye, their condition has essentially slipped from more or less stable to critical.

The most significant challenge of our time is to preserve and protect our biotic legacy. CI's mission to defend biodiversity places its staff in some 40 countries around the world, in partnership with an amazing diversity of institutions and individuals from various backgrounds and cultures. The strategies they have applied are informed by sound, independent science. They have developed broad experience in determining how best to respond to crisis situations, while at the same time planning for the future in incremental steps.

I wish you good reading and hope that this book helps broaden your perspective and understanding of the challenge of conserving the natural world.

HARRISON FORD

EARTH'S BIOLOGICALLY RICHEST AND MOST

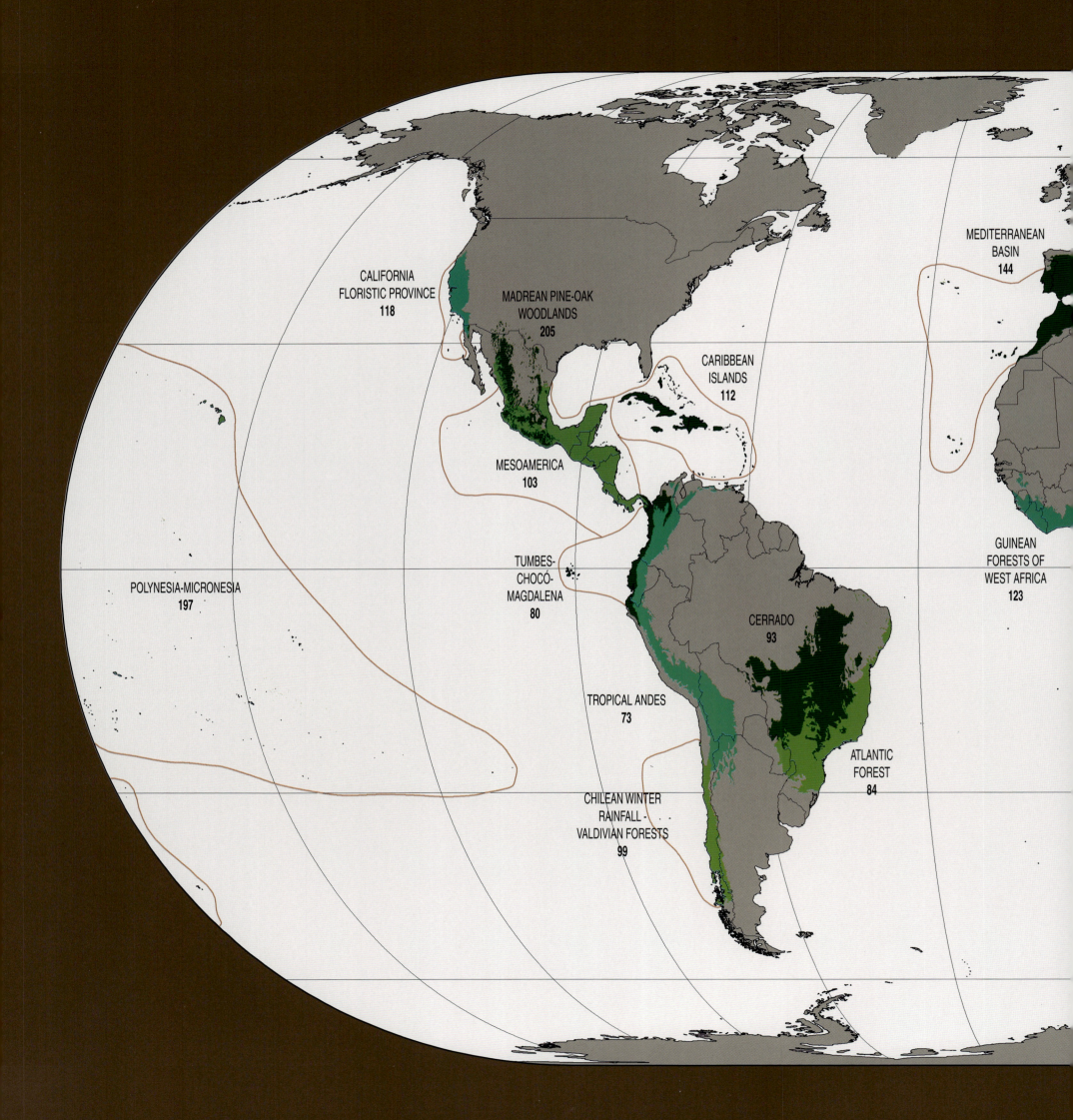

CALIFORNIA
FLORISTIC PROVINCE
118

MADREAN PINE-OAK
WOODLANDS
205

MEDITERRANEAN
BASIN
144

CARIBBEAN
ISLANDS
112

MESOAMERICA
103

TUMBES-
CHOCÓ-
MAGDALENA
80

POLYNESIA-MICRONESIA
197

GUINEAN
FORESTS OF
WEST AFRICA
123

CERRADO
93

TROPICAL ANDES
73

ATLANTIC
FOREST
84

CHILEAN WINTER
RAINFALL -
VALDIVIAN FORESTS
99

ENDANGERED TERRESTRIAL ECOREGIONS

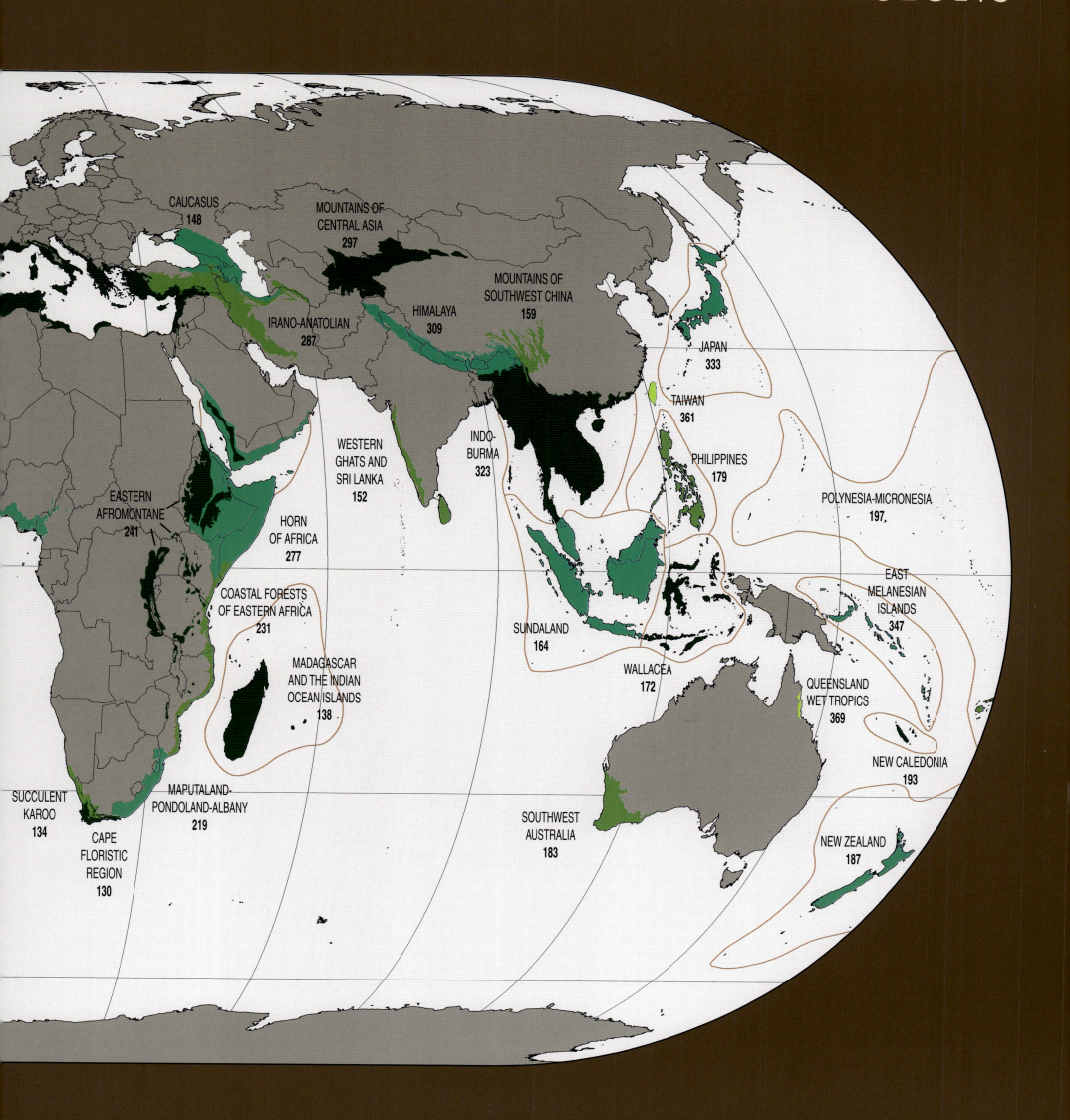

INTRODUCTION

Global Priority Setting for Biodiversity Conservation

Life on Earth faces a crisis of historical and planetary proportions. Unsustainable consumption in many northern countries and crushing poverty in the tropics are destroying wild nature. Expanding agriculture, industry, and urbanization are fragmenting and eliminating natural environments; accidental and deliberate introduction of exotic species is wreaking havoc on native communities; pollution is altering complex biogeochemical and climate cycles through the land, air, and water; and hunting, trade, and overfishing are decimating the last populations of large vertebrate species (Vitousek et al. 1997). Biodiversity is besieged.

Extinction is the gravest aspect of the biodiversity crisis: it is irreversible. While extinction is a natural process that is part of the history of this planet, the fossil record indicates that, in the absence of humans, the life span of a species averages one million years (May et al. 1995). Now, however, human impacts have elevated the rate of species extinction by at least a thousand, possibly several thousand times the natural background rate (Pimm et al. 1995). Mass extinctions of this magnitude have only occurred five times before in the history of our planet; the last, probably caused by a cataclysmic asteroid impact 65 million years ago, brought the end of the dinosaur age (Álvarez et al. 1980).

It is easy to imagine the disasters that humanity would face if the rate of other natural processes, such as the frequency of floods or disease transmission rates, increased a thousand-fold. The world as we know it would be devastated. But what exactly do we lose with the catastrophic extinction of other species? Foreclosing future resource-use options is perhaps the most obvious consequence. Scientists have recognized only a fraction (maybe less than 10%; perhaps even as little as 1%) of the species with which we share our planet, and know the biology of even fewer (Novotny et al. 2002). Thus, with species extinction we destroy a vast genetic storehouse (Myers 1983) that could one day be found to hold, for instance, a cure for AIDS. Current developments in the treatment of malaria, one of the world's biggest killers, use artemisinin-based compounds derived from the plant *Artemisia annua* (Sachs 2002). The biodiversity crisis could be compared with burning down the world's libraries without knowing the titles of 90% of the books or the content of most of the pages of the known books. Less tangibly, but no less importantly, species extinction inflicts a deep cultural, spiritual, and moral wound on humanity. All of the world's societies value species for their own sake, over and above any utilitarian purpose, and wildlife —especially the larger vertebrates and many plants— are an integral part of the fabric of all human cultures (Wilson 1984; Wilson and Kellert 1993).

The road to extinction is also perilous to people. For example, the destruction of montane forests causes frequent, massive landslides with dreadful human cost —witness the tragic mudslides that killed 10 000 people following Hurricane Mitch in Honduras in 1998 (Hellin et al. 1999)— while the Severe Acute Respiratory Syndrome (SARS) outbreak in East Asia has been directly linked to the trade in wildlife for human consumption (Guan et al. 2003). Other consequences of biodiversity loss are more subtle and cumulative, but equally significant, such as the progressive deterioration of the natural basis for sustainable economic growth. A number of high-profile studies (e.g., Costanza et al. 1997) have placed the annual economic value of ecosystem services such as climate and water regulation, pollination, and recreation in the tens of trillions of dollars —costs that society would have to bear if these generally free but unaccounted services were no longer accessible. A significant fraction of such services can be attributed directly to biodiversity. Balmford et al. (2002) concluded that conversion of natural ecosystems to anthropogenic landscapes roughly halves their economic value.

In order to stem the extinction crisis most effectively, we must prioritize where we should act first. To a large extent conservation is, and always will be, local. People care most about what is happening in their own backyards. We believe that all biodiversity is important and that all nations and communities, large or small, should do everything possible to conserve the biological riches on which they depend. However, some local efforts have planetary consequences and thus justify priority allocation of scarce financial resources.

The establishment of priorities for biodiversity conservation is a complex issue (Margules and Pressey 2000). The problem can best be framed by a question: In which areas would a given conservation dollar contribute the most towards slowing the current rate of extinction of global biodiversity? Species are distributed unevenly around the world (Gaston 2000), which means that mapping this variation is essential if we are to address the question. However, we can not simply measure the numbers of species living in particular areas. This is because several species-rich areas might hold a large fraction of the same species, meaning that the overall number that could be conserved within such areas might be rather small (Pressey and Nicholls 1989). Instead, we must measure not species richness but endemism: the degree to which species are only found in a given place. This can be thought of as a measure of irreplaceability —in essence, the number of geographic options one has for the conservation of the

On p. 1, in the State of Coahuila, Mexico, there is a conservation model that has been carried out by ranchers in the Serranías del Burro for forty years. It has facilitated the recovery of biodiversity in these lands.
© **Patricio Robles Gil**/*Sierra Madre*

On p. 2, Eungella National Park is one of Queensland's most ecologically diverse parks with 860 plant species, including the Alexandra palm (Archontophoenix alexandrae). This mountain refuge lies close to the boundary between subtropical and tropical rainforests.
© **Günter Ziesler**

On pp. 4-5, the Sumatran orangutan (Pongo abelii), here seen in Gunung Leuser National Park, is now considered a full species, distinct from the Bornean orang-utan. It is one of the most threatened great apes.
© **Anup Shah**/naturepl.com

On p. 6, laurisilva forest in the Frontera Rural Park (El Hierro Island, Canary Islands), comprised mainly of flowering laurel (Laurus azorica), Indian bay (Persea indica), Canarian laurel (Ilex canariensis), tilo tree (Ocotea foetens), faya or firetree (Myrica faya), and delfino (Myrsine canariensis).
© **Francisco Márquez**

On pp. 8-9, the Maderas del Carmen Protected Area for Flora and Fauna in the El Carmen Mountains in the State of Coahuila (Mexico), part of CEMEX's comprehensive program in this region.
© **Patricio Robles Gil**/*Sierra Madre*

On the opposite page, the spectacular and Endangered golden lion tamarin (Leontopithecus rosalia) is found only in forest fragments in the lowlands of the State of Rio de Janeiro, and is perhaps Brazil's best-known monkey species. Along with Brachyteles, it represents one of the two primate genera endemic to the hotspot.
© **Frans Lanting**/*Minden Pictures*

19

species found in a given area (Pressey et al. 1994). Since we can not conserve a species that is endemic to a given area anywhere except in that area, the area is wholly irreplaceable at a global scale.

A further problem concerns which species we should evaluate. We know that we can not map all species because we have not even named most of them. Quite fortuitously, vascular plants and vertebrate animals —the species we know best— tend to be large, and play prominent roles in structuring ecosystems (Terborgh 1988), although species that we know less about are also vital for ecosystem processes (Wilson 1987). Whether or not the distributions of plants and vertebrates are mirrored by the myriad of unknown terrestrial invertebrate species remains an open question, although some evidence suggests that they may be (Howard et al. 1998). Some taxa, such as tiger beetles, seem to exhibit excellent congruence with many other groups (Pearson and Cassola 1992; Carroll and Pearson 1998), while others show less clear patterns (Van Jaarsveld et al. 1998). These comparisons are also heavily dependent on scale (Reid 1998). At regional scales we often see much greater congruence than at fine scales (Pearson and Carroll 1999). Thanks to recent advances in bioinformatics, we will soon be able to use massive datasets on invertebrate species distributions to delimit the boundaries of biologically unique areas more precisely than ever (Meier and Dikow 2004). One of the largest gaps in our current knowledge remains in the aquatic realm, which is in critical need of effective conservation action. Distributions of marine and freshwater species remain largely unknown, although ongoing projects are addressing this issue.

Our ultimate goal is to keep nature intact, which means that we must stop anthropogenic species extinctions. To approach this goal, we must slow the *rate* of species extinction as much as possible (over and above simply conserving as many species as we can) with whatever conservation resources we have at our disposal, which requires incorporating threats (or *vulnerability*) and costs into priority setting. Like species, threats are hard to measure. The extent of habitat destruction is one useful metric, given the well-documented relationship between the size of an area of habitat and the number of species it retains (Brooks et al. 1997). Other measures, such as human population density (Balmford et al. 2001), are also used.

Threats and costs are generally related to each other; the more threatened an area is, the more it will cost to conserve (Ando et al. 1997). However, the relationship is not always linear, as it depends in large part on the economic conditions of the country and immediate locale in which the priority area is located (Balmford et al. 2003). Some extremely threatened areas can still be conserved at low cost (e.g., much of Madagascar and some areas in Southeast Asia), often by addressing underlying poverty simultaneously with biodiversity conservation, while others tend to be quite expensive (e.g., the California Floristic Province and New Caledonia).

However, because economic opportunity costs vary dramatically across the landscapes of hotspots and wilderness areas, there still exist areas of relatively low cost in all hotspots, offering great conservation opportunities, as well as areas of high cost in wilderness areas requiring immediate attention to threats (Chomitz et al. 2004).

We still face a paradox in determining how to incorporate threats, costs, and opportunities into conservation priorities. Intuitively, we want to conserve the most threatened areas first, to avoid losing them the soonest. But we also want to get the greatest return for our conservation dollar, which in theory would mean targeting the areas of lowest cost, greatest opportunity, and least threat first. This paradox can be resolved by the measurement of irreplaceability —or the degree of endemism (Mittermeier et al. 2003a). Thus, we identify those areas that hold species found nowhere else and that are guaranteed to lose species if the areas are not conserved. Among these, we rank our actions based on threats, with the most threatened biodiversity receiving the most urgent action. Wherever we have choices, or equal levels of endemism, we should select opportunities for attending to areas that are the least expensive to conserve (and often the least threatened). In effect, we need a dual conservation strategy that always prioritizes endemic-rich areas and ensures that we protect the most threatened places with species that we will otherwise lose, while preemptively protecting equally unique places that are not yet under extreme threat.

History of the Hotspots Concept

A seminal paper by Norman Myers (1988) first articulated the principles of irreplaceability and threat to inform terrestrial conservation priorities on a global scale. Myers identified ten tropical forest "hotspots" characterized both by exceptional levels of plant endemism and by uncommon rates of habitat loss, although without quantitative criteria as to what exactly constituted a hotspot. Subsequently, Myers (1990) added a further eight hotspots, including four Mediterranean-type ecosystems. Conservation International adopted Myers' hotspots as its institutional blueprint in 1989, making minor modifications and additions over the next seven years. In 1996, Conservation International made the decision to undertake a reassessment of the hotspots concept, including an examination of whether key areas had been overlooked. This was done in collaboration with Myers and took three years. A preliminary report (Mittermeier et al. 1998) was followed by an extensive global review (Mittermeier et al. 1999), a scientific analysis (Myers et al. 2000), and a detailed online publication (www.biodiversityhotspots.org). These efforts introduced quantitative thresholds for the designation of hotspots. To qualify as a hotspot, a region had to meet two strict criteria: it had to contain at least

1 500 species of vascular plants (>0.5% of the world's total) as endemics, and it had to have 30% or less of its original vegetation (extent of historical habitat cover) remaining. This analysis identified 25 hotspots, collectively holding as endemics no less than 44% of the world's plants and 35% of terrestrial vertebrates (mammals, birds, reptiles and amphibians) in an area that formerly covered only 11.8% of the Earth's land surface. However, the fulcrum around which these startling results were presented was that this land area had been reduced by 87.8% of its original extent, such that this amazing wealth of biodiversity was restricted to only 1.4% of Earth's land surface.

Concurrent with the development of the hotspots strategy was the recognition of the advantages to investing in the least threatened —and cheapest— highly biodiverse areas. In fact, Myers (1988) was the first to notice that three endemic-rich regions of tropical forest remained largely intact —he called these "good news areas." Similarly, Mittermeier (1988) called attention to several high biodiversity tropical rainforest regions that were still in relatively intact condition. He later broadened the concept to address three regions —Amazonia, the Congo Forests of Central Africa, and the island of New Guinea— and referred to them as "major tropical wilderness areas" (McNeely et al. 1990; Mittermeier et al. 1998). While threatened to a much lesser extent than the hotspots, these areas are nevertheless under growing pressure from human activities.

Recently, the emphasis on biodiversity-rich wilderness has been reassessed against the background of all of Earth's wilderness areas, quantitatively defined as retaining at least 70% of their original habitat and holding human population densities of less than five people per square kilometer (Mittermeier et al. 2002, 2003b). This analysis found that while 44% of Earth's land area can still be considered wilderness, only five of these regions (covering just 6.1% of that area) are "high biodiversity wilderness areas" with more than 1 500 plant species as endemics. These are Amazonia, the Congo Forests of Central Africa, the island of New Guinea, the North American Deserts of the Southwestern United States and Northern Mexico, and the Miombo-Mopane Woodlands and Savannas of Southern Africa. Together, they hold 17% of the planet's plants and 8% of terrestrial vertebrates as endemics.

Based on these analyses, Conservation International uses a two-pronged strategy for global conservation prioritization, simultaneously focusing on the threatened and irreplaceable hotspots and on the high biodiversity wilderness areas, which are irreplaceable but still largely intact, and as such represent important conservation opportunities. The decision, at any given point in time, as to whether we should allocate particular resources to a hotspot or to a high biodiversity wilderness area depends on numerous factors, including donor interest, immediate political, economic or social opportunity or need, and other conservation benefits (e.g., protection of major ecosystem services). However, all of these areas —the hotspots and the high biodiversity wilderness areas combined— are on Conservation International's priority list, and the organization's programs employ a strategic mix of both.

A consistent concern for conservation practitioners is that data for aquatic species have yet to be synthesized at a global scale across many taxa and aquatic habitats. It was not until 2002 that the first comprehensive global assessment of conservation priorities for an aquatic system —coral reefs— was published (Roberts et al. 2002). This analysis identified 18 centers of endemism (across four assemblages —1 700 coral reef fish, all 804 scleractinian coral species, three mollusk families, and 69 lobster species) and highlighted ten of these regions as hotspots facing high threats. Remarkably, the study found that eight of the ten reef hotspots (and 14 of the 18 centers of endemism) lie adjacent to terrestrial hotspots, raising an intriguing possibility that terrestrial hotspots may actually reflect aquatic ones rather well. The publication of Roberts et al. (2002) has attracted much-needed attention to marine hotspots, although data on these areas remains sparse compared with information on terrestrial systems (Lambshead 1993). Our lack of knowledge about freshwater systems is even more pronounced —where even a first look at global conservation prioritization has yet to be carried out. These areas constitute one of the world's most endemic-rich and threatened biomes (McAllister et al. 1997), making such an analysis most urgent.

Impact of Hotspots

The impact of the hotspots concept has been astounding. One measure of this is scientific. Searching the Web of Science for all citations including the word "hotspot" in the title yields numerous scientific papers. While many of these concern geology, astronomy, or genetics (and a few, behavioral ecology or remote sensing), nearly 100 citations use the word "hotspot" to refer to biodiversity conservation priorities. Analyzing these citations over time reveals a clear pattern of gradual increase following Myers' (1988, 1990) original work, a rapid acceleration with the publication of Myers et al. (2000), and an increasing number of publications on marine hotspots following Roberts et al. (2002). In addition, the number of times that Myers et al. (2000) has been cited in the peer-reviewed scientific literature has shown a steady increase since its publication, and by January 2004 totaled 438 instances.

More importantly, the impact of the hotspots concept in terms of investment in conservation has been dramatic (Myers and Mittermeier 2003). As indicated above, Conservation International adopted hotspots as its central strategy in 1989. In the same year, the Chicago-based John D. and Catherine T. MacArthur Foundation adopted hotspots as its primary global investment strategy (Mittermeier et al. 1998). In 2000, the World Bank and the Global Environment Facility joined Conservation

International to establish the Critical Ecosystem Partnership Fund, a conservation finance mechanism focused explicitly on the hotspots (Dalton 2000; www.cepf.net); the MacArthur Foundation and the Japanese Government have since joined the partnership, bringing the total amount available to $125 million. Conservation International's $100-million Global Conservation Fund, supported by the Gordon and Betty Moore Foundation, also uses hotspots (along with high biodiversity wilderness areas) to guide its investments. More than $750 million has been devoted to saving hotspots over the last 15 years, perhaps the largest financial investment in any single conservation strategy (Myers 2003). The hotspots concept has also entered the mainstream as a tool for forward-thinking private sector businesses that have adopted biodiversity conservation policies for their operations and supply chain systems. For example, Office Depot explicitly gives preference to pulp and paper vendors that protect natural forests in the biodiversity hotspots and high biodiversity wilderness areas.

Biodiversity conservation efforts in hotspots often require the ability to withstand and adapt to a rapidly changing socio-political climate. While it can be tempting to write off high-risk areas, experience demonstrates both the importance and the potential for operating and maintaining a conservation presence in hotspots that are undergoing political difficulties. Madagascar, one of the most important hotspots, was almost abandoned by conservationists in the early to mid-1980s, and again during a brief period of political strife in 2001 and 2002. Fortunately, several organizations persevered, notably the World Wildlife Fund, USAID, and the World Bank and, beginning in the early 1990s, Conservation International and the Wildlife Conservation Society. This resolve paved the road for a positive environment for the new President, Marc Ravalomanana, to give conservation a high priority in his government's development plans. At the Fifth World Parks Congress in September 2003, President Ravalomanana committed to tripling the country's protected area network over the next five years, and just five months after this pledge he announced the establishment of 14 new areas increasing coverage by 65%. At the time of his announcement, President Ravalomanana also requested the involvement of the international community in creating a $50-million trust fund for conservation over the next five years; seven months later, a total of $24 million in commitments has already been made. Liberia, one of the most important countries in the heavily impacted Guinean Forests of West Africa Hotspot, has, until very recently, been written off by most of the international conservation community. Nonetheless, Fauna and Flora International and Conservation International operated there through some of the worst periods of instability and violence. Largely because of their efforts, the Liberian Senate in 2003 enacted legislation expanding the country's protected areas network, and the stage is now set to make forest policy re-

form and conservation a priority for Liberia's reconstruction. Such cases provide excellent illustrations of the conservation return on investment produced by the hotspots strategy.

An Updated Hotspots Analysis

The hotspots analysis is in constant evolution. There are two major ways in which hotspots can change over time. The first is a real effect. Threats and their impacts change, meaning that some places may become more threatened, while others, if conservation efforts are successful, may eventually recover. The second is that our knowledge of biodiversity, threats, and costs is continually improving; new species are discovered, new populations are found, and higher-resolution land cover data is collected. Over the last few years, in concert with the information revolution and the emergence of the Internet, this data has become better compiled (Sugden and Pennisi 2000). Now, several years after the publication of the reassessment of the hotspots strategy (Mittermeier et al. 1999; Myers et al. 2000), it is time to revisit the hotspots themselves in light of new data regarding species distributions and changing conditions of the planet's ecosystems.

We should emphasize from the outset that the current effort is not a reworking of the entire hotspots concept. Rather, the aims of this analysis are to revisit the status of the existing hotspots, refine their boundaries, update the information associated with them and, most importantly, consider a number of potential hotspots that may qualify as additions to the existing list of 25. Consequently, the criteria for what qualifies as a hotspot remain unchanged. There continues to be much debate in the literature concerning total vascular plant diversity, with lower estimates ranging from 270 000 to 320 000 (May 1992; Prance et al. 2000), and higher estimates ranging up to 422 000 (Govaerts 2001; Bramwell 2002). For now, we have retained the lower figure of 300 000 used by Myers et al. (2000), given that the higher figure remains controversial (Thorne 2002).

When Myers et al. (2000) published the results of their analysis, they noted that a number of areas harbored exceptional plant endemism and were also under unusual threat, but were insufficiently documented to meet the hotspots criteria: the Ethiopian Highlands, the Angola Escarpment, southeastern China, Taiwan, and the forests of the Albertine Rift. The Queensland Wet Tropics in northeastern Australia were also mentioned as having a remarkably high species-to-area ratio, but insufficient endemic plant species to qualify as a hotspot. Additional data on Taiwan and the Queensland Wet Tropics now confirm that neither reaches the threshold of being a hotspot. However, because both are globally important and come so close to meeting the criteria, we include special treatment of them in this book (pp. 361 and 369, respectively). Furthermore,

investigation of the definition of a hotspot for the rain-forests of eastern Australia continues, and it is likely that an expanded interpretation of this region will result in confirmation of its hotspot status in the future. New data also demonstrates the hotspot status of the Ethiopian Highlands and Albertine Rift (discussed below). Finally, the Angola Escarpment and southeastern China remain little known, and thus it is still not possible to ascertain whether or not the regions qualify as hotspots.

One major finding of this updated analysis is that six previously overlooked areas qualify for hotspot status. These are the Madrean Pine-Oak Woodlands of northern Mexico and the southwestern United States (p. 205), southern Africa's Maputaland-Pondoland-Albany region (p. 219), the Horn of Africa (p. 277), the Irano-Anatolian region (p. 287), the Mountains of Central Asia (p. 297), and Japan (p. 333). In addition, one existing hotspot is divided into two. Mittermeier et al. (1998) first suggested the Himalaya (p. 309) and Indo-Burma (p. 323) regions as separate hotspots. In Mittermeier et al. (1999) and Myers et al. (2000) these were combined, but data is now sufficient to show that they contain quite distinctive biotas. That a number of these changes are in Asia is explained partly by the fact that biodiversity data for the continent has historically been less thoroughly synthesized than has data for the Americas and Africa, and partly because much of the data that does exist for key countries such as China and Japan has, at least until recently, been inaccessible to conservation scientists outside of these regions.

An important modification to the hotspots strategy presented here is the reconfiguration of several African hotspots. One problem we have always grappled with is that the combination of the East African Coastal Forests (Burgess and Clarke 2000) with Tanzania's Eastern Arc Mountains (Lovett and Wasser 1993) as a single hotspot is somewhat incongruous biogeographically (Myers et al. 1999). Furthermore, recognition by Myers et al. (2000) of the potentially high levels of endemism in the Ethiopian Highlands and Albertine Rift meant these regions needed to be re-evaluated with better data. It is now apparent that none of the montane areas —the Ethiopian Highlands, Albertine Rift, or Eastern Arc Mountains— qualify as hotspots on their own, because they do not meet the cut-off of 1 500 endemic plants. However, the classic work on African biogeography by Frank White (1983) provides a simple solution. The biogeographic affinities of these regions suggest that they are best considered as a single unit, the Afromontane Region, despite their fragmented geography. Thus, we identify this region as the Eastern Afromontane Hotspot, encompassing the Eastern Arc Mountains and Southern Rift (p. 245), the Albertine Rift (p. 255), the Ethiopian Highlands (p. 262), and a few outliers. This leaves the Coastal Forests of Eastern Africa, running from southern Somalia south through Kenya, Tanzania, and Mozambique, as a unique hotspot in its own right (p. 231).

The final change revealed in our reassessment of the hotspots is truly terrifying. Less than a decade ago, the islands of eastern Melanesia —the Bismarcks, Solomons, and Vanuatu— while known to be extremely endemic-rich, still held largely intact habitat. Since then, rampant logging and establishment of oil palm plantations have devastated these islands, leaving only 30% of their forests remaining, a situation mirroring the fate of Indonesia's forests a decade ago (Holmes 2000). Thus, the primary cause of the identification of the East Melanesian Islands Hotspot (p. 347) is a worsening threat over a very short period of time.

In revisiting the boundaries of the hotspots, we have tried to achieve a balance between what is scientifically defensible, and what is pragmatically acceptable. The hotspots are based on plant endemism, and so, as far as possible, our decision regarding where or whether to include a particular area or island within a hotspot is determined by the floristic affinities of the region in question. As before, the landmark publication *Centers of Plant Diversity* (Davis et al. 1994-1997) has been instrumental in guiding and influencing some of our decisions in this regard. However, in some cases, we have seen fit to deviate from this ideal, in order to accommodate tropical islands —many of which have very high proportions of threatened species— that might otherwise slip through the net of conservation priorities. For this reason, we have grouped certain islands with their closest-lying hotspots including, for example, Galápagos and Malpelo with Tumbes-Chocó-Magdalena, Juan Fernández with the Chilean Winter Rainfall-Valdivian Forests, the Azores and Cape Verde Islands (both part of the Macaronesian Islands along with the Canaries and Madeira) with the Mediterranean Basin; and Lord Howe and Norfolk islands with New Zealand. This is done solely for purposes of pragmatic convenience, and with full recognition that the floristic affiliations of these islands with their associated landmasses are tenuous at best.

Synthesis of the Updated Hotspots Data

In total, this updated analysis reveals the existence of 34 biodiversity hotspots, each holding at least 1 500 endemic plant species, and having lost at least 70% of its original habitat extent. Overall, the 34 hotspots once covered a land area of 23 490 101 km^2, 15.7% of the Earth's land surface, an area equivalent in size to Russia and Australia combined. Their individual areas spanned two orders of magnitude. Three of the regions historically covered more than two million square kilometers each (Indo-Burma, the Mediterranean Basin, and the Cerrado), and a further six, more than a million. The smallest, New Caledonia, covered only 18 972 km^2, and three others were smaller than 100 000 km^2. The average original size was 690 885 km^2, and the median size 385 316 km^2. This extent of habitat has now been reduced to 3 379 246 km^2, a mere 2.3% of the planet's

TABLE 1. Original extent, remaining habitat, and percentage of remaining habitat for each hotspot (determined using an equal-area projection) and its predominant biome type (Olson et al. 2001)

Hotspot	Original extent (km²)	Remaining habitat (km²)	Percentage remaining habitat	Predominant biome type
Tropical Andes	1 542 644	385 661	25	Tropical and Subtropical Moist Broadleaf Forests; Montane Grasslands and Shrublands
Tumbes-Chocó-Magdalena	274 597	65 903	24	Tropical and Subtropical Moist Broadleaf Forests
Atlantic Forest	1 233 875	99 944	8	Tropical and Subtropical Moist Broadleaf Forests
Cerrado	2 031 990	432 814	22	Tropical and Subtropical Grasslands, Savannas, and Shrublands
Chilean Winter Rainfall-Valdivian Forests	397 142	119 143	30	Mediterranean Forests, Woodlands, and Shrubs; Temperate Broadleaf and Mixed Forests
Mesoamerica	1 130 019	226 004	20	Tropical and Subtropical Moist Broadleaf Forests
Madrean Pine-Oak Woodlands	461 265	92 253	20	Tropical and Subtropical Coniferous Forests
Caribbean Islands	229 549	22 955	10	Tropical and Subtropical Dry Broadleaf Forests
California Floristic Province	293 804	73 451	25	Mediterranean Forests, Woodlands, and Shrubs; Temperate Coniferous Forests
Guinean Forests of West Africa	620 314	93 047	15	Tropical and Subtropical Moist Broadleaf Forests
Cape Floristic Region	78 555	15 711	20	Mediterranean Forests, Woodlands, and Shrubs
Succulent Karoo	102 691	29 780	29	Deserts and Xeric Shrublands
Maputaland-Pondoland-Albany	274 136	67 163	25	Tropical and Subtropical Moist Broadleaf Forests; Montane Grasslands and Shrublands
Coastal Forests of Eastern Africa	291 250	29 125	10	Tropical and Subtropical Moist Broadleaf Forests
Eastern Afromontane	1 017 806	106 870	11	Tropical and Subtropical Moist Broadleaf Forests; Montane Grasslands and Shrublands
Horn of Africa	1 659 363	82 968	5	Tropical and Subtropical Grasslands, Savannas, and Shrublands
Madagascar and the Indian Ocean Islands	600 461	60 046	10	Tropical and Subtropical Moist Broadleaf Forests
Mediterranean Basin	2 085 292	98 009	5	Mediterranean Forests, Woodlands, and Shrubs
Caucasus	532 658	143 818	27	Temperate Broadleaf and Mixed Forests
Irano-Anatolian	899 773	134 966	15	Temperate Broadleaf and Mixed Forests
Mountains of Central Asia	863 362	172 672	20	Temperate Grasslands, Savannas, and Shrublands; Montane Grasslands and Shrublands
Western Ghats and Sri Lanka	189 611	43 611	23	Tropical and Subtropical Moist Broadleaf Forests
Himalaya	741 706	185 427	25	Tropical and Subtropical Coniferous Forests; Montane Grasslands and Shrublands
Mountains of Southwest China	262 446	20 996	8	Temperate Coniferous Forests
Indo-Burma	2 373 057	118 653	5	Tropical and Subtropical Moist Broadleaf Forests
Sundaland	1 501 063	100 571	7	Tropical and Subtropical Moist Broadleaf Forests
Wallacea	338 494	50 774	15	Tropical and Subtropical Moist Broadleaf Forests
Philippines	297 179	20 803	7	Tropical and Subtropical Moist Broadleaf Forests
Japan	373 490	74 698	20	Temperate Broadleaf and Mixed Forests
Southwest Australia	356 717	107 015	30	Mediterranean Forests, Woodlands, and Shrubs
East Melanesian Islands	99 384	29 815	30	Tropical and Subtropical Moist Broadleaf Forests
New Zealand	270 197	59 443	22	Temperate Broadleaf and Mixed Forests
New Caledonia	18 972	5 122	5	Tropical and Subtropical Moist Broadleaf Forests
Polynesia-Micronesia	47 239	10 015	21	Tropical and Subtropical Moist Broadleaf Forests
Total	**23 490 101**	**3 379 246**		

land surface. Its size is slightly more than the country of India or a fraction less than the five largest American states combined (Alaska, Texas, California, Montana, and New Mexico = 3 392 950 km²). In all, 86% of the hotspots' habitat has already been lost, and only 14% remains. Table 1 details these statistics hotspot-by-hotspot.

The distribution of the hotspots among biomes is greatly skewed towards tropical forests (Table 1). Of the 34 hotspots, 22 (65%) are predominantly tropical forest biomes, ranging from very wet hotspots (like the East Melanesian Islands) to sparsely wooded savanna and grassland (as in the Cerrado). Six hotspots (18%) primarily hold temperate forest, five (15%) Mediterranean-type ecosystems (two of which also have temperate forest elements), and one (3%) is desert.

Among them, the hotspots hold no less than 150 000 plant species as single-hotspot endemics (Table 3). That is 50% of the world's total. By far, the two hotspots with the most endemics are the Tropical Andes and Sundaland, with no less than 15 000 endemic plant species (Table 2). Two other hotspots —the Mediterranean Basin, and Madagascar and the Indian Ocean Islands— also exceed 10 000 endemic plant species; and five more exceed 5 000. The four hotspots richest in endemic plants are also the most speciose, with 20 000 or more plant species occurring in each. Plant numbers per hotspot are derived from specialist estimates rather than from species-by-species lists, which makes it impossible to calculate the total number of endemics or even the number of species occurring in hotspots (Table 3). This is because these estimates do not account for the plants that are shared between hotspots. In other words, if we were to attempt to produce such totals, we would underestimate overall plant endemism by failing to include species confined to multiple hotspots while inflating total hotspot richness by single occurrences counted more than once.

Hotspot	Plants E	Plants O	Mammals E	Mammals O	Birds E	Birds O	Reptiles E	Reptiles O	Amphibians E	Amphibians O	Freshwater fishes E	Freshwater fishes O
Tropical Andes	15 000 (50)	30 000	75 (13)	569	584 (34)	1 728	275 (45)	610	664 (57)	1 155	131 (35)	380
Tumbes-Chocó-Magdalena	2 750 (25)	11 000	10 (4)	283	112 (13)	892	98 (30)	325	29 (14)	204	115 (46)	251
Atlantic Forest	8 000 (40)	20 000	71 (27)	263	148 (16)	936	94 (31)	306	286 (60)	475	133 (38)	350
Cerrado	4 400 (44)	10 000	14 (7)	195	16 (3)	605	33 (15)	225	26 (10)	251	200 (25)	800
Chilean Winter Rainfall-Valdivian Forests	1 957 (50)	3 892	14 (22)	65	12 (5)	226	27 (66)	41	29 (67)	43	24 (56)	43
Mesoamerica	2 941 (17)	17 000	66 (15)	440	213 (19)	1 124	240 (35)	686	353 (61)	575	340 (67)	509
Madrean Pine-Oak Woodlands	3 975 (75)	5 300	6 (2)	328	23 (4)	525	37 (10)	384	50 (23)	218	18 (21)	84
Caribbean Islands	6 550 (50)	13 000	41 (46)	89	167 (28)	607	468 (94)	499	164 (99)	165	65 (40)	161
California Floristic Province	2 124 (61)	3 488	18 (12)	151	8 (2)	341	4 (6)	69	25 (46)	54	15 (21)	73
Guinean Forests of West Africa	1 800 (20)	9 000	67 (21)	320	75 (9)	793	52 (25)	206	83 (34)	246	143 (28)	512
Cape Floristic Region	6 210 (69)	9 000	4 (4)	90	6 (2)	324	22 (22)	100	16 (31)	51	14 (41)	34
Succulent Karoo	2 439 (38)	6 356	2 (3)	74	1 (0)	227	15 (16)	94	1 (3)	29	0 (0)	28
Maputaland-Pondoland-Albany	1 900 (23)	8 100	5 (3)	193	0 (0)	541	36 (18)	205	12 (15)	80	20 (27)	73
Coastal Forests of Eastern Africa	1 750 (44)	4 000	11 (5)	198	12 (2)	636	54 (22)	250	8 (8)	102	32 (15)	219
Eastern Afromontane	2 356 (31)	7 598	104 (21)	490	110 (8)	1 325	93 (27)	347	79 (28)	285	617 (69)	893
Horn of Africa	2 750 (55)	5 000	20 (9)	219	25 (4)	704	93 (33)	284	7 (13)	53	10 (10)	100
Madagascar and the Indian Ocean Islands	11 600 (89)	13 000	144 (93)	155	183 (58)	313	367 (96)	381	226 (99)	228	97 (59)	164
Mediterranean Basin	11 700 (52)	22 500	25 (11)	224	32 (6)	497	77 (34)	228	27 (31)	86	63 (29)	216
Caucasus	1 600 (25)	6 400	18 (14)	130	2 (1)	381	20 (23)	87	4 (24)	17	12 (9)	127
Irano-Anatolian	2 500 (42)	6 000	10 (7)	141	0 (0)	364	13 (11)	116	4 (19)	21	30 (33)	90
Mountains of Central Asia	1 500 (27)	5 500	6 (4)	143	0 (0)	493	1 (2)	59	4 (44)	9	5 (19)	27
Western Ghats and Sri Lanka	3 049 (52)	5 916	18 (13)	140	35 (8)	457	176 (66)	265	138 (77)	179	139 (73)	191
Himalaya	3 160 (32)	10 000	12 (4)	300	15 (2)	979	49 (28)	177	41 (33)	124	33 (12)	269
Mountains of Southwest China	3 500 (29)	12 000	5 (2)	237	1 (0)	611	15 (16)	94	40 (41)	98	23 (25)	92
Indo-Burma	7 000 (52)	13 500	73 (17)	433	73 (6)	1 277	204 (39)	518	139 (45)	311	553 (44)	1 262
Sundaland	15 000 (60)	25 000	173 (45)	381	146 (19)	771	244 (54)	449	172 (71)	242	350 (37)	950
Wallacea	1 500 (15)	10 000	127 (57)	222	265 (41)	650	99 (45)	222	32 (55)	58	50 (20)	250
Philippines	6 091 (66)	9 253	102 (61)	167	185 (35)	535	160 (68)	235	74 (75)	99	67 (24)	281
Japan	1 950 (35)	5 600	46 (51)	91	15 (4)	368	28 (44)	64	44 (76)	58	52 (24)	214
Southwest Australia	2 948 (53)	5 571	12 (21)	57	10 (4)	285	27 (15)	177	19 (58)	33	10 (50)	20
East Melanesian Islands	3 000 (38)	8 000	39 (45)	86	154 (42)	365	54 (47)	114	38 (86)	44	3 (6)	52
New Zealand	1 865 (81)	2 300	2 (50)	4	89 (45)	198	37 (100)	37	4 (100)	4	25 (64)	39
New Caledonia	2 432 (74)	3 270	6 (67)	9	23 (22)	105	62 (89)	70	0 (—)	0	9 (11)	85
Polynesia-Micronesia	3 074 (58)	5 330	11 (73)	15	170 (57)	300	31 (51)	61	3 (100)	3	20 (21)	96

While data for most invertebrate groups remains sparse, we can produce much more accurate summary statistics for terrestrial vertebrates (Table 2). The growing accuracy of the figures provided for terrestrial vertebrates in the hotspots is largely due to major advances in the reliability of species distribution data. We have relied on two main sets of data here: the IUCN (the World Conservation Union) Red List partnership and data synthesized across terrestrial ecoregions by the World Wildlife Fund-U.S. (Olson et al. 2001). The new data presented for amphibians per hotspot derives entirely from the former, namely the groundbreaking work of the Global Amphibian Assessment. Mammal data is based on work initiated by the Global Mammal Assessment, conducted through the same partnership, and mapped to ecoregions. Distribution data for birds has always been the most advanced of the four terrestrial vertebrate groups, thanks to the pioneering research of BirdLife International, another member of the IUCN Red List partnership, and was likewise expanded to synthesize the distributions of non-threatened species across ecoregions. Reptile data remains poor (only crocodilians, turtles, and tortoises having been relatively well assessed), but a comprehensive online taxonomic reference exists (www.embl-eidelberg.de/~uetz/LivingReptiles.html), preliminary data has been compiled across ecoregions, and a Global Red List Assessment is expected to commence in 2005. Species regularly occurring in a given hotspot were included in the analysis, and so vagrants or passage migrants were not incorporated. Since seabirds spend significant time on land where they nest, their nesting ranges were included, while marine mammals and marine reptiles were wholly excluded. Thus, a number of wide-ranging seabirds are considered endemic to hotspots in which their entire breeding ranges are confined.

Overall, the total number of terrestrial vertebrates endemic to a single hotspot is 10 413, representing 36% of all terrestrial vertebrate species. With rapid increases in data quality and synthesis, we can now derive species lists for each hotspot, above and beyond estimated species numbers. We are, therefore, able to sum not only single-hotspot endemics but also those species that are confined to multiple hotspots: thus, 12 066 species in total, 42% of all terrestrial vertebrates, are endemic to the 34 hotspots combined. Finally, we list the exact number of species occurring in these hotspots (i.e., species occurring within the boundaries of, but not endemic to, the hotspots): 22 319 —77% of the planet's total. We break these numbers down by class —mammals, birds, reptiles, and amphibians— in Table 3. Clearly, reptiles and, especially, amphibians, are more prone to hotspot endemism than are the more wide-ranging mammals and birds, but the overall similarity between taxonomic groups is reassuring. All of these are truly astounding numbers, demonstrating the extremely high concentration of life-forms in hotspots.

The current analysis includes the first assessment of inland fishes across all hotspots, thereby completing the coverage of vertebrates. In order to achieve this advance, we have relied on William Eschmeyer's excellent *Catalogue of Fishes* (1998; www.calacademy.org/research/ichthyology) and an increasing number of atlases and checklists for large fish faunas (e.g., Reis et al. 2003). In some cases, we assembled preliminary lists for the hotspots from country lists available in the FishBase online database (Froese and Pauly 2003; www.fishbase.org). Distributions of species in the country lists were then checked against the boundaries of the hotspots. The data given in Table 2 for fishes reflects species considered valid in the *Catalogue of Fishes* as of February 2004; all inland fishes native to the hotspots are included, without regard to their salinity preferences. This is clearly a significant underestimate of the actual number of fishes in the hotspots, given that new species of freshwater fishes are being discovered at a rate of close to two hundred species per year. Future analyses will include estimates of undiscovered species and will increasingly be based on species mapping, as is already the case for most other vertebrates. Overall, 28% of the world's 12 070 recognized freshwater fishes (3 418) are endemic to individual hotspots; 3 550 (29%) are endemic to all hotspots; and 6 689 species (55%) occur in the hotspots.

There are only two invertebrate groups for which comprehensive global data allow assessment across hotspots. These are tiger beetles (Pearson and Carroll 1998), for which 1 326 (58% of all species) are endemic to individual hotspots, and *Nasutitermes* termites (Abe et al. 2000), among which 194 (30% of all species) are single-hotspot endemics, 229 (36%) are endemics overall, and 439 (69%) occur in the hotspots (Table 4). These proportions are remarkably similar to those found for vertebrates and plants, and endemism to individual hotspots is also highly congruent. More generally, however, an acceleration of efforts to provide conservation practitioners with data is under way for invertebrate taxa, with global taxonomic and distribution databases of selected invertebrate groups now available (e.g., for ants www.antbase.org, katydids, www.tettigonia.com, and beetles www.coleoptera.org), and numerous others

On pp. 34-35, a buttress tree (Dracontomelon vitiense) *and a large hanging vine in the Vatthe Conservation Area, Espiritu Santo, Vanuatu Islands, Melanesia Hotspot.*
© **Patricio Robles Gil**/*Sierra Madre*

On the opposite page, an orchid of the genus Sobralia, *which is native to Central and South America, in Corcovado National Park on the Osa Peninsula, Costa Rica.*
© **Kevin Schafer**

TABLE 3. Numbers of plant and vertebrate species endemic to single hotspots, endemic to any hotspot(s), and occurring in any hotspot(s). The first row gives the total global number of species in each group, following Myers et al. (2000) for plants, and the World Wildlife Fund-U.S. database of terrestrial vertebrates in ecoregions and relevant IUCN assessments for terrestrial vertebrates

	Plants	*Mammals*	*Birds*	*Reptiles*	*Amphibians*
Total number worldwide	300 000	4 932	10 253	8 163	5 454
Single-hotspot endemics	150 000	1 357	2 910	3 305	2 841
% of all species in taxon	50	27	28	40	52
Endemic to any hotspot(s)	—	1 569	3 551	3 723	3 223
% of all species in taxon	—	32	35	46	59
Occurring in any hotspot(s)	—	3 744	8 385	5 779	4 411
% of all species in taxon	—	76	82	71	81

TABLE 4. Numbers of tiger beetle and *Nasutitermes* termite species endemic to (E) and occurring in (O) each of the 34 hotspots

Hotspot	Tiger beetles (n = 2 304)		Nasutitermes *termites* (n = 640)	
	E	O	E	O
Tropical Andes	48	63	7	29
Tumbes-Chocó-Magdalena	28	42	3	7
Atlantic Forest	63	88	11	67
Cerrado	23	64	28	103
Chilean Winter Rainfall-Valdivian Forests	1	5	0	0
Mesoamerica	107	149	17	34
Madrean Pine-Oak Woodlands	43	71	0	3
Caribbean Islands	9	23	7	14
California Floristic Province	5	19	0	0
Guinean Forests of West Africa	15	52	2	23
Cape Floristic Region	4	21	0	2
Succulent Karoo	2	10	0	3
Maputaland-Pondoland-Albany	15	36	0	7
Coastal Forests of Eastern Africa	2	11	1	8
Eastern Afromontane	19	38	3	20
Horn of Africa	28	46	0	2
Madagascar and the Indian Ocean Islands	211	213	7	9
Mediterranean Basin	24	46	0	1
Caucasus	—	—	0	0
Irano-Anatolian	0	18	0	0
Mountains of Central Asia	—	—	0	0
Western Ghats and Sri Lanka	101	139	15	26
Himalaya	34	72	10	15
Mountains of Southwest China	—	—	0	0
Indo-Burma	167	279	15	39
Sundaland	96	149	47	81
Wallacea	79	106	3	8
Philippines	113	132	16	31
Japan	6	24	0	0
Southwest Australia	39	43	0	17
East Melanesian Islands	11	20	1	7
New Zealand	14	14	0	1
New Caledonia	15	16	0	1
Polynesia-Micronesia	4	5	1	1

can, cautiously, use taxonomy as a surrogate for phylogeny. Genera tend to be more distinct from one another than are species, families more distinct than genera, and so on, although the exact phylogenetic difference between taxonomic levels varies considerably within and between classes (Avise and Johns 1999).

Table 5 presents the numbers of plant and vertebrate genera and Table 6, the numbers of plant and vertebrate families endemic to and occurring in hotspots. Table 7 emphasizes those hotspots holding endemic genera and families. The results are remarkable: the hotspots hold particularly large numbers of endemic genera and families (Table 8), even relative to their high levels of species endemism (Table 2). Indeed, simulation tests (for birds) show levels of generic and familial endemism in the hotspots to be significantly higher than expected given their numbers of endemic species (Brooks et al. 2004). At the higher level, the distantly isolated hotspots like Madagascar and the Indian Ocean Islands, New Caledonia, New Zealand, Polynesia-Micronesia, and the Caribbean Islands stand out in particular (Table 7). The exceptional nature of Madagascar and the Indian Ocean Islands, with a total of 24 endemic families (eight plant families, 16 endemic vertebrate families) can not be overemphasized; its closest competitors are New Zealand, Southwest Australia, and the Chilean Winter Rainfall-Valdivian Forests, each with seven endemic families. The same is true of endemic genera, with Madagascar and the Indian Ocean Islands topping the world list with 478 (310 plant genera, 168 vertebrate genera); the Caribbean Islands are second with 269 and Sundaland third with 199 (although here it should be noted that data is incomplete for some of the most diverse hotspots, e.g., the Tropical Andes and the Atlantic Forest, for which comprehensive information on endemic plant genera were simply not available).

are at different stages of development. Recently, Conservation International has launched an Invertebrate Diversity Initiative to help initiate and coordinate efforts to gather and share data on invertebrate distributions, as well as to develop innovative tools for invertebrate identification.

While the 34 hotspots clearly hold astounding levels of species endemism, this is not sufficient to describe the extent to which they represent the history of life. This is important because it could be argued that another measure of biodiversity, phylogenetic diversity (the length of time of independent evolution of a given species), better represents evolutionary potential, ecological diversity, and the range of options for future human use than does species endemism per se. Sechrest et al. (2002) provided the first test of this for two mammalian lineages —primates and carnivores—, and found that hotspots hold more unique evolutionary history than expected given their numbers of endemic species. Phylogenetic data of this kind is not yet available for most groups of species, but for terrestrial vertebrates we

On the opposite page, a large fern in the Hengduan Shan Mountains, in Yunnan Province, China.
© **Patricio Robles Gil**/*Sierra Madre*

Threats and Responses in the Hotspots

Threats to hotspots are similar to, although more intense than, the threats facing biodiversity worldwide. Habitat destruction, by definition, is a pervasive threat affecting hotspots, and is already causing extinctions in many (Brooks et al. 2002). Accelerating anthropogenic climate change will undoubtedly magnify the effects of habitat destruction and fragmentation (Thomas et al. 2004), although its specific effects on biodiversity have yet to be assessed for most hotspots (Midgely et al. 2002). Predatory invasive species have already had a devastating impact on the island hotspots, where species evolved in the absence of animals such as cats and rats (Steadman 1995). Introduction of exotic plant species into hotspots, particularly those of Mediterranean-type vegetation, is also having massive ecosystem effects, wholly changing hydrology, biogeochemical cycles and, ultimately, biodiversity (Groves and Di Castri 1991). Direct exploitation of species for food, medi-

TABLE 11. Numbers of threatened mammal, bird, and amphibian species endemic to and occurring in (in parentheses) individual hotspots, following IUCN (2003) and provisional 2004 listings for amphibians. VU-Vulnerable; EN-Endangered; CR-Critically Endangered

Hotspot	Mammals			Birds			Amphibians		
	VU + EN + CR	EN + CR	CR	VU + EN + CR	EN + CR	CR	VU + EN + CR	EN + CR	CR
Tropical Andes	15 (68)	8 (22)	4 (6)	101 (149)	58 (68)	12 (13)	255 (315)	177 (200)	75 (84)
Tumbes-Chocó-Magdalena	6 (30)	1 (5)	1 (2)	21 (48)	10 (16)	5 (6)	7 (31)	4 (15)	0 (5)
Atlantic Forest	20 (37)	13 (17)	5 (7)	63 (86)	39 (45)	10 (14)	54 (58)	36 (37)	15 (15)
Cerrado	4 (21)	1 (4)	0 (0)	7 (24)	3 (8)	3 (5)	3 (4)	3 (3)	2 (2)
Chilean Winter Rainfall-Valdivian Forests	3 (10)	0 (3)	0 (0)	6 (8)	1 (2)	1 (1)	14 (17)	7 (9)	4 (5)
Mesoamerica	29 (48)	20 (27)	4 (5)	32 (42)	15 (17)	5 (5)	178 (231)	123 (155)	59 (67)
Madrean Pine-Oak Woodlands	2 (25)	2 (12)	0 (3)	2 (10)	2 (3)	1 (1)	39 (99)	32 (69)	13 (24)
Caribbean Islands	18 (18)	8 (8)	2 (2)	48 (52)	28 (28)	10 (10)	135 (135)	101 (101)	39 (39)
California Floristic Province	4 (7)	3 (3)	1 (1)	4 (9)	2 (3)	2 (3)	7 (12)	0 (3)	0 (0)
Guinean Forests of West Africa	31 (48)	19 (26)	3 (3)	31 (36)	12 (13)	4 (4)	41 (60)	32 (47)	11 (14)
Cape Floristic Region	1 (10)	1 (5)	1 (2)	0 (9)	0 (0)	0 (0)	7 (11)	4 (6)	2 (3)
Succulent Karoo	1 (11)	0 (4)	0 (2)	0 (9)	0 (0)	0 (0)	1 (2)	0 (0)	0 (0)
Maputaland-Pondoland-Albany	2 (21)	1 (6)	0 (1)	0 (10)	0 (2)	0 (0)	6 (10)	5 (7)	1 (2)
Coastal Forests of Eastern Africa	6 (20)	6 (11)	2 (4)	2 (17)	2 (5)	0 (0)	3 (16)	2 (4)	0 (0)
Eastern Afromontane	48 (78)	20 (28)	14 (14)	35 (45)	15 (22)	2 (3)	39 (59)	20 (27)	2 (4)
Horn of Africa	10 (27)	4 (10)	3 (5)	9 (21)	5 (5)	3 (3)	1 (1)	0 (0)	0 (0)
Madagascar and the Indian Ocean Islands	50 (51)	27 (27)	11 (11)	54 (55)	30 (30)	15 (15)	58 (58)	28 (28)	8 (8)
Mediterranean Basin	15 (40)	5 (11)	4 (5)	7 (17)	5 (8)	2 (4)	12 (15)	5 (5)	1 (1)
Caucasus	2 (14)	2 (3)	1 (1)	0 (8)	0 (2)	0 (1)	2 (1)	1 (1)	0 (0)
Irano-Anatolian	3 (16)	3 (5)	0 (0)	0 (9)	0 (1)	0 (0)	4 (5)	1 (1)	0 (0)
Mountains of Central Asia	3 (19)	1 (7)	0 (2)	0 (9)	0 (1)	0 (0)	1 (2)	1 (1)	0 (0)
Western Ghats and Sri Lanka	14 (35)	11 (16)	3 (4)	10 (25)	2 (6)	0 (2)	95 (100)	79 (81)	33 (33)
Himalaya	4 (46)	3 (17)	2 (3)	8 (43)	2 (6)	1 (2)	21 (30)	5 (7)	1 (1)
Mountains of Southwest China	3 (39)	3 (16)	1 (1)	1 (23)	0 (1)	0 (0)	25 (35)	8 (11)	2 (2)
Indo-Burma	25 (70)	17 (31)	9 (12)	16 (70)	9 (18)	2 (4)	41 (66)	10 (18)	3 (4)
Sundaland	60 (81)	34 (40)	12 (14)	40 (59)	14 (18)	10 (12)	54 (57)	13 (13)	3 (3)
Wallacea	44 (50)	14 (16)	1 (1)	49 (51)	27 (27)	7 (7)	5 (7)	0 (0)	0 (0)
Philippines	47 (49)	20 (21)	7 (7)	55 (61)	21 (22)	11 (11)	13 (14)	4 (4)	0 (0)
Japan	21 (24)	15 (17)	3 (3)	10 (27)	3 (9)	2 (2)	14 (14)	13 (13)	2 (2)
Southwest Australia	6 (10)	3 (4)	1 (1)	3 (5)	1 (1)	0 (0)	3 (3)	1 (1)	1 (1)
East Melanesian Islands	20 (23)	5 (5)	4 (4)	32 (35)	6 (6)	2 (2)	3 (3)	0 (0)	0 (0)
New Zealand	2 (2)	0 (0)	0 (0)	57 (62)	22 (22)	5 (5)	4 (4)	2 (2)	1 (1)
New Caledonia	3 (3)	2 (2)	0 (0)	7 (10)	7 (7)	3 (3)	—	—	—
Polynesia-Micronesia	7 (8)	6 (6)	4 (4)	88 (93)	45 (46)	21 (21)	1 (1)	1 (1)	0 (0)

to— hotspots. For the three groups for which assessments of distribution and conservation status have been conducted, we can measure these proportions with a high level of accuracy (Table 11). The groups show rather different patterns of threat across the hotspots. Threatened birds are concentrated in the island hotspots (although the Tropical Andes and Atlantic Forest are very important as well), with the Caribbean Islands, Madagascar and the Indian Ocean Islands, Sundaland, Wallacea, and the Philippines all having large numbers of threatened species present and endemic. Not surprisingly, the same holds true for threatened mammals, but forested mainland regions also harbor large proportions of threatened mammals, especially the Atlantic Forest, Mesoamerica, the Guinean Forests of West Africa, and the Eastern Afromontane Hotspot. The hottest hotspots for threatened amphibians are tropical mountains, especially in the Neotropics —the Tropical Andes and Mesoamerica— although the Caribbean Islands and the Western Ghats and Sri Lanka also hold major concentrations of threatened amphibians. Table 12 summarizes the overall numbers and percentages of Extinct, Critically Endangered, Endangered, and Vulnerable mammals, birds, and amphibians endemic to single hotspots, endemic to any hotspot(s), or occurring in any hotspot(s). In all cases, there are many more threatened species occurring within or endemic to the hotspots than we expect based on the equivalent statistics for all species. Consistently, more than two-thirds of threatened species are single-hotspot endemics, and approaching 90% of threatened species occur in at least one hotspot. Throughout the book, we include annotation of threat status (VU, EN or CR) in parentheses following

TABLE 12. Numbers and percentages of threatened mammal, bird, and amphibian species endemic to single hotspots, endemic to any hotspot(s), and occurring in any hotspot(s), following IUCN (2003) and provisional 2004 listings for amphibians. VU-Vulnerable; EN-Endangered; CR-Critically Endangered; EX-Extinct

	Mammals				Birds				Amphibians			
	VU + EN + CR	EN + CR	CR	EX	VU + EN + CR	EN + CR	CR	EX	VU + EN + CR	EN + CR	CR	EX
Total number worldwide	1 128	514	180	74	1 186	513	182	129	1 543	891	341	25
Single-hotspot endemics	529	278	103	53	798	386	139	107	1 143	718	278	18
% of all species in taxon	47	54	57	72	67	75	76	83	74	81	82	72
Endemic to any hotspot(s)	564	288	107	53	867	401	142	107	1 221	756	288	18
% of all species in taxon	50	56	59	72	73	78	78	83	79	85	84	72
Occurring in any hotspot(s)	809	366	119	53	1 039	439	152	107	1 367	823	307	18
% of all species in taxon	72	71	66	72	88	86	84	83	89	92	90	72

IUCN (2003), although using provisional 2004 listings for amphibians.

Overall, 56% of the world's EN and CR mammals are endemic to the hotspots (59% of just the CR mammals). The equivalent percentages for birds are 78%, and for amphibians 85%. This represents three-quarters of all Critically Endangered and Endangered terrestrial vertebrates; in absolute numbers, this adds up to 1 445 CR and EN terrestrial vertebrate species found only in the hotspots. These numbers emphasize the need for immediate conservation action to take place in the hotspots if the rate of extinction is to be slowed.

Beyond Hotspots: Identifying Conservation Targets on the Ground

While hotspots and other global prioritization systems are extremely important in informing the flow of conservation resources, they do not provide any guidance as to how and where within these large regions conservation should be focused on the ground. Thus, a further crucial advantage bestowed by the IUCN-SSC species assessments is the ability to move from the global to the local scale of conservation planning. In Conservation International, this planning process is known as establishing targets for conservation outcomes (Conservation International 2004). We define conservation outcomes at three scales of ecological organization: species (where we strive for "Extinctions Avoided" outcomes); sites (where the targets are "Areas Protected" outcomes); and landscapes (at which our aims are "Corridors Consolidated" outcomes).

Targets for "Extinctions Avoided" outcomes apply to those species facing the highest risk of extinction, and are listed as threatened on the IUCN Red List. The establishment of targets for "Areas Protected" outcomes is more complex, and requires the careful evaluation of sites that are actually or potentially managed for conservation against a set of standard criteria (based on vulnerability and irreplaceability) that focus on the threatened species identified above. The sites meeting these criteria are called "key biodiversity areas," and become targets for conservation action on the ground. An important characteristic of the process of defining key biodiversity areas is that it is a locally led process —although strictly following global standards— and is, therefore, a "bottom-up" process organizationally as well as ecologically. A further advantage is that this process links to BirdLife International's *Important Bird Areas* process, which has been under way for more than a decade (e.g., Fishpool and Evans 2001), and covers the identification of key biodiversity areas for birds. To date, processes for identifying key biodiversity areas have been initiated in more than half the hotspots.

A small, but extremely important, subset of key biodiversity areas are those that hold threatened species as endemics to a single site. To tackle these extraordinarily high-site conservation priorities, an *Alliance for Zero Extinction* (AZE; www.zeroextinction.org) of conservation organizations has formed over the last year. AZE aims to identify and conserve all sites holding the entire global population of one or more Critically Endangered or Endangered species. An initial draft of site identification has now been completed for terrestrial vertebrate species, revealing 365 AZE sites worldwide. A very high proportion of these sites —nearly 80%— fall within the hotspots. The AZE sites therefore represent refugia for species that could potentially repopulate areas of restored habitat. So ensuring the continued existence of these unique, highly threatened nodes is a vital component of conserving the overall biodiversity of each hotspot.

While the achievement of species- and site-scale conservation outcomes is essential if conservation is to succeed, it is not sufficient. A large body of ecological literature demonstrates that conservation action is also necessary at the landscape scale, for the purposes of maintaining ecological and evolutionary processes on which species and sites depend, mitigating regional-scale threats (Sanderson et al. 2003), and more efficiently exploring conservation and development

On pp. 62-63, the Critically Endangered golden-crowned sifaka (Propithecus tattersalli) at the edge of an area devastated by gold mining activities in the Daraina region of northeastern Madagascar. This species, which was not described by science until 1988, now has a very small remaining range, but has been the focus of a comprehensive protected area program by the Malagasy conservation organization Association Fanamby.
© **Pete Oxford**/naturepl.com

options. The Wildlife Conservation Society has been making some progress with the measurement of landscape-scale conservation targets for wide-ranging species through their "landscape species" concept (Sanderson et al. 2002), while other work is beginning to address abiotic ecological processes (e.g., Cowling et al. 1999).

Coda: Hotspots as a Line in the Sand

Overall, three major conclusions emerge from this updated hotspots analysis. First, while the importance of the additions to the hotspots list and of the advances provided by matching hotspots to ecoregion boundaries and by updated species data are not to be underestimated, it is clear that the hotspots concept is solidifying. Compared to the initial conceptual advances of Myers (1988) and the data synthesis of Myers et al. (2000), this update results in few major modifications to the broad global picture of hotspots. While the 25 hotspots identified by Myers et al. (2000) held 44% of all plants and 35% of terrestrial vertebrates as single-hotspot endemics, the sum of single-hotspot endemics to the 34 hotspots considered here gives increases of only 6% and nearly 2% respectively, to yield totals of 50% of all plants and 37% of all terrestrial vertebrates.

Second, the amount of biodiversity contained in the hotspots is extremely high. More than half of the planet's species are endemic to only 16% of its land area. Based on the evidence from terrestrial vertebrates, it seems that the overall number of species occurring in the hotspots is much greater —approaching four-fifths. If we consider only the extent of remaining habitat —2.3% of the planet's land surface— these numbers are even more remarkable, although it must be kept in mind that in the long term we aim to attempt to restore much of this degraded land, in addition to the immediate priority of conserving that habitat which still persists. By any measure, the hotspots stand out from the rest of the world: even the high biodiversity wilderness areas, the next greatest concentrations of biodiversity (and, admittedly, less well known than the hotspots), hold only 17% of plants and 8% of terrestrial vertebrates as endemics, in 6.1% of Earth's land area. Hotspots hold a concentration of endemics about three times as great for plants and nearly five times greater for vertebrates. Clearly, if the conservation community is to succeed in preventing extinctions and maintaining the full range of global biodiversity, a very strong focus on hotspots is essential.

Finally, and most importantly, hotspots provide us with the real measure of the conservation challenge. Unless we succeed in conserving this small fraction of the planet's land area, we will lose more than half of our natural heritage —regardless of how successful conservation is outside of the hotspots. While conservation in the hotspots is complex, expensive, and difficult, it is not optional. We utterly reject a triage approach of abandoning the hotspots —it would signal the end of half of our biodiversity. Instead, we see the successes of the last fifteen years as a rallying cry for a tenfold increase in conservation attention, resources, and funding received by the hotspots. Nothing less than the diversity of life on Earth hangs in the balance.

RUSSELL A. MITTERMEIER[1]
PATRICIO ROBLES GIL[4]
MICHAEL HOFFMANN[2]
JOHN PILGRIM[2]
THOMAS BROOKS[2]
CRISTINA G. MITTERMEIER[1]
JOHN LAMOREUX[3]
GUSTAVO A.B. DA FONSECA[1, 2, 13]

KEITH ALGER[1]
FREDERICK BOLTZ[1, 14]
KATRINA BRANDON[2]
AARON BRUNER[2]
JOSÉ MARIA CARDOSO DA SILVA[5]
ASSHETON CARTER[1]
ROBERTO CAVALCANTI[1, 15]
DON CHURCH[1]
MATTHEW FOSTER[2]
CLAUDE GASCON[1]
LARRY GORENFLO[2]
BRIAN GRATWICKE[6]
MARIANNE GUERIN-MCMANUS[1]
LEE HANNAH[2]
DAVID KNOX[2]
WILLIAM R. KONSTANT[1, 7]
THOMAS LACHER[2]
PENNY LANGHAMMER[2]
OLIVIER LANGRAND[1]
NICHOLAS LAPHAM[1]
DAN MARTIN[1]
NORMAN MYERS[8]
PIOTR NASKRECKI[2, 9]
MICHAEL PARR[10]
DAVID PEARSON[11]
GLENN PRICKETT[1]
DICK RICE[2]
ANTHONY RYLANDS[2]
WES SECHREST[2, 12]
MICHAEL LEONARD SMITH[2]
SIMON STUART[12]
JORGEN THOMSEN[1]
MICHAEL TOTTEN[1]
JUSTIN WARD[1]

Note: The authors' addresses are listed on p. 390.

On pp. 66-67, Tijuca National Park, the largest urban forest in the world, is entirely surrounded by the city of Rio de Janeiro, one of the largest cities in the world. More than 300 million people live within 10 km of protected areas in the biodiversity hotspots.
© **Frans Lanting**/*Minden Pictures*

On the opposite page, a young Tibetan woman in the northern part of China's Yunnan Province.
© **Patricio Robles Gil**/*Sierra Madre*

AN UPDATE
OF EXISTING HOTSPOTS

In our last review of the hotspots (Mittermeier et al. 1999; Myers et al. 2000), we presented information on 25 hotspots. However, we also noted that there were a number of regions that were possible hotspot candidates which could not be included due to a lack of adequate information at that time. In this reanalysis of the hotspots, which began in 2000, we have assessed a number of these areas and have found that some of them qualify for hotspot status. In addition, we have reassessed and updated the previously defined 25 hotspots, providing new data and making minor changes in the borders of several. For the most part, however, 23 of them have remained the same.

In the case of the remaining two hotspots included in Mittermeier et al. (1999) and Myers et al. (2000), we have made changes significant enough to warrant their inclusion as new chapters. The original Eastern Arc Mountains and Coastal Forests of Tanzania and Kenya Hotspot has undergone major changes. The Coastal Forests have been separated out as a new hotspot and extended considerably to the north into northern Kenya and Somalia, and south into southern Mozambique (p. 231). The Eastern Arc Mountains, which on their own do not qualify as a hotspot, have now been included in a more extensive Eastern Afromontane Hotspot based on botanical affinities first recognized by White (1983) in his classic work on the botany of Africa. This new hotspot also incorporates the Southern Rift, the Albertine Rift, and the Ethiopian Highlands, and is presented on p. 241.

The original Indo-Burma Hotspot also warranted redefinition to recognize the two distinct, although overlapping, regions that it contained. Consequently, it, too, was modified to such an extent that the two areas had to be separated as new hotspots. The bulk of this hotspot, including Myanmar (Burma), Vietnam, Cambodia, Laos, Thailand, extreme northern Malaysia north of the Kangar-Pattani Line, the karst region of extreme southeastern China, and the island of Hainan, remains in what we continue to call the Indo-Burma Hotspot. Areas to the northwest in northeast India, Bhutan, Nepal, and southwestern China have now been included in a new Himalaya Hotspot, which also extends further to the west into Pakistan and northeast Afghanistan than did the Himalayan section of the original Indo-Burma Hotspot. These two new hotspots are covered on pp. 309 and 323.

For the other 23 original hotspots, we present here a review of their geographic extent, with details of minor changes in borders, a small map, their principal distinguishing characteristics, their biodiversity, threats to their survival, and a discussion of conservation measures already in place —with particular emphasis on protected area coverage. In particular, we provide updated information on their species richness and endemism in vascular plants, mammals, birds, reptiles, and amphibians; add new information on freshwater fishes; and, for the first time, also include data on endemism at the genus and family levels. This data is combined with data on the new hotspots and presented in the text and tables of the Introduction.

On the opposite page, the orang-utans are endemic to the Sundaland Hotspot, and are declining everywhere. The Sumatran orang-utan is now considered a distinct species from the Bornean orang-utan and is Critically Endangered.
© Anup Shah/naturepl.com

TROPICAL ANDES

José Vicente Rodríguez-Mahecha [25] • Paul Salaman [25]
Peter Jørgensen [26] • Trisha Consiglio [26]
Eduardo Forno [107] • Antonio Telesca [105] • Luis Suárez [27]
Fabio Arjona [25] • Franklin Rojas [106]
Robert Bensted-Smith [27] • Victor Hugo Inchausty [107]

The Tropical Andes Hotspot is the richest and most diverse biodiversity hotspot on Earth. The Andes Mountain Range, its different cordilleras, its vast array of slopes and peaks, and its isolated valleys provide for a multiplicity of microhabitats and climatic conditions that have led to the evolution of an incredible number of plant and animal species. The hotspot covers a total of 1 542 644 km² in the countries of Venezuela, Colombia, Ecuador, Peru, and Bolivia, and extends a very short distance into extreme northwestern Argentina. The centerpiece of the hotspot is the tropical portion of the Andes mountain chain, which runs north to south in Bolivia, Peru, and Ecuador, then splits into three major cordilleras in Colombia, and extends still further to the northeast into the northwestern corner of Venezuela. The hotspot is bounded roughly by the Tropic of Capricorn to the south and by the natural termini of the Andes to the north in Colombia and Venezuela (including the isolated Sierra Nevada de Santa Marta in Colombia and the Cordillera de la Costa montane forests in Venezuela). The western border of the hotspot is marked by the eastern edge of the Tumbes-Chocó-Magdalena Hotspot, while on the eastern slope of the Andes, in Ecuador, Peru, and Bolivia, the border extends down to 500 m, a realistic cutoff point between the Andean slopes and the Amazonian lowlands. The hotspot is also taken to include the inter-Andean valleys of the northern cordilleras in Colombia.

The Tropical Andes is sometimes divided into northern and southern zones, with the border between them being an arid, east-west valley that coincides roughly with the Ecuador-Peru border in the far northern portion of Peru (Piura) and extending north into neighboring Ecuador. At this nexus, called the Marañón Gap or Huancabamba Depression, altitudes drop to around 500 m, creating one of the most important barriers to faunal and floral migration in the Andes. This gap also serves as an east-west corridor between the Amazon and the Pacific (Gentry 1977, 1990).

The vegetation of the Tropical Andes Hotspot follows a gradient from lowlands to highlands, with tropical wet and moist forests occurring at 500-1 500 m; cloud forest formations of various kinds, variously referred to as *yunga*, *ceja de selva*, or *ceja de montaña*, which can range in altitude from 800 to 3 500 m (and covering an area of approximately 250 000 km² in Peru alone); and grassland and scrubland systems, which are mainly paramos in the northern Andes and the drier *puna* in the southern Andes. Both of the latter begin at 3 000 to 3 800 m and extend up to between 4 200 and 4 800 m, usually ending at the snowline. Beginning in the lowlands of the eastern slopes at around 500 m altitude, the sub-Andean forests are similar to those of the hot, Amazonian lowlands, but have fewer palm species, fewer lianas, and fewer buttresses, although the canopy can reach as high as 45 m. Within the sub-Andean forest belt, vegetation begins to transition at around 1 500 m, at which point the plant family Lauraceae becomes the dominant element (Cuatrecasas 1958; Langendoen and Gentry 1991; Dodson and Gentry 1991). Andean forests then begin at approximately 2 000 m, and are characterized by shorter trees and more abundant epiphytes such as mosses, lichens, ferns, and algae. At 3 000 to 3 800 m, Andean forests then give way to paramos in the north and *puna* in the south.

In addition to the main Andean vegetation types, other systems such as dry forests and arid, warm to cool non-forest environments —including woodlands, cactus stands, thornscrub, and matorral— occur adjacent to the wet montane, paramo and *puna* formations, in dry intermontane basins or along the dry Andean slopes of Peru in particular, usually at altitudes of 2 000 to 3 000 m. *Polylepis* forests represent another vegetation type unique to the Andes, this tree genus being restricted to the montane areas of western South America, and a conspicuous element of some high-elevation tropical habitats.

In terms of plants and vertebrates, the Tropical Andes Hotspot leads virtually all others in both species diversity and endemism. Perhaps the most impressive figures are those for vascular plants, with an estimated 30 000-35 000 species, or approximately 10% of the world's species, occurring in this hotspot. In fact, the Tropical Andes contains 20%-80% of the total plant species occurring in Bolivia, Ecuador, Peru, and Venezuela. Endemism is equally impressive, with an estimated 50% (and perhaps 60% or higher) of species endemic to the hotspot (around 15 000 species), and peaks in the number of endemic species occurring in

The adult male Andean cock-of-the-rock (Rupicola peruviana)*, a spectacular species found in the Andean Mountains from Venezuela south to Bolivia, spends much of its time at communal courtship sites, called leks, where it puts on displays for females.*
© **Patricio Robles Gil**/*Sierra Madre*

On the opposite page, violet-tailed sylph (Aglaiocercus coelestis)*, one of the many hummingbird species found in the Andes, the world's center of hummingbird diversity.*
© **Patricio Robles Gil**/*Sierra Madre*

the Andean regions of each country (Jørgensen and León-Yánez 1999; Kessler 2000, 2002; Van der Werff and Consiglio 2004). For example, almost 3 000 of Ecuador's 4 000 endemic plant species and around 3 650 of Peru's 5 400 endemic species are Andean; over 25% of total endemic species for Peru and Ecuador occur in the 2 500-3 000-m elevation zone alone. These figures are likely to be an underestimate, especially as new taxa are being described; for example, there have been about 440 plant species described between 1999 and 2003 from the Ecuadorian portion of the Tropical Andes Hotspot alone (out of a total of 532 for the country as a whole) (D. Neill, pers. comm.). In addition, for the Orchidaceae, the largest family in Peru and one that has its peak of endemism in the Tropical Andes, it is estimated that an increase of almost 50% of known species has occurred in the last 10 years (C. Dodson, pers. comm.). It is likely that we need five times the number of plant collections that have been carried out to date to be reasonably certain of the region's plant diversity. Several flagship plant species also occur in the Tropical Andes. Among the list of endemics is a high Andean bromeliad species (*Puya raimondii*) that takes as long as a century to reach maturity and has the tallest inflorescence of any plant on Earth, reaching as much as six meters in height.

The Tropical Andes also has the highest bird diversity and endemism of any hotspot, perhaps not surprising given that Colombia, Peru, and Ecuador hold the first, second, and fourth positions on the global list of countries with the most avian species. Furthermore, these high numbers of birds derive largely from the Andean portions of these countries (Stotz et al. 1996; Mittermeier et al. 1997). The total number of regularly occurring bird species for the Tropical Andes Hotspot is 1 728, of which an astounding 584 species are endemic. Furthermore, 69 genera are endemic. It is not surprising, then, that BirdLife International recognizes around 21 different Endemic Bird Areas (EBAs) lying partly or entirely within this hotspot, among which the Colombian East Andes, with 34 species endemic, is the most important, having one Extinct (Colombian grebe, *Podiceps andinus*) and four Critically Endangered species: the gorgeted wood-quail (*Odontophorus strophium*), chestnut-bellied hummingbird (*Amazilia castaneiventris*), Niceforo's wren (*Thryothorus nicefori*), and Colombian mountain grackle (*Macrogelaius subalaris*). Flagship bird species occurring in this hotspot include the yellow-eared parrot (*Ognorhynchus icterotis*, CR), an enigmatic macaw-sized species that depends on the Quindío wax palm (*Ceroxylon quindiuense*, VU), which is the national tree of Colombia; the Andean condor (*Vultur gryphus*), one of the largest flying birds on Earth; and the diminutive hummingbirds (Trochilidae), a family of tiny, jewel-like birds that reaches its greatest diversity in the Tropical Andes.

Endemism and diversity among amphibians and reptiles in the Tropical Andes exceed even the amazing figures for birds and plants. The Tropical Andes have by far the highest amphibian diversity of any hotspot on Earth, with a total of 1 155 species (1 088 frogs and toads; 28 salamanders, newts and sirens; and 39 caecilians), of which 664 species are endemic. Some of the amphibian genera reach amazing levels of diversity in the Tropical Andes, the best example being the widespread genus *Eleutherodactylus* of the family Leptodactylidae, with 343 species present and 244 endemic. There are also 10 endemic genera (of the 79 represented). Unfortunately, this is also a hotspot for amphibian extinctions, with several taxa already having disappeared in recent years, particularly some beautiful harlequin toads of the genus *Atelopus* that tend to be stream-dwelling species and appear highly sensitive to local climate change and habitat loss, and are susceptible to disease (Ron et al. 2003). In terms of reptiles, there are 610 species native to the Tropical Andes Hotspot (304 lizards, 294 snakes, eight turtles and tortoises, and four crocodilians), of which 275 species and three genera are endemic.

Mammal diversity and endemism are also noteworthy. Of a total of 569 species, some 75 are endemic. As elsewhere, rodents are the most diverse mammal group with 220 species, followed by bats with 181 species. There are curious pockets of higher endemism within certain habitats of this hotspot, with both the *puna* and *paramo* formations having high mammal endemism. There are also six endemic genera, each represented by single species: Garlepp's mouse (*Galenomys garleppi*), the Andean rat (*Lenoxus apicalis*), little or mountain coati (*Nasuella olivacea*), puna mouse (*Punomys lemminus*), and fish-eating rat (*Anotomys leander*, EN), a species known only from the Andes of northern Ecuador and highly specialized for an aquatic existence. The sixth endemic genus is one of the most important mammal flagship species for the Tropical Andes, the yellow-tailed woolly monkey (*Oreonax flavicauda*, CR). It is the largest mammal endemic to Peru, and is only one of three primate genera in the Neotropics to be endemic to a single country. It is restricted to a small area of cloud forest in the northern Peruvian departments of Amazonas and San Martín. Other important large mammal flagships include the spectacled bear (*Tremarctos ornatus*, VU), woolly or mountain tapir (*Tapirus pinchaque*, EN), and vicuña (*Vicugna vicugna*), a camelid that lives at altitudes of 3 000 to 4 800 m, mainly in the *puna* ecosystem.

Freshwater fishes are represented by 380 documented species, although many more are expected as explorations extend onto the Amazonian flanks of the mountains. A total of 131 fish species are endemic to the hotspot, a surprising number for an area centered on the crest of a mountain range. One major component of endemism consists of members of the cyprinodont genus *Orestias*, which has undergone a significant radiation in Lake Titicaca and nearby drainages, resulting in a cluster of 43 species endemic to the southern end of the hotspot. Most remarkable perhaps are the naked sucker-mouth catfishes (family Astroblepidae) that

inhabit torrential streams from one end of the hotspot to the other. With the exception of a species in Panama and a few species that extend to lower elevations, the family's 90 species are endemic to the region.

Humans have lived in the Andes for many millennia, and the region was home to one of the world's great past civilizations, the Empire of the Incas. However, the degree of human impact varies considerably within this region, from areas that have lost almost all of their original vegetation (e.g., some of the inter-Andean valleys in Colombia and Ecuador) to some that are still largely pristine (e.g., parts of the eastern slopes of the Andes in Bolivia and Peru). Broadly speaking, the most disturbed portions of the hotspot are the dry inter-Andean valleys, where the original forests have largely disappeared and, on average, less than 10% remains. The inter-Andean valleys provide the most hospitable environment for humans in the region, and these areas have been densely populated since pre-Columbian times.

Other heavily impacted ecosystems within the Andes are the paramos and the *puna*. Both have been greatly modified by seasonal burning and grazing, agriculture, and mining. The *puna* also suffers from over-exploitation of certain slow-growing woody plant species for firewood, especially around urban centers such as Arequipa, while *puna* ecosystems of both Peru and Bolivia are also affected by the mining industry, with toxic runoff and water contamination being a major concern.

An additional threat that has emerged in recent years, especially in the high Andean forests of Colombia, is the cultivation of the opium poppy, in clearings cut within montane forests to grow this highly profitable illegal crop. Unfortunately, the programs designed to control illegal crops use chemical defoliants that cause even more damage to biodiversity, as well as allowing harmful chemical herbicides to enter into highland ecosystems and trickle into lower altitudes through the rivers and streams, a factor that may have contributed to amphibian and freshwater fish die-offs in these regions.

As a result of all these pressures, a large portion of the natural vegetation of the Tropical Andes Hotspot has already been lost, and it is estimated that the area remaining in fully intact condition is likely no more than 25%, or 385 661 km^2, and probably much less. The eastern slopes of the Andes in Peru and Bolivia have the most extensive areas of largely intact natural vegetation.

Despite the bleak picture painted above, protected areas today are conserving some of the most important remnants of the Tropical Andes Hotspot. In total, these protected areas cover some 16% of its original extent. However, many of these protected areas are small and ineffective, and only 7.9% of the hotspot is protected in reserves or parks in IUCN categories I to IV. This has led to the recognition for the need not only to create new and better-managed parks, but also to interconnect existing parks through what are commonly referred to as "corridors." An example of a "corridor" project, and a model for using corridors as a conservation strategy in the Andean region, can be found in the Amazon-Andes interface in southern Peru and adjacent portions of Bolivia. One of the first and most important components of this corridor is Manú, the largest rainforest biosphere reserve on Earth at 18 812 km^2, and which protects major areas of *puna*, cloud forest, and lowland forest. Another major piece of this string-of-pearls of Andean slope ecosystems is the Tambopata-Madidi protected area complex straddling the Peru-Bolivia border, representing fully 22 250 km^2 of new parks created in the richest portion of the most diverse biodiversity hotspot on Earth, an area larger than El Salvador and a very significant accomplishment for biodiversity conservation.

The Tropical Andes has benefited from a series of major conservation investments in the last several years. For example, the Critical Ecosystem Partnership Fund has made a commitment to invest some $6 million in the Vilcabamba-Amboró Corridor in Peru and Ecuador over the past three years, with the specific objective of building civil society capacity to carry out biodiversity conservation activities in this important region. At the same time, the Global Conservation Fund (GCF), based at Conservation International, has invested $1.273 million in projects in Bolivia, Colombia, Peru, and Ecuador. These projects have helped to stimulate the creation of some nearly 3 million hectares of new protected areas in some of the highest-priority regions of these countries. Included among the projects supported by the GCF were two debt-for-nature swaps in Peru in 2003 and in Colombia in 2004. Both of these were carried out in partnership with the World Wildlife Fund, The Nature Conservancy, and the United States Government; they will provide $10.6 million to 10 sites in Peru and $10 million to five sites in Colombia over a 12-year period. These are just a few examples of the direct support given to conservation in recent years.

Other conservation activities in the region are focusing directly on amelioration of some of the most dangerous threats to the environment, e.g., infrastructure development, while several on-the-ground efforts to conserve key threatened species (such as the recent recovery of the yellow-eared parrot) are also under way. In conclusion, looking at this region as a whole, there is considerable room for optimism. Although portions of the Tropical Andes have been heavily impacted, extinctions have been relatively few, and there is still enough time to design and implement conservation areas at a scale which is likely to ensure the survival of the vast majority of life-forms that exist in this, the richest of the planet's terrestrial hotspots.

On pp. 76-77, Machu Picchu Historic Sanctuary, located within the Vilcabamba-Amboró Conservation Corridor, is surrounded by striking mountains. Machu Picchu receives more than 400 000 visitors per year, who come to enjoy one of the most magical landscapes in the Peruvian Andes.
© **Haroldo Castro**

On the opposite page, the spectacled bear (Tremarctos ornatus) is the only representative of the bear family in South America, and is distributed in forested habitats at higher elevations from Venezuela and Colombia south through the Andean mountain range to Bolivia.
© **Patricio Robles Gil**/*Sierra Madre*

Above, the booted racket-tail (Ocreatus underwoodii) is a fairly common and widespread hummingbird species occurring from Colombia to Peru.
© **Patricio Robles Gil**/*Sierra Madre*

TUMBES-CHOCÓ-MAGDALENA

José Vicente Rodríguez-Mahecha [25] • Paul Salaman [25]
Peter Jørgensen [26] • Trisha Consiglio [26] • Luis Suárez [27]
Fabio Arjona [25] • Robert Bensted-Smith [27]

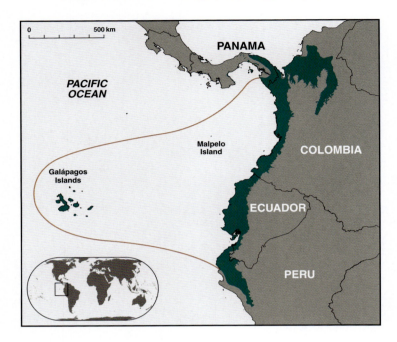

The Tumbes-Chocó-Magdalena Hotspot was previously referred to as the Chocó-Darién-Western Ecuador Hotspot in Mittermeier et al. (1999). It has now changed its name and expanded its boundaries to include several new areas, most notably the Magdalena Valley in Colombia. As we now define this hotspot, it originally covered 274 597 km² in the northwestern corner of South America. It begins east of the Panama Canal in the wet and moist forests of Panama's Darién Province, extends south through the Chocó region of western Colombia, and then on into the moist forests of northwestern Ecuador, where it is bounded by the Pacific Ocean to the west and the western slope of the Andes to the east. It then also extends still further south to include the dry forests of western Ecuador and those in Tumbes, Piura, and La Libertad departments in the extreme northwestern corner of Peru, south as far as Huacho. In northern Colombia, the hotspot also follows the forests of the Chocó as they go east around the northern Andean termini and into the Magdalena Valley. In addition to the mainland portion of the hotspot, we also include here the island of Malpelo (8 km²), located around 500 km off the coast of Buenaventura, Colombia, and the Galápagos Islands (7 882 km²), lying some 960 km west of Ecuador in the Pacific Ocean and including 13 large islands and six smaller islands lying right on the equator. Although these islands are volcanic in origin, they do have some floristic affinities with the mainland, and therefore are included here with the geographically nearest hotspot.

This hotspot is characterized by a great variety of habitats ranging from extensive mangrove areas, beaches, rocky shorelines, and coastal wilderness and dry forests, to the world's wettest rainforests. The dry forest region of western Ecuador and Tumbes and Piura in Peru is especially diverse, with habitats ranging from arid scrub and desert through deciduous tropical thornscrub forest and deciduous *Ceiba trichistandra* forest, to semievergreen *C. pentandra* forest, semievergreen lowland and premontane tall forest, to deciduous to semievergreen intermontane scrub. Punctuating the otherwise flat coastal plain, this hotspot also contains numerous smaller mountain systems, including the Serranía del Sapo, Serranía de los Saltos, and Serranía del Baudo, which run parallel to the coast in extreme western Colombia; the Cordillera de San Blas and Serranía del Darién in southeastern Panama; the Serranía de Abibe and Serranía de San Lucas in northern Colombia; the Cordillera de la Costa in Ecuador; and the Cerros de Amotape in Peru, all of which represent "islands" of endemism that add to the wide spectrum of biodiversity in this top-priority ecosystem.

Broadly speaking, the Tumbes-Chocó-Magdalena Hotspot can be divided into two major phytogeographic regions: the wet and moist forest Chocó and Darién biogeographic zones in the north and the Ecuadorian and Peruvian dry forest zone in the south, with a number of subtle geographic and biological barriers within these. The variety of ecosystem types in such a limited geographic area has given rise to high levels of diversity and endemism, and overall plant diversity in the hotspot is estimated at 11 000 species; plant endemism is estimated at 25%, which gives a figure of 2 750 endemic species of vascular plants for this hotspot. Plant diversity in the Colombian portion of the hotspot alone reaches an estimated 5 000 total species (G. Galeano, pers. comm.), and it is thought that the Colombian Chocó is likely to be the most floristically diverse site in the Neotropics. Based on an assessment of the Missouri Botanical Garden's TROPICOS Database, it has been estimated that we need five times the number of plant collections that have been made to date to be reasonably certain of the region's plant diversity. The flora of the Galápagos Islands is represented by 699 species of vascular plants, of which at least 177 species are endemic (25.3%), and there are six endemic genera of flowering plants (Jørgensen and León-Yánez 1999; Valencia et al. 2000).

In terms of vertebrate diversity and endemism, the Tumbes-Chocó-Magdalena Hotspot is impressive. Bird diversity in the mainland portion of the hotspot is 892 regularly occurring species, with 112 endemics. There are also 13 endemic bird genera, 10 of which are monotypic and, with the exception of the spiny-faced antshrike (*Xenornis setifrons*, VU), all are represented by species considered not threatened by BirdLife International, which is surprising. BirdLife International also considers this region to be a very high priority, and recognizes six Endemic Bird Areas (EBAs) in the hotspot as here defined, including the Nechi Lowlands, the Darién Lowlands, the Darién Highlands, the Tumbesian Region, and the Chocó. The Tumbesian Region EBA, with 17 threatened bird species confined entirely to this EBA

(such as the white-winged guan, *Penelope albipennis*, and the Peruvian plantcutter, *Phytotoma raimondii*), is considered one of the three EBAs most critically in need of conservation action. The Chocó EBA has a total of 51 species confined to it, a total second only to the Atlantic Forest Lowlands EBA (Stattersfield et al. 1998). The Galápagos Islands form an EBA in their own right, with 22 endemic terrestrial species including the 12 species of Darwin's finches so important to Darwin's Theory of Evolution. Flagship species include the bizarre long-wattled umbrella bird (*Cephalopterus penduliger*, VU) and the blue-black grass quit (*Volatinia jacarina*), the latter being the common ancestor of the Galápagos finches.

Mammal diversity and endemism are also high in this hotspot, with 283 species, of which 10 are endemic, five of them on the Galápagos. The rice rats of the genus *Nesoryzomys* are confined entirely to the Galápagos Islands. The location of this hotspot at the transition zone between Central and South America results in the occurrence of some largely Central American mammal species (for instance, pocket gophers of the family Geomyidae) that can not be found elsewhere in the South American continent. Also among the mammals of this hotspot are a number of important primate flagships, including three species of spider monkey of the genus *Ateles* (*A. fusciceps*, *A. geoffroyi*, and *A. hybridus*, CR) and three species of bare-faced tamarins of the genus *Saguinus*: the cotton-top tamarin or *mono tití blanco* (*S. oedipus*, EN), the rufous-naped or Panamanian tamarin or *bichichi* (*S. geoffroyi*), and the white-footed tamarin or *tití del Chocó* (*S. leucopus*, VU). On the Galápagos Islands, the most recognizable flagship is the Galápagos Islands fur seal (*Arctocephalus galapagoensis*, VU), the smallest of the pinnipeds, with an adult length of about 1.5 m.

Reptile diversity is quite high in this hotspot, with an estimated 325 species, of which 98 are endemic (including 21 species on the Galápagos). The lizard genus *Anolis* is particularly well represented, with 42 species present, 30 of them endemic). There are also five endemic genera including *Emmochliophis*, for which the two species, *E. fugleri* and *E. miops*, are known only from a single male and a single female specimen from western Ecuador; *Teuchocercus*, with a single species, *T. keyi*, from Ecuador; and *Trachyboa*, represented by two species of snakes. The remaining two endemic genera are also among the hotspot's most remarkable flagship species, and both occur in the Galápagos: the marine iguana (*Amblyrhynchus cristatus*, VU) and the two threatened species of land iguana (*Conolophus* spp.).

Amphibian diversity is even more impressive, with 204 mainland species, of which 29 are endemic, including two species of caecilians (*Caecilia antioquiaensis* and *C. tenuissima*). There are no native amphibians on the Galápagos, although Fowler's snouted tree frog (*Scinax quinquefasciata*) has become established on Santa Cruz. Among the amphibians, the poison arrow or poi-

son dart frogs (*Dendrobates* spp.) of the family Dendrobatidae are important flagships. These beautiful, brightly colored little animals secrete toxic alkaloids through their skin, their bright aposematic coloration serving to warn predators that they are off limits. One species, the golden poison frog (*Phyllobates terribilis*, EN), a bright yellow species found only in the Río Saija Basin in the southern portion of the Colombian Chocó, is among the three most poisonous vertebrates in the world, and its toxicity is such that the local Emberá Indians poison their blowgun darts simply by rubbing them along the backs of these little frogs. Unfortunately, many of the known amphibian endemics have very limited ranges such as isolated ridge tops only a few square kilometers in extent, making them particularly vulnerable to extinction.

The coastal watersheds of northwestern South America have rather sparse fish faunas compared to the great watersheds of the Atlantic versant, and the hotspot contains only 251 species in 54 families. Miocene fossils from the Magdalena Basin show that the fauna was richer in the past and that many characteristic elements of the Amazon/Orinoco fauna were present prior to uplift of the Andes. Isolation following uplift has contributed to a moderate level of endemism, with 115 endemic species and seven endemic genera, centered primarily in the Magdalena and Atrato basins. There is also a single endemic species (*Ogilbia galapagosensis*) on the Galápagos.

As a whole, it is estimated that natural vegetation remaining in more or less pristine condition in this hotspot is approximately 24% of the original extent, with much of what remains occurring in the Colombian Chocó and parts of the Darién. Current threats to the region are the same as in most other hotspots, and range from direct conversion of land for both large- and small-scale agriculture, such as banana and African oil palm, to climate change and elevated ultraviolet radiation impacting amphibians and perhaps other species as well. Many different kinds of infrastructure development (such as roads, dams, and canals) are also planned for this region, and colonization is on the rise in many areas. Finally, hunting continues to be an issue in some parts of the hotspot, especially for several of the larger bird and mammal species.

The degree of threat varies considerably from region to region. The Ecuadorian portion of this hotspot is under the gravest threat at present, with only about 2% of the original forest cover remaining. The situation in the Panamanian Darién is substantially better, with some 65% of original forest cover still remaining, while the Chocó region of Colombia, and especially the Department of Chocó, remains largely intact. Mangrove ecosystems are under threat throughout this hotspot due to overexploitation for timber and fuelwood, and because they are cleared to give way to shrimp aquaculture, an activity that has already destroyed many Ecuadorian mangroves. The Galápagos Islands are severely impacted by invasive alien

On the opposite page, broad-billed motmot (Electron platyrhynchum), a widespread species. This photo was taken in Río Ñambí Nature Reserve, Colombia.
© **Patricio Robles Gil**/*Sierra Madre*

Above, Galápagos land iguana (Conolophus subcristatus) on Isla Plaza, one of two species of land iguanas endemic to the Galápagos.
© **Cristina G. Mittermeier**

species, and only three of the larger islands are considered unaltered by humans.

Portions of this hotspot, and especially the Chocó and western Ecuador, have been considered among the planet's highest priorities for conservation for more than twenty years (e.g., Gentry 1977, 1979). This has resulted in a wide range of conservation projects by national governments, multilateral and bilateral funding agencies, and international and national conservation organizations, which have led to the creation of a range of protected areas and many other conservation efforts of varying success. Presently, approximately 12.5% of the hotspot is considered protected; however, only 6.9% of the hotspot is conserved in IUCN categories I to IV. A large network of indigenous reserves and *comunas* (communal Black ancestral lands) exists throughout the hotspot, an example being that of several Awá Indigenous Reserves straddling the Colombia-Ecuador border. Although indigenous reserves do not necessarily protect the full range of biodiversity as well as a fully protected national park or biological reserve, they do have great significance for conservation and ensure more sustainable use of natural resources than Western forms of development. The Global Conservation Fund at Conservation International is currently supporting several initiatives in northwestern Ecuador, focused on protection of remaining intact lowland forests in and around the Cotacachi Cayapas Ecological Reserve and Awá Ethnic Reserve. Key interventions in this area include community-supported land acquisitions, purchase of logging concessions, community land titling, and development of community-based incentive agreements for conservation.

The Critical Ecosystem Partnership Fund (CEPF) has also made considerable investments in the Chocó-Manabí portion of this hotspot. Since this program began in January, 2002, some $3.3 million have been awarded to 24 different projects focused on field activities and strengthening local NGO capacity.

Elsewhere, other significant areas have been proposed for protection as well, including such biologically important zones as the Naya Corridor in the south-central Colombian Chocó (Departments of Valle and Cauca), the protection of which would help conserve an altitudinal transect from the peaks of the western Andean cordillera to the sea, and represent perhaps the last, best chance to conserve a representative sample of the Chocoan forest ecosystems.

Last, but not least, the Galápagos have long been a focus of conservation activity and investment, and the vast majority of this unique archipelago is now recognized as both a World Heritage Site and a Biosphere Reserve.

In summary, the Tumbes-Chocó-Magdalena Hotspot presents several challenges and opportunities. Given the relatively intact nature of the Chocó and the Darién, there is a better possibility of setting aside large blocks of forest habitat than in most other hotspots. At the same time, in the Ecuadorian portion of this hotspot, in both the wet and moist forests and the dry

forests, there exists the need for the same kind of immediate salvage-type operations required in some of the other highly degraded, endemic-rich hotspots like the lowland forests of the Philippines and the northeastern portion of Brazil's Atlantic Forest Region, which are also at or under 3% of their original extent. There is no doubt that the future of these Ecuadorian forests hangs in the balance, and that they must be placed at or near the top of any list of global biodiversity conservation priorities.

ATLANTIC FOREST

Gustavo A.B. da Fonseca[1, 2, 13] • Anthony Rylands[2]
Adriano Paglia[5] • Russell A. Mittermeier[1]

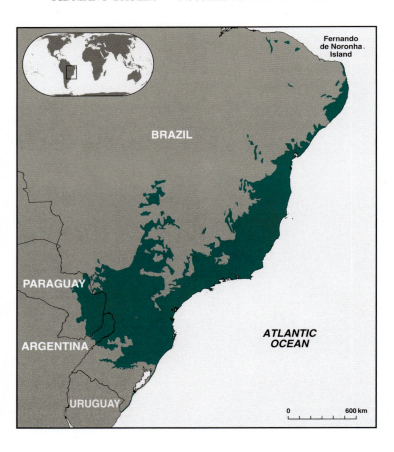

The Atlantic Forest, or *Mata Atlântica*, is a unique series of South American rainforest ecosystems quite distinct from the more extensive Amazonian Forests. It once extended almost continuously from the states of Rio Grande do Norte and Ceará in northeastern Brazil south to Rio Grande do Sul, and included the typical Atlantic coastal forest on the narrow, low-lying coastal plain, the forests on the foothills of the Serra do Mar and related mountain ranges that run roughly parallel to the coast, and the forests on the slopes of the Serra do Mar itself, reaching up to 1 800-2 000 m. In northeastern Brazil, these forests covered only a narrow coastal strip, rarely exceeding 50-100 km in width, and were replaced inland by drier Caatinga and Cerrado formations typical of the Brazilian interior. The Atlantic Forest also extends into eastern Paraguay, Misiones in extreme northern Argentina, and narrowly along the coast into Uruguay. Due to its widespread destruction, rampant even in the early sixteenth century, it is now difficult to

Agrias claudina photographed in the State of Santa Catarina, Brazil. Butterfly species reach a high level of diversity and endemism in the Atlantic Forest.
© **Luiz Claudio Marigo**

On the opposite page, the Critically Endangered northern muriqui monkey (Brachyteles hypoxanthus), here seen drinking from a stream on the forest floor, is one of Brazil's most threatened primate species, and one of two primate genera endemic to the Atlantic Forest Hotspot.
© **Luciano Candisani**

Although the Mexican portion of the hotspot accounts for the largest relative area of land under protection (41 835 km^2), this represents only 6.7% of the total 625 700 km^2 of the area of the hotspot in Mexico.

Conservation action to counter the ongoing threats to the Mesoamerica Hotspot concentrates on the creation and maintenance of the Mesoamerican Biological Corridor, as well as numerous other initiatives to integrate sustainable development with biodiversity conservation. Adopted by a host of donors, the region's governments, and four major international conservation groups —Conservation International, the World Wildlife Fund, The Nature Conservancy, and the Wildlife Conservation Society— during the 1980s, the Mesoamerican Biological Corridor has three objectives: to maintain the integrity of the protected areas that already exist in the Mesoamerica Hotspot; to determine where new protected areas need to be created in order to extend the corridor concept; and to connect these new and existing protected areas through the establishment of high conservation value forestry plantations and agroforestry systems that run between the corridor's existing parks, refuges, and biosphere reserves. This large-scale corridor strategy has gained wide support because it presents a simple, yet elegant structure on which to promote a wide range of conservation activities, such as biodiversity protection, buffer zone management, regional planning, and sustainable private enterprises based on regional development goals. This region is particularly important strategically for food security, since it is home to wild relatives of important crops such as maize, cacao, beans, and others.

A regional perspective such as the Mesoamerican Biological Corridor, among others, offers a much broader perspective concerning the natural range of variability seldom captured by national policy and within political borders. Planning should seek to combine local policy with the specific objectives of habitat connectivity for area-sensitive species, such as the jaguar; habitat-specialists, such as the resplendent quetzal; and narrow-ranging species, such as some *Atelopus* toad species. Equally important is the representation of the full range of the wide variety of ecosystems within protected areas. There is great potential to develop a regional network of transboundary protected areas, such as exists between Costa Rica and Panama (La Amistad International Park), a concept which is emerging elsewhere as well. The Critical Ecosystem Partnership Fund (CEPF) is facilitating a regional approach to promote conservation by supporting bi- and tri-national initiatives that rely on cooperation of governments and NGOs. The fact that there are eight countries in this hotspot, each with disparate political agendas and motivations, makes this a great challenge.

The Mesoamerica Hotspot also has within it a globally recognized model for the value of ecotourism as a foreign exchange earner and as an alternative to harmful extractive industries. For a variety of reasons, Costa Rica recognized early on the great potential for ecotourism and structured itself to take advantage of this source of income. As a result, Costa Rica earned $1.25 billion in tourism-related industries in 2000, and it is estimated that 70.7% of tourists visit natural protected areas —an enormous figure for a small country with a population of only 3.9 million people. On the other hand, there remains a very delicate balance between tourism potential and agriculture-based revenue generation.

In conclusion, although the problems in this region are many and the commitment to conservation varies from country to country, there exists in Mesoamerica a variety of mechanisms for regional-level government dialogue on the environment which are far better than in many other hotspots that spread over several sovereign nations. Other positive indicators include the shared vision of the Mesoamerican Biological Corridor; the high percentages of national territory already in parks and reserves in four of the eight nations (Costa Rica, Guatemala, Panama, Belize); the strong and growing local capacity that exists within the region; the proven value of alternatives like ecotourism and non-timber forest products; the development of several national-level institutions for biodiversity research and conservation; the promotion of sustainable use initiatives; and the continuing interest and involvement of a variety of donor agencies and international conservation organizations.

CARIBBEAN ISLANDS

MICHAEL LEONARD SMITH [2] • S. BLAIR HEDGES [117]
WILLIAM BUCK [118] • ARLO HEMPHILL [1]
SIXTO INCHAUSTEGUI [119] • MICHAEL A. IVIE [120]
DON MARTINA [121] • MICHAEL MAUNDER [122]
JAVIER FRANCISCO ORTEGA [122, 123]

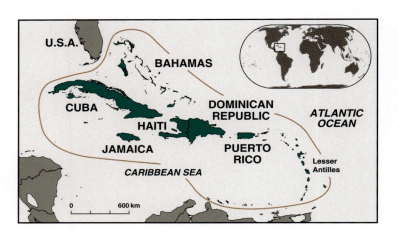

The Caribbean Islands Hotspot consists mainly of three large groups of islands between North and South America: the Bahamas, the Greater Antilles, and the Lesser Antilles. In contrast to the previous definition under the name Caribbean Hotspot, we now exclude southern Florida and its islands on the North American Continental Shelf because that area has greater floristic affinity to the rest of the continent, has few endemics, and has had only a marginal role in the phytogeographic history of the Antilles (Graham 2003). The Caribbean Islands themselves vary in their floristic affinities, but have in common a history of limited contact with the diverse biotas

A red-billed streamertail (Trochilus polytmus), a hummingbird species endemic to the island of Jamaica.
© **Mike Read**/naturepl.com

On the opposite page, Ricord's iguana (Cyclura ricordi), a Critically Endangered iguana species that is endemic to a very small area in the southern part of the Dominican Republic on the border with Haiti. It is sympatric with the more widespread rhinoceros iguana (C. cornuta), from which it can be readily distinguished by its red eyes.
© **Cristina G. Mittermeier**

of the continents. As a result, their biotas share an "oceanic" character marked by a relatively low representation of higher taxa, but also having extraordinary diversity within those higher phyletic groups that are present.

The Caribbean Islands Hotspot is commonly referred to as the West Indies in the English-language literature. Our definition differs only in a few minor details from a biotic region formally defined by James Bond in his *Birds of the West Indies* (1936). The islands of the West Indies have a terrestrial surface area of only 229 549 km². The four largest islands, Cuba (105 806 km²), Hispaniola (73 929 km²), Jamaica (11 190 km²), and Puerto Rico (9 100 km²) make up over 90% of the land area of the hotspot, but the myriad smaller islands harbor large numbers of endemic species far out of proportion to their size. Geologically, the West Indies are a mix of old regions of the Caribbean Tectonic Plate (Cuba, Jamaica, Hispaniola, Puerto Rico, the Virgin Islands, and their satellite islands), the tops of volcanoes (the active volcanic arc from Saba to Grenada), and slightly raised limestone platforms (the Caribees from Sombrero to Barbados, plus the Bahamas, the Cayman Islands, southern Dutch islands, and Aves Island). Elevations range from over 3 000 m (the formerly glaciated summit of Pico Duarte) to a desert depression 40 m below sea level, both on Hispaniola.

Politically, this is a very diverse hotspot, with thousands of islands governed by 18 nations. Twelve of these are independent island nations (Commonwealth of the Bahamas, Republic of Cuba, Jamaica, Republic of Haiti, Dominican Republic, Federation of St. Kitts and Nevis, Antigua and Barbuda, Commonwealth of Dominica, Barbados, St. Lucia, St. Vincent and the Grenadines, and Grenada). Fifteen polities are dependencies of, in free association with, or integral parts of: the United States of America (Puerto Rico, U.S. Virgin Islands, Navassa); the United Kingdom (Cayman Islands, Turks and Caicos Islands, British Virgin Islands, Anguilla, Montserrat); the Kingdom of the Netherlands (Aruba and the Netherlands Antilles including Curaçao, Bonaire, Saba, St. Eustatius, and St. Maarten); the Republic of France (Departments of Martinique and Guadeloupe, including its dependencies St. Martin and St. Barthelemy); the Republic of Honduras (Swan Islands), or the Bolivarian Republic of Venezuela (Aves Island west of Dominica, and oceanic islands from Blanquilla to Islas las Aves).

The vegetation of the Caribbean Islands is variable due to the influences of climate and Earth history. Low-lying islands tend to be semiarid, and most were originally dominated by dry evergreen bushland and dry evergreen thicket, with savanna occurring on parts of Barbuda, Jamaica, and Puerto Rico (where the average rainfall at low elevations is only 300-600 mm per year). On the other hand, wetter environments occur where trade winds encounter the higher Caribbean mountains, giving rise to a variety of moist tropical forest types including marsh forest, various types of seasonal forest, montane forest, and elfin woodland (Beard 1955). In moister areas, around lagoons and river mouths, permanent brackish and freshwater swamps give way to extensive mangrove forests. The previously extensive lowland rainforests have mostly been destroyed.

Plant diversity and endemism in the Caribbean Islands Hotspot are both very high, with a total of 13 000 species estimated to occur in the Caribbean region (Davis et al. 1997), including perhaps 6 550 single-island endemics. Cuba's flora is particularly rich, with an estimated 6 505 vascular plant species, of which 3 224 are endemic (Davis et al. 1997); this represents 54% of the endemic plants for the hotspot as a whole, and indeed would qualify Cuba as a hotspot in its own right. Plant endemism at the generic level is also high in these islands. Of an estimated 2 500 genera of seed plants in the Caribbean, 204 angiosperm genera and one gymnosperm genus (*Microcycas*) are endemic to the Greater Antilles. Of these, fully 118 are restricted to single islands. Important families with endemic genera include Asteraceae (32), Rubiaceae (30), Euphorbiaceae (14), and Leguminosae (13). There is one endemic plant family, the Goetziaceae (Davis et al. 1997). Even mosses, with notoriously broad distributions, have around 500 species in the Caribbean Islands, with about 10% endemism (Delgadillo et al. 1995).

Vertebrate diversity and endemism in this hotspot are noteworthy. Mammals are represented by 89 extant species, of which 41 are endemic, including two endemic families: the solenodons (*Solenodon* spp.), with two species of rare giant shrews, and a large radiation of rodents called hutias (family Capromyidae), which are related to guinea pigs. The region hosts 15 endemic genera, including the fruit-eating bat genus *Brachyphylla*, with two species.

Birds are represented by 607 species, of which 167 are endemic, with many of those restricted in total range to small areas within islands. A remarkable 35 genera are endemic, and there are also two endemic families: the palmchat (*Dulus dominicus*) of the family Dulidae, and the todies (Todidae). The bird list includes some important flagship species, such as the St. Vincent parrot (*Amazona guildingii*, VU) from the island of St. Vincent, the St. Lucia parrot (*A. versicolor*, VU) from the island of the same name, and the imperial parrot (*A. imperialis*, EN) from Dominica; the bee hummingbird (*Mellisuga helenae*) from Cuba, the world's smallest bird; and the ivory-billed woodpecker (*Campephilus principalis*, CR), last recorded with any certainty in Cuba in 1987.

The Caribbean Islands Hotspot is particularly rich in reptiles with 499 native species, of which 468 are endemic. There are several large evolutionary radiations of lizards, such as the anoles (*Anolis*; 154 species, 150 endemic) with their colorful dewlaps used in displays; dwarf geckos (*Sphaerodactylus*; 86 species, 82 endemic) that include the world's smallest lizards (e.g., *S. ariasae*, with a body length of 18 mm); and curly tails (*Leiocephalus*; 23 species, all endemic) that hold their tails in a coil as they run. There are 11 species of rock iguanas (*Cyclura*), including some measuring more than one meter in length, and one that is blue (*C. lewisi*); one of these species, the Jamaican iguana (*C. collei*, CR), is confined to the Hellshire Hills in Jamaica. A species considered to be an

On pp. 114-115, Los Haitises National Park in the Dominican Republic, one of an extensive network of protected areas in this small island nation.
© **Patricio Robles Gil**/*Sierra Madre*

Above, besides a population recently discovered on Isla de la Juventud, the Endangered Cuban crocodile (Crocodylus rhombifer) is known only from the Zapata Swamp, also in Cuba. Three other highly threatened species are found only in this extremely important national park.
© **Neil Lucas**/naturepl.com

ancient relict in the lizard family Xantusiidae, *Cricosaura typica*, occurs only in a remote part of eastern Cuba. Major radiations of snakes include the large boas (*Epicrates*, nine species); a genus of boldly patterned snakes that change colors (*Tropidophis*; 26 species, all endemic); fast-moving racers (*Alsophis*; 13 species, all endemic); and some pencil-thin and smaller burrowing snakes (*Typhlops* and *Leptotyphlops*) that include the smallest snake in the world (*L. bilineata*; 108 mm). The Aruba Island rattlesnake (*Crotalus unicolor*, CR) is found only on Aruba.

All 165 native species of amphibians present in the hotspot are frogs, of which 164 (99%) are endemic to the region. All but a few are endemic to single islands. The frog fauna is dominated by those of the genus *Eleutherodactylus* (139 spp.), which are forest frogs that lay eggs on land and hatch into miniature adults with no tadpole stage. One Cuban species (*E. iberia*, CR) is the smallest tetrapod in the Northern Hemisphere, with a length of only 10 mm, while a golden-colored species in Puerto Rico, possibly Extinct, is one of only a few species of frogs in the world known to be live-bearing. One of the largest tree frogs (Hylidae) in the world, the Jamaican snoring frog (*Osteopilus crucialis*, EN), has a length of about 120 mm and occurs in Jamaica, where males of this declining species make a loud snoring call from within giant, hollow trees. The toads (*Bufo*; 11 species) have also radiated in the West Indies, and captive-breeding programs have been implemented for the Puerto Rican crested toad (*B. lemur*, CR). An edible species of frog endemic to Dominica and Montserrat, the "mountain chicken" (*Leptodactylus fallax*, CR), is one of the largest frogs in the Western Hemisphere, but has been rapidly declining in numbers due to human consumption, habitat loss, and an outbreak of chytridiomycosis on Dominica.

The hotspot's inland fishes include 161 species, of which 65 are endemic to one or a few islands. Nearly half of the endemics are restricted to very small ranges, often consisting of a single lake or springhead, and these sites constitute the sole opportunities for conservation of these species in nature. As in other hotspots that are composed of islands, the freshwater fish fauna consists of two distinctive elements. The smaller and younger islands have faunas dominated by species that are widespread in marine waters, but that enter fresh water to some degree, especially when obligate freshwater species are absent or few in number. This component accounts for the relatively high diversity at the family level. The larger and older islands of the Greater Antilles differ in having faunas dominated by several groups that are old enough to have occupied inland waters of the proto-islands and continental coasts prior to extensive plate tectonic movements. These groups (e.g., gars, killifishes, silversides, and cichlids) include significant local radiations, which account for the hotspot's moderate number of endemic species. The hotspot's five endemic fish genera all have distributions that overlap in western Cuba, apparently the oldest part of the hotspot that has remained continuously above sea level.

Humans first populated the islands about 4 000 years ago, and there is evidence that even the early inhabitants were involved in modifying the biota through direct use or, perhaps more far-reaching, through the introduction of species from the continents. Early species introductions include the agouti on Dominica, tortoises on many islands, and possibly even large animals such as white-tailed deer (*Odocoileus virginianus*) on Curaçao. Introductions of species were enormously accelerated after the arrival of Europeans, whose transportation technologies led to the import of species —both intentionally and accidentally— from all parts of the globe. The introduction of the Indian mongoose (*Herpestes auropunctatus*) from Asia in 1872 resulted in a series of extinctions as it was moved from island to island. Even small, uninhabitable islands such as Navassa and Sombrero now have floras dominated by continental weed species, and throughout the hotspot native amphibian, reptile, and bird faunas have been devastated by rats and domestic cats and dogs. In total, some 36 vertebrate species are considered to have gone extinct in the region since 1500, including species like the Cuban macaw (*Ara tricolor*), Jamaican giant galliwasp (*Celestus occiduus*), and four species of *Nesophontes* (relatives of the solenodons).

The islands have been subject to Western-style development including extensive monoculture for five hundred years, longer than any other part of the New World. For most of this period, the exploration and development of the islands' natural resources were carried out by colonial centers outside the Caribbean Basin. In many cases, Caribbean natural resources were simply liquidated (e.g., semiprecious hardwoods of Haiti and many other states). The widespread cultivation of sugarcane (*Saccharum officinarum*) was also conducted for the benefit of foreign economies and, similarly, resulted in broad transformation of island landscapes. Consequently, as a result of changes that have taken place since European arrival, only a small portion of the vegetation that once existed still remains in more or less pristine condition, and it is estimated that intact vegetation covers no more than 10% of the original extent of the land area. Interestingly, although less than 15% of Cuba's original forests remain intact, they still represent the largest forested areas remaining in the Antilles.

According to the World Database on Protected Areas, some 12.9% of the hotspot is officially protected in a variety of different conservation units, although only 7.1% is conserved in protected areas classified in IUCN categories I to IV. In the largest Caribbean country, Cuba, about 15% of the total land area falls within protected areas, including the 300-km^2 Zapata Swamp, home to the Cuban crocodile (*Crocodylus rhombifer*, EN), the Zapata rail (*Cyanolimnas cerverai*, EN), the Zapata wren (*Ferminia cerverai*, EN), and the dwarf hutia (*Mesocapromys nanus*, CR), all threatened species found nowhere else. The country of Dominica leads in percentage coverage, with 21.4% of its territory designated for protection, while other countries also report relatively high protection (for example, the Dominican

A handful of hatchling Cuban crocodiles from a breeding facility in Cuba. This Endangered species is endemic to Cuba and is now restricted to the Zapata Swamp and Isla de la Juventud.
© **Cristina G. Mittermeier**

Republic, with 15%). However, in many of these countries, the existing protected area network is ineffective and poorly managed, while in other nations in the Caribbean protected areas are almost nonexistent. Haiti and Grenada, for example, both have only 1.7% of their respective land areas under protection, while Barbados and Aruba Island each have less than 1%. Indeed, in a recent global gap analysis, the Caribbean Islands emerge as a region of high urgency for expansion of the protected areas network (Rodrigues et al. 2003).

Prospects for the protection of biodiversity have been greatly enhanced by the development of alliances between major industries, such as tourism, and the governmental and private organizations that carry out conservation on the ground. Protected area systems are now being designed for the dual goals of safeguarding biodiversity and contributing to island livelihoods. A significant advance occurred in 2000, when the Protocol for Specially Protected Areas and Wildlife (SPAW) came into force. Created at the initiative of the Caribbean countries themselves, this protocol provides region-wide standards and mechanisms for harmonizing conservation efforts across the hotspot's diverse cultures and political systems.

CALIFORNIA FLORISTIC PROVINCE

WILLIAM R. KONSTANT [1, 7] • DEAN TAYLOR [100]
DAVID A. WAKE [101] • SCOTT ROBBINS LOARIE [102]
ROXANNE BITTMAN [103] • BARBARA ERTTER [104]

On the opposite page, rhododendrons in bloom, Redwood National Park, California, U.S.A.
© **Carr Clifton**/*Minden Pictures*

The California Floristic Province is one of the five Mediterranean-type hotspots and the only hotspot that occurs largely within the borders of the United States of America. Stretching nearly 1 800 km along the western coast of North America, most of its 293 804 km² are found within the State of California, with extensions into southwestern Oregon and northwestern Baja California, Mexico. All areas west of the peaks of the Cascade and Sierra Nevada ranges are included within its boundaries, as are a handful of islands off California's southwestern coast, including the Channel Islands (913 km²), and Isla Guadalupe (264 km²), located some 300 km west of Baja California.

As its name implies, the California Floristic Province is an ecological construct based on plant species composition, a unique mixture of northern temperate and southern xeric elements fostered by a Mediterranean climate of hot, dry summers and cool, wet winters. Four other hotspots share this climate: Central Chile, the Cape Floristic Region, Southwestern Australia, and the Mediterranean Basin (Barbour et al. 1993; Dallmann 1998).

Four subregions within the Province stand out as centers of exceptionally high plant diversity: the Sierra Nevada, Transverse Ranges, Klamath-Siskiyou region, and Coast Ranges (Stebbins 1978; Davis et al. 1997). Rare plant communities of the southern Sierra Nevada include the giant sequoia (*Sequoiadendron giganteum*) forest, piute cypress woodland, and lone manzanita shrubland (Grossman et al. 1994). The Transverse Ranges are a narrow strip that runs east to west in southern California, separating the Coast Ranges to the north from the Peninsular Ranges to the south. At least 10 rare plant communities have been recorded from this region. The Klamath-Siskiyou region bridges the coastal mountain ranges of California and Oregon, and is home to approximately 20 rare plant communities, including the most diverse temperate coniferous tree community in the world (Vance-Borland et al. 1995-1996). This region also represents the contact zone between the Pacific Northwest Floristic Province and the California Floristic Province. The Coast Ranges comprise a wide variety of habitats, including coastal dune, coastal salt marsh, maritime chaparral, coastal cypress forest, redwood forest, mixed evergreen forest, mixed hardwood-redwood forest, northern yellow pine forest, southern oak forest, *Calocedrus* forest, mixed hardwoods, valley oak savanna, coastal prairie scrub, vernal pools, and freshwater marshes, within which at least a dozen rare plant communities can be found (Steinhart 1994; Davis et al. 1997). The unusually high plant diversity in the Coast and Transverse ranges, coupled with the disproportionate human habitat preference for lowlands and foothills near the coast, puts these regions at special risk (Seabloom et al. 2002).

Some of the highest levels of plant diversity within the California Floristic Province are found in the southern part of the Sierra Nevada Range and in the Klamath-Siskiyou region (Davis et al. 1997). In addition, serpentine soil habitats occur along fault zones in the Central and North Coast and Cascade ranges, from sea level to an elevation of 2 900 m. Due to specific chemical and physical characteristics of the soils, these habitats are nutrient-poor, and this has led to the

establishment of a highly specialized and diverse flora (Davis et al. 1997). It has been estimated that serpentine endemic plant species represent 10% of the California Floristic Province's endemics (Kruckeberg 1984).

High levels of species diversity and endemism have developed within this region due to its varied topography, climate zones, geology, and soils. Plant diversity is exceptional, with 3 488 native vascular species, including 2 124 endemics. Fifty-two of the region's plant genera are also unique. The total number of plant species is greater than that for the central and northeastern United States and adjacent portions of Canada, an area almost 10 times as large (Raven and Axelrod 1978; Raven 1988; Davis et al. 1997).

The region's impressive endemism is a mixture of outstanding relicts and newly derived species (Stebbins and Major 1965). Many of the relicts once had much larger ranges in the Tertiary, but during the cooling and drying trends that accompanied the ice age in North America, these species became restricted to the California region's relatively mild climate. Because many of these relicts have no extant close relatives, they are particularly important botanically. The most famous relicts that best symbolize the region are the giant sequoia and coastal redwood (*Sequoia sempervirens*). The giant sequoia, known to reach more than 75 m in height and 30 m in circumference, is believed to be the largest species that ever lived. Although coastal redwoods are among the world's tallest trees, with record specimens surpassing 105 m, they are far less massive than their relatives. Other noteworthy relict trees include the ironwood trees (*Lyonothamnus floribundus*) endemic to Santa Cruz and Santa Catalina islands, and the California bay laurel (*Umbellularia californica*). The region's newly produced species result from recent outbursts of speciation within certain genera —primarily annual herbaceous dicots— in response to climate fluctuations since the Middle Pliocene in areas increasingly diverse geographically (Raven and Axelrod 1978). Genera such as *Clarkia*, *Lasthenia*, and *Phacelia* have undergone remarkable radiations. The above-mentioned serpentine endemic species represent examples of such newly produced endemics.

While plant endemism is impressive, vertebrate diversity and endemism are less so. Of approximately 341 resident, breeding, and migrant bird species, only eight are endemic, as are 18 of the 151 native terrestrial mammals. Four of the 69 native reptiles are endemic, including two species found only on Cedros Island, 12.9 km off the Baja California Peninsula: the Cedros Island diamond rattlesnake (*Crotalus exsul*) and Cedros Island horned lizard (*Phrynosoma cerroense*).

The highest levels of endemism are found among the amphibians, with 25 endemic species out of a total of 54. The salamander fauna of California is especially noteworthy for the high degree of endemism and its uniqueness: 38 described species, 24 of which are endemic. The region contains one of the two best-understood complexes, the ensatina (*Ensatina eschschol-*

tzii), which demonstrate stages in the pattern and process of species formation. It also contains the arboreal salamanders (genus *Aneides*, with three endemic species), which ascend to the tops of the tallest redwoods. The slender salamanders of the genus *Batrachoseps* are especially diverse, and only one of the 18 currently recognized species does not occur in the hotspot. Included in this genus are the only truly desert-adapted fully terrestrial salamanders (two species), as well as the distinctive San Gabriel Mountains slender salamander (*B. gabrieli*), discovered recently in mountains in the Los Angeles Metropolitan Area.

Isolated from the large eastern North American fish fauna by the western mountains and deserts, the California Floristic Province Hotspot has a relatively small fauna of inland fishes comprising 73 native species. One of the most distinctive elements is a concentration of lamprey species that includes a cluster of localized landlocked species in the northern mountains. Lampreys represent the deepest offshoot of living vertebrates, and eight of the world's 43 surviving species occur in this hotspot. Together with two sturgeons that represent another of the deepest vertebrate lineages, these species cause the hotspot to rank with Japan as global leaders in phyletic rarity for fishes.

Among vertebrates, there are some important flagship species. The grizzly bear (*Ursus arctos*) has been the California state symbol for more than 150 years, and is immortalized in the names of creeks, mountains, peaks, and valleys throughout California. Some might consider it a classic flagship species for this hotspot, despite the fact that it has been extirpated; the last California grizzly was shot sometime in the 1920s (Wirka 1994). Also, of the world's 13 subspecies of elk or wapiti, two —Roosevelt's elk (*Cervus elaphus roosevelti*) and the tule elk (*C. e. nannodes*), the largest and the smallest of the North American subspecies, respectively— are native to the California Floristic Province and served as flagships for conservation throughout the last century. One species that has received a great deal of attention is the endemic California tiger salamander (*Ambystoma californiense*, VU), currently a major point of contention in rapidly growing Sonoma and Santa Barbara counties. Animals perhaps less well-known, but very effective symbols for local action, include the San Francisco garter snake (*Thamnophis sirtalis tetrataenia*), California gnatcatcher (*Polioptila californica*), and island fox (*Urocyon littoralis*), the latter with six subspecies all confined to the six largest of the eight California Channel Islands. In salt marshes around San Francisco Bay, the salt-marsh harvest mouse (*Reithrodontomys raviventris*, VU) faces dual pressures from encroaching development and feral house cats.

The most important flagship, however, remains the California condor (*Gymnogyps californianus*, CR), North America's largest bird, and a strong symbol for wildlife conservation in the western part of the continent. Native Americans considered the condor a sacred animal with supernatural powers, but westward-moving

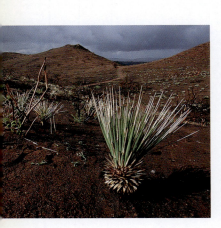

Chaparral yucca (Yucca whipplei), *or Our Lord's Candle as it is also known, in an area of burn recovery in dry coastal sage scrub following fires in San Diego County, California, October 2003. There is an interesting symbiotic relationship between this species and the California yucca moth* (Tegeticula maculata).
© Richard Herrmann

On the opposite page, coreopses (Coreopsis spp.) *and California poppies* (Eschscholzia californica), *the state flower, in Antelope Valley California Poppy Reserve.*
© Carr Clifton/Minden Pictures

pioneers shot these birds for target practice, collected their eggs, and poisoned the animals upon which they fed. The species was a hair's breadth away from extinction. Today, however, thanks to a collaborative captive-breeding and reintroduction effort involving the U.S. Fish and Wildlife Service, California Department of Fish and Game, National Audubon Society, Zoological Society of San Diego, Los Angeles Zoo, and The Peregrine Fund, captive-bred California condors are being returned to the wild.

California is the most populated (estimated at 35 million people in 2002; U.S. Census Bureau) and fastest-growing state in the United States, and this severely impacts biodiversity within the hotspot (Jensen et al. 1993). Urbanization, air pollution, agricultural expansion, logging, strip mining, oil extraction, road construction, livestock grazing, the spread of non-native plants, an increasing use of off-road vehicles, and the suppression of natural fires all pose significant threats. Human population pressures have rendered California one of the four most ecologically degraded states in the country, with all or part of the nation's eight most threatened ecosystems represented: beach and coastal strand, southern California coastal sage scrub, large streams and rivers, California riparian forests and wetlands, California native grasslands, old-growth ponderosa pine forests, cave and karst systems, and the ancient forests of the Pacific Northwest, which include the coastal redwoods (Noss 1994; Noss and Peters 1995).

Today, native grasslands and vernal pool habitats have been reduced to perhaps 1% of their original extent (Holland and Jain 1990), and wetlands, riparian woodlands, and southern maritime sage scrub to 10% or less. Saltwater and freshwater wetlands once covered almost two million hectares in California, but have since declined by about 90% due largely to landfilling and the diversion of river systems. As a result, so have significant shellfish, fish, and waterfowl populations (Barbour et al. 1993). Along California's lowland rivers, riparian forests provide essential wildlife habitat. However, the 4 000 km^2 or more of riparian forests found two centuries ago in California's Central Valley have been reduced by 90% due to logging, grazing, and industrial development. Along the coast, redwoods evolved to thrive in a mild, foggy maritime climate until logging began in earnest in the mid-nineteenth century, largely to supply construction needs in San Francisco. Mechanized timber extraction has effectively reduced original stands by 85% since cutting began, although, as *Sequoia* is one of the only stump-sprouting conifers, many of these stands have regenerated. In total, we estimate that no more than 25% of the California Floristic Province remains in pristine condition.

California has a long history of conservation. In 1864, U.S. President Abraham Lincoln established California's Yosemite Valley and the Mariposa Grove of Giant Sequoias as the first national area to receive protection explicitly for public use (Turner 1991).

Together with Sequoia National Park, it offers protection for outstanding biodiversity within the southern Sierra Nevada. Redwood National Park, officially established in 1968 (and expanded in 1978), has evolved over more than 35 years of intensive conservation effort. By contrast, the 1 010-km^2 Channel Islands National Park provides protection for nesting colonies of seabirds and breeding populations of seals and sea lions. In total, approximately 37% of this hotspot has some form of official protection, although protected areas offering a stricter level of protection (IUCN categories I to IV) cover only 10.2% of the hotspot's surface area. The creation of many protected areas was brought about largely through the actions of groups such as the Sierra Club, Wilderness Society, and The Nature Conservancy. Unfortunately, while a considerable degree of protection has resulted for the high-elevation flora, much less, if any, protection has been accomplished for the serpentine or vernal pool subsets of the endemic flora.

In conclusion, while the California Floristic Province lies largely within one of the world's richest nations and contains some of Earth's most famous and most popular national parks, it suffers from threats similar to those operating in hotspots found within countries that are much more disadvantaged economically. Furthermore, a great deal remains to be done in order to ensure that the unique and threatened biodiversity of this hotspot is adequately safeguarded in suitable protected areas. Biodiversity loss clearly is not a problem unique to developing tropical nations.

GUINEAN FORESTS OF WEST AFRICA

Mohamed Bakarr[55] • John F. Oates[56] • Jakob Fahr[57]
Marc Parren[58] • Mark-Oliver Rödel[59] • Ron Demey[60]

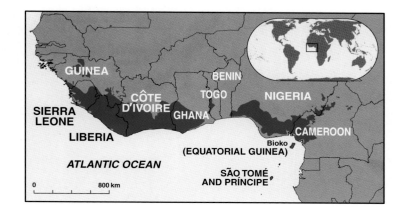

On the opposite page, West African forests still harbor many species new to science, such as this attractive unnamed toad of the Bufo togoensis *complex.*
© Piotr Naskrecki

The Guinean Forests of West Africa Hotspot extends from Guinea and Sierra Leone eastwards to the Sanaga River in Cameroon. These forests originally covered an estimated 620 314 km^2 and form the westerly part of the Guineo-Congolian Regional Center of Endemism defined by White (1983). Although biogeographically distinct, the hotspot comprises two forest blocks: the

Upper Guinea block, which extends from Guinea to Togo; and the Nigeria-Cameroon block, extending to the Sanaga River. The two units are separated by the Dahomey Gap in Benin, an area that is now a mixture of farmland, derived savanna woodland, and relict patches of dry forest.

Although the West African forest region traditionally is separated from the Central African forests by the Cross River in eastern Nigeria, the hotspot as here defined extends into Cameroon as far as the Sanaga River (Oates 1986; Martin 1991; IUCN 1996), and includes such high-priority areas as Korup National Park and the Cameroon Highlands. The Nigeria-Cameroon border region is under a level of threat comparable to that of Upper Guinea. The hotspot also includes several important montane regions, such as the aforementioned Cameroon Highlands (the high point being Mount Cameroon, at 4 095 m) and the Upper Guinea, or Greater Nimba, Highlands, between Guinea, Sierra Leone, Liberia, and Côte d'Ivoire.

The two major forest blocks in this hotspot also correspond to two important centers of endemism: Upper Guinea, which corresponds to that portion of the hotspot west of the Gap, and the Nigeria-Cameroon border region plus Bioko Island. The region from Ghana to the Cross River is transitional and supports overlapping generalist species shared by the two forest blocks, such as the mona monkey (*Cercopithecus mona*) and chimpanzee (*Pan troglodytes*, EN).

Also included in this hotspot are four islands located in the Gulf of Guinea to the west of the southern limits of the region (and sometimes referred to as the "Galápagos of Africa"): Bioko (Fernando Po; 2 017 km²) and Annobon (Pagalu; 17 km²), both now part of Equatorial Guinea; and São Tomé (857 km²) and Príncipe (139 km²), which together constitute an independent nation. Bioko is a continental-shelf island, supporting a much more diverse flora and fauna, but with a relatively low rate of endemism at the species level, whereas the remaining three are oceanic and relatively depauperate because of their isolation, but rich in endemic taxa (Jones 1994).

The Guinean forests include a range of distinct vegetation zones varying from moist forests along the coast, freshwater swamp forests (for example, around the Niger Delta), to dry, semi-deciduous forests inland with prolonged dry seasons. Of all West African countries, only Liberia lies entirely within the moist forest zone, although a substantial portion of Sierra Leone also falls within the boundaries. In Ghana, derived savanna reaches the coast around Accra, where the average annual rainfall falls below 1 200 mm. This savanna merges into the highly threatened dry forest of the Togo-Volta Highlands and the Dahomey Gap, which ends in eastern Benin. Moist forest continues from there —originally uninterrupted— through the Cross River region in southern Nigeria to Cameroon.

Vascular plant diversity for the entire Guinea-Congolian phytochorion has been estimated to be close to 12 000 species, with 6 400 endemics (Davis et al. 1994). Upper Guinea alone holds about 2 800 species, of which nearly 25% are lianas, while some 530 vascular plants are endemics (Poorter et al. 2004). Site-specific studies such as those of Cable and Cheek (1998), who recorded 2 435 plant species from Mount Cameroon (49 of them endemic), suggest that overall plant diversity in the Guinean forest ecosystem may be as high as 9 000 species. Based on these figures, knowledge of the 185 endemics recorded from the Gulf of Guinea, and using endemism in the Upper Guinea block as an indication of endemism overall, the figure for vascular plant endemism for the region as a whole is estimated at 20%, or 1 800 species.

The Guinean Forests Hotspot also contains a rich and unique faunal assemblage. An important feature of the Guinean forest fauna is that many of the endemic species tend to have highly restricted ranges within the hotspot, making many of these species extremely vulnerable to forest destruction. For example, the Upper Guinea Highlands are home to an exceptionally high number of endemic bats and amphibians with restricted ranges, all of which are Critically Endangered or Endangered.

About 63 of the estimated 320 mammal species are endemic to the region; in addition, there are seven endemic genera, including monotypic genera such as the Liberian mongoose (*Liberiictis kuhni*, EN). Another monotypic genus, the pygmy hippo (*Hexaprotodon liberiensis*, VU), an appealing miniature of its huge cousin, is endemic to Guinean forests, with one subspecies in Upper Guinea and one in the Niger Delta. This hippo is an important flagship species, as are a handful of other Upper Guinea endemics such as Jentink's duiker (*Cephalophus jentinki*, VU), the zebra duiker (*C. zebra*, VU), the Diana monkey (*Cercopithecus diana*, EN), and Preuss' guenon (*C. preussi*, EN).

Avian diversity is also particularly high, with an estimated 793 species that are considered to occur regularly in this hotspot, of which 75 species and six genera are endemic. BirdLife International recognizes most of the Guinean Forests as a conservation priority for birds, with five Endemic Bird Areas (EBAs) lying partly or entirely within the hotspot. These include the Upper Guinea Forests, with 15 species confined entirely to this EBA, including the Liberian greenbul (*Phyllastrephus leucolepis*, CR); and the Cameroon Mountains, with a remarkable 27 endemic species, among them the enigmatic Mount Kupe bush-shrike (*Telophorus kupeensis*, EN). São Tomé, Príncipe, and Annobon are all considered distinct EBAs.

Reptile and amphibian diversity is less well documented. Preliminary minimum estimates indicate 206 species of reptiles and 246 species of amphibians, of which roughly 52 reptiles and 83 amphibians are endemic to the region as defined. There are also seven

On pp. 124-125, a small stream flowing along the floor of the rainforest in the Guinean Forests of West Africa Hotspot.
© Piotr Naskrecki

Above, a hingeback tortoise (Kinixys erosa) in Tai National Park, Cote d'Ivoire. Hingebacks are widely distributed in sub-Saharan Africa, especially in forested areas, but are rarely seen.
© Patricio Robles Gil/Sierra Madre

On the opposite page, Lowe's guenon (Cercopithecus lowei) in the Tai Forest region of Cote d'Ivoire. This species is endemic to the Guinean Forests of West Africa Hotspot.
© Patricio Robles Gil/Sierra Madre

endemic amphibian genera, and a single endemic reptile genus (*Cophoscincopus*) comprising three lizard species. Many more species are likely to be discovered; for example, during the last ten years, 11 new frog species have been described from the region and many more still await description. Spectacular species in this region are the goliath frog (*Conraua goliath*, EN), the world's largest anuran; and the Mount Nimba toad (*Nimbaphrynoides occidentalis*, CR), a species outstanding for its reproductive biology in that, following a gestation period of nine months, they give birth to fully developed toadlets.

There are an estimated 512 species of freshwater fishes in this hotspot, about 35% of which are endemic, making it a truly remarkable area for fish biodiversity. About 25% of the world's 350 species of killifish occur in this hotspot, and about half of these are endemic. Cichlid fishes also feature prominently in this hotspot, with 37 (out of 62) endemic species and five endemic genera. Four of these endemic genera (*Konia*, *Myaka*, *Pungu*, and *Stomatepia*) are known only from Lake Barombi Mbo, a crater lake in northwest Cameroon.

The Guinean Forests Hotspot is one of the most severely threatened forest systems in the world, with extreme habitat fragmentation and degradation throughout most of the region. According to Forest Resources Assessment 2000 figures, remaining forest cover in each of the countries within the hotspot totals 716 200 km², although this includes all of Cameroon, which falls only partly in the hotspot. Other earlier estimates put remaining forest cover at 15% for the entire Guinean forest ecosystem, including the islands (Sayer et al. 1992; WRI 1992; Parren and De Graaf 1995). Taking the more or less pristine forests into consideration, we believe that the total is considerably less, but in the absence of more solid figures we use the figure of 15% in our global analysis.

Presently, the major threat is deforestation, due to commercial logging and slash-and-burn agriculture, both of which are prevalent in all Guinean forest countries. Plantation agriculture (e.g., oil palm, rubber, bananas, and cacao) has been very significant in replacing forest in Côte d'Ivoire, parts of Ghana, southern Nigeria, western Cameroon, and Bioko. There is already a negative feedback of deforestation on the regional and local climate, resulting in decreased annual precipitation and prolonged dry seasons. Most of the moist and dry forests within the Guinean region are already at the climatic margin where the respective forest types can persist. The coupled effects of global and regional climate change seriously threaten vast stretches of the remaining areas that today are still forested.

Both small-scale and industrial-scale mining are also serious threats to the remaining Guinean forests. In many of the countries, particularly in the Upper Guinea Highlands, forests are located on substrates that are often rich in high-grade iron ore, diamonds, gold or bauxite. In addition, the Gulf of Guinea harbors one of the richest oil fields on a global scale.

Bushmeat hunting is one of the major threats to larger animal species in the Guinean forests. Although bushmeat has long been an important component of the diet of rural West Africa, growing urban populations, improved road networks, and increased access to forests have created a huge commercialized trading system for it both nationally and internationally. Numerous studies have indicated that the bushmeat trade in the region is enormous; estimates of its value in Ghana run as high as US$400 million per year and for Côte d'Ivoire, $500 million (see Bakarr et al. 2001). Although it is unlikely that the bushmeat trade can ever be completely controlled in an area where it is such an integral part of the culture, efforts should be made to curb or eliminate hunting of the most extinction-prone species, such as red colobus monkeys (Oates et al. 2000). If such efforts are not promoted, then we will likely see full realization of an "Empty Forest Syndrome" whereby, structurally, forest looks rather undisturbed, but in which the larger mammals are either reduced to very small numbers or completely extirpated (see, for example, Oates 1999).

The region's political instability has also contributed to forest destruction. In the 1990s, the United Nations High Commissioner for Refugees documented over a million refugees fleeing civil wars and persecution in Liberia and Sierra Leone and seeking safety in Guinea, Côte d'Ivoire, and Ghana. This number has increased significantly in recent years with the outbreak of conflict in Côte d'Ivoire. Refugee communities impact forests by settling in uninhabited areas, placing increasing pressure on resources through demands for fuelwood and food resources such as bushmeat. Environmental impacts of refugees do not necessarily end when peace accords are signed, and indeed can be exacerbated. Many times, there is a need for more land during repatriation and resettlement. Very often the only uninhabited land available is in forest parks and reserves.

Weak and inefficient governance constitutes a problem in most of the countries in this region, again meaning that laws and protected areas on paper may not be well enforced. One of the outcomes is that illegal logging is on the rise since timber is becoming scarce. For instance, Ghana is able to produce one million cubic meters sustainably from its forest reserves and the wider agricultural landscape. However, in 2002, Ghana's Minister for Lands and Forestry admitted that "the total quantity of logs removed in 1999 amounted to 3.7 million cubic meters, four times the annual allowable cut."

Since the late 1960s, efforts have been under way in all the countries to establish more strictly controlled,

On the opposite page, an African palm civet (Nandinia binotata) sold for food by a roadside vendor near Monrovia, Liberia. A wide range of species are sold for the bushmeat trade in this region.
© **Haroldo Castro**

Above, a family of lowland gorillas (Gorilla gorilla gorilla) killed for meat in Cameroon. The bushmeat trade is widespread in West and Central Africa and is a major threat to wildlife throughout the region.
© **Karl Ammann**/naturepl.com

and effectively managed, protected areas. However, the area of forest incorporated into strict protected areas is still small compared to the area of closed forest cover remaining in each of the countries. An analysis of the protected areas coverage in this hotspot yields some interesting results. Approximately 17% of the original extent of the hotspot is considered to have some form of protection; however, when one considers only those classified in IUCN categories I to IV, then the percentage drops to just 3%. The management of protected areas such as national parks has been almost universally lax, with rampant hunting still occurring, except in limited areas where there are long-term wildlife research projects.

To ensure long-term survival of many forest species, it is imperative that remaining forest areas be given more adequate protection and that as many existing forest reserves as possible be elevated to National Park status. While this is being done, it is also important to consider broader landscape approaches, identifying mechanisms like corridors, in order to connect these fragmented protected areas with one another through whatever means possible (Parren et al. 2002). In 1999, Conservation International held a priority-setting workshop in Elmina, Ghana, which defined priority actions and areas for the Upper Guinea forest block (Bakarr et al. 2001). The following year, the U.S.-based World Wildlife Fund organized and led a similar process for the Congo Basin forests, and extended it to the Nigeria-Cameroon forest block. The two workshops have together established a regional vision for biodiversity conservation in the entire Guinean forests, and should stimulate transboundary conservation initiatives and foster integration among West African countries.

Although civil strife in Côte d'Ivoire, Liberia, and Sierra Leone continues to pose major constraints for conservation investment in the hotspot, moderate progress has been made with the regional conservation vision. With the five-year, $5-million investment in the Upper Guinea forest block from the Critical Ecosystem Partnership Fund (CEPF), most priority areas and actions identified in the region are already being addressed. The CEPF investment has been particularly crucial in mobilizing locally based conservation organizations as well as civil society groups, mainly through partnerships with international organizations. In addition, CEPF investment has also catalyzed new investments from bilateral donors and the private sector. For example, CI and local partners are implementing conservation activities in the Upper Guinea Highlands with support from the U.S. Agency for International Development (USAID) and Rio Tinto. The Global Conservation Fund at CI is also contributing significantly through innovative mechanisms to increase the area of forests under protection across the hotspot.

The South African bowsprit or angulate tortoise (Chersina angulata) is the most common of the endemic tortoises of South Africa, and is particularly abundant in parts of the Cape Floristic Region.
© **Tony Heald**/naturepl.com

On the opposite page, a spring bloom at Ramskop Nature Reserve in the Clanwilliam area of the Western Cape. Namaqualand's spectacular flowers attract visitors from around the world every September.
© **Gerald Cubitt**

CAPE FLORISTIC REGION

RICHARD M. COWLING [28] • SHIRLEY M. PIERCE [29]

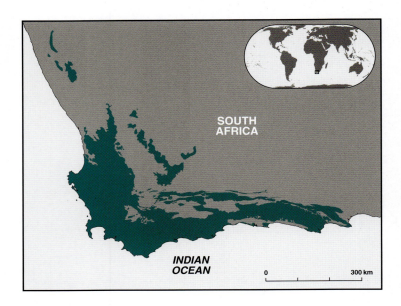

The Cape Floristic Region is located at the southwestern tip of the African Continent and lies entirely within the borders of South Africa. It is one of the five Mediterranean-type systems on the hotspots list, and is one of only two hotspots that encompass an entire floral kingdom (the other being New Caledonia). Indeed, despite having extremely infertile soils, this region has the greatest extratropical concentration of plant species in the world, with 9 000 plant species, 6 210 of them endemics, crammed into just 78 555 km². Furthermore, diversity and endemism are impressive not just at the species level, but at the generic and familial levels as well, with this region accounting for five of South Africa's 12 endemic plant families. Among the hotspots, only Madagascar and the Indian Ocean Islands (8) and New Caledonia (5) have comparable family-level endemism.

The characteristic and most widespread vegetation of the Cape, covering some 46 000 km², is *fynbos*, an Afrikaans word that translates as "fine bush" (Kruger 1979). Fynbos is a shrubland comprising hard-leafed, evergreen, fire-prone shrubs, which are, in geological terms, a relatively recent feature (Cowling and Richardson 1995). Before the predominance of these shrublands, the region was covered with a lush rainforest of mixed Gondwanan-Paleotropical affinities (Linder et al. 1992). With the development of the cold Benguela Current along the Cape west coast about 15 million years ago, there was a subsequent deterioration in climate, resulting in a retreat of the forests. They were replaced by flammable sclerophyllous plants, relatives of the ancient lineages that had persisted on locally dry sites since the birth of flowering plants.

Many different fynbos vegetation types have been described by plant ecologists (Cowling et al. 1997), and fynbos is characterized by four major plant types: restioids, ericoids, proteoids, and bulbs. Restioids, mainly members of the Gondwanan family Restionaceae,

are evergreen rush or reed-like plants that are the uniquely diagnostic plant type of fynbos. The ericoids include more than 3 000 species of small-leafed shrubs (0.5-2 m tall), which give fynbos a heath-like appearance. The proteoids are the tallest fynbos shrubs (2-4 m), and comprise showy members of the Proteaceae, another Gondwanan family, among them the king protea (*Protea cynaroides*), South Africa's national flower. Finally, fynbos includes more than 1 500 species of bulbs or geophytes, many of which have been developed worldwide as valuable horticultural plants, e.g., freesias, agapanthus, gladioli, and ixias.

The Cape also includes several non-fynbos vegetation types. Of these, *Renosterveld* (Afrikaans for "rhinoceros veld," referring to the presence of the black rhinoceros [*Diceros bicornis*], that used to browse there but is now extinct in this region) is the most extensive, covering some 20 000 km². This community comprises a low shrub layer (1-2 m tall) of mainly ericoids, usually dominated by the renosterbos (*Elytropappus rhinocerotis*, Asteraceae), with a ground layer of grasses and seasonally active bulbs.

Trees are very rare in pristine Cape landscapes and true forests occupy a mere 3 850 km², mostly in moist, fire-protected sites on the southern coastal forelands and lower mountain slopes. The Cape forests, 10-30 m tall, are essentially outliers of the Afromontane forests of the high mountains of tropical Africa, but also include relics from the mesic Tertiary times. A form of dwarf forest, 3-5 m tall and locally known as thicket, occupies about 4 500 km² of fire-protected habitat (mainly coastal dunes and river valleys) in drier areas; thicket is compositionally related to the subtropical forests of the Indian Ocean coastline (Vlok et al. 2003). In contrast to the plants of the fynbos and renosterveld, forest and thicket plants are not chemically and structurally adapted to burn, and new individuals that germinate from bird-dispersed fruits establish only over extended, fire-free periods.

The Cape owes its status as a distinct floral kingdom to the presence of five endemic plant families (of a total of 164), and 160 endemic genera (17% of 942 genera). Certain genera have undergone massive diversification —the 10 largest genera account for 21.5% of the flora—, with the two most speciose being *Erica* (Ericaceae: 658 species) and *Aspalathus* (Fabaceae: 257 species). Species richness and local endemism is greatest in the southwest; the Cape Peninsula (471 km²) alone supports 2 256 species (including 90 endemics).

Diversity and endemism among the fauna of the Cape Floristic Region appears to be much lower than in plants, although very little is known about some invertebrate groups (Johnson 1992). There are 90 mammal species recorded from the Cape Floristic Region, of which four are endemic. The list of endemic species includes two species of golden moles: the Fynbos golden mole (*Amblysomus corriae*) and Van Zyl's golden mole (*Cryptochloris zyli*, CR). The best mammal flagship in the region is the bontebok (*Damaliscus pygargus pygargus*, VU), a beautiful animal whose name in Afrikaans means

"brightly colored antelope" and which was saved from extinction only by the foresight of conservationists.

Bird diversity, too, is not particularly high, owing to the structural uniformity of the vegetation and the shortage of food (McMahon and Fraser 1988). Only 324 regularly occurring species have been recorded from the region, and just six of these are endemics. Nonetheless, the area is considered an Endemic Bird Area by BirdLife International (Stattersfield et al. 1998), and is home to a number of true fynbos species such as the Cape sugarbird (*Promerops cafer*), one of only two species in the family Promeropidae; the orange-breasted sunbird (*Nectarinia violacea*); and the Protea canary (*Serinus leucopterus*).

Reptile diversity, on the other hand, is moderately high at 100 species, of which 22 are endemic. Among reptiles, the tortoises are the best flagship species, with five species occurring almost entirely within the Cape Floristic Region, including the South African bowsprit or angulate tortoise (*Chersina angulata*), the leopard tortoise (*Geochelone pardalis*), and the geometric tortoise (*Psammobates geometricus*, EN). The latter is among the most threatened tortoises in the world, having already lost some 97% of its original habitat to extensive agricultural development; its remaining habitat amounts to no more than 5 000 ha, and its population is estimated at only 2 000-3 000 individuals in 31 different localities (Baard 1997).

Amphibians and freshwater fish, though low in overall diversity, exhibit high endemism. In all, there are 51 species of amphibians (in 16 genera), 16 of them endemic (although no genera or families are endemic), and they include species like the enchanting arum lily frog (*Hyperolius horstocki*, VU) which, as its name suggests, lives within the flower of the arum lily (*Zantedeschia aethiopica*). In addition, two amphibian genera are endemic, both represented by single species: the micro frog (*Microbatrachella capensis*, CR), which is found in sandy, coastal fynbos heathland, and the montane marsh frog (*Poyntonia paludicola*), a species of mountain fynbos heathland. Of the 34 native fish species, 14 are endemic. Some distinctive fishes in the clear mountain streams characteristic of this region are the Cape galaxias (*Galaxias zebratus*), a peculiar, elongated and scaleless fish, as well as several endemic species of redfin minnows (*Pseudobarbus* spp.) (Skelton 1993).

Much less is known about the invertebrate fauna of the Cape. However, the few groups that have been studied suggest very high levels of endemism. For example, of the 234 species of butterflies in the region, 72 are endemic (Rebelo 1992). One regional study, carried out on the Cape Peninsula, recorded 111 invertebrate endemics in 471 km², a higher number than for plant endemics (Picker and Samways 1996).

The Cape Floristic Region is seriously threatened by a battery of human activities that have seen the Coast Renosterveld and Sandplain Fynbos, both lowland habitats, reduced by 48% and 83% of their original extent, respectively; much of what remains exists in small and

On the opposite page, George or Scarborough lily (Cyrtanthus elatus), Outeniqua Mountains, South Africa.
© **Haroldo Castro**

Above, a succulent, Crassula columnaris, *from the Western Cape.*
© **Gerald Cubitt**

isolated fragments in a matrix of chemically treated agriculture (Rouget et al. 2003a). Even in the mountains, where impoverished soils previously limited agriculture, farming based on indigenous crops such as rooibos tea (*Aspalathus linearis*), honeybush tea (*Cyclopia* spp.), and cut flowers (mainly Proteaceae) is rapidly encroaching on natural habitat. Nonetheless, the greatest threat to the Cape Flora overall is undoubtedly the invasion of alien plants (Richardson et al. 1992), mainly originating from other Mediterranean-type climate regions such as southern Australia (wattles [*Acacia* spp.], myrtle [*Leptospermum laevigatum*]), the Mediterranean Basin (*Pinus halepensis, P. pinaster*), and California (*P. radiata*). Originally introduced to supplement the meager Cape tree flora, these fire-adapted species have invaded about 70% of both mountain and lowland fynbos. Overall, some 33% or 23 600 km^2 of the Cape Floristic Region has been transformed by agriculture, urbanization, and dense stands of alien plants (Rouget et al. 2003a). However, of the remaining area, only about 20% can be regarded as pristine in the sense that it is entirely free of alien plants and subjected to appropriate fire and grazing regimes.

An analysis of the World Database on Protected Areas reveals that approximately 14% of the hotspot has some level of protection, of which at least 13% of the hotspot area is classified in IUCN categories I to IV. However, according to Rouget et al. (2003b), approximately 25%, or 19 350 km^2, of the Cape Floristic Region (including the Little Karoo enclave) is conserved in 189 protected areas. Statutory conservation areas (protected areas with secure organizational and institutional support) comprise 49% of this area, whereas non-statutory reserves (mainly private conservation initiatives) comprise the remainder. Despite a relatively healthy proportion under some form of conservation management, these reserves were established in an *ad hoc* manner and are not entirely representative of the Cape's biota. Thus, some 50% of mountain landscapes are conserved, exceeding targets for many individual habitat types, whereas only 9% of the lowlands are conserved. Furthermore, the conservation area does a relatively poor job in protecting the ecological and evolutionary processes that maintain the Cape's unique biodiversity. Obvious priorities include remnant habitat in the highly vulnerable and poorly conserved lowlands, as well as the expansion of upland reserves to accommodate the full spectrum of species and processes.

However, there have been some positive developments on the conservation front, including: the successful initiation of the "Working for Water Programme," which aims to deliver a major fynbos ecosystem service —clean and plentiful supplies of water— cost-effectively by removing all alien plants from mountain catchments; the expansion of protected areas through proclamation of the Cape Peninsula National Park and the Cape Agulhas National Park; and investment by the Critical Ecosystem Partnership Fund (CEPF) and the Global Environmental Facility (GEF) to develop and implement a

strategic plan for the sustainable conservation of the Cape Flora and associated biota (Cowling and Pressey 2003). Of particular interest within CEPF's $6-million investment portfolio is support for the region's three mega-reserves: Baviaanskloof, Cederberg, and Gouritz, where funds have been used to prepare strategic management and business plans to ensure that these areas will be able to meet future conservation challenges. Emphasis has also been placed on building the capacity of previously disadvantaged local conservationists through a $1-million CEPF small-grants fund administered by the Table Mountain Fund. If the programs mentioned above continue to be successful, then there is every hope that future generations will be able to benefit from and marvel at this most extraordinary biological phenomenon.

SUCCULENT KAROO

PHILIP DESMET [37] • RICHARD M. COWLING [133]

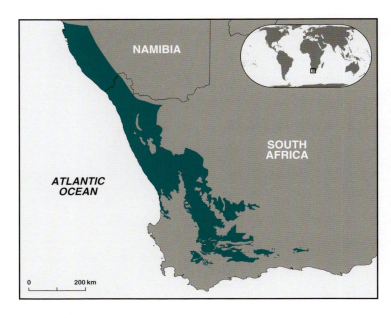

Arid lands tend to have highly endemic floras and faunas, but are usually relatively species poor. The Succulent Karoo is an extraordinary exception, and is one of only two arid regions in the world that can be considered a true biodiversity hotspot (the other being the Horn of Africa, which is recognized here as a new hotspot). It harbors a staggering 6 356 plant species (in 168 families and 1 002 genera) (Driver et al. 2003) and the richest succulent flora in the world (Van Jaarsveld 1987).

This predominantly winter-rainfall desert, which occupies 102 691 km^2 on the arid fringes of the Cape Floristic Region, has been divided by biogeographers into two zones, the strongly winter-rainfall Namaqualand-Namib Domain of the Cape west coast and southern Namibia (generally known as Namaqualand) and the Southern Karoo Domain, where rainfall often peaks in the spring and autumn months (Jürgens 1991). In broad phytogeographical terms, the Succulent Karoo forms part of the Karoo-Namib Regional Center of Endemism (White 1983). However, the area is largely transitional between the Cape Floristic Region and the Nama-Karoo, and shows a particularly strong floristic

Succulents reach amazing levels of diversity in the Succulent Karoo, and include a wide range of tiny species such as this Crassula congesta, *photographed near Oudtshoorn in the Little Karoo region.*
© **Olivier Langrand**

On the opposite page, aloes are very diverse in the Succulent Karoo, and are often very restricted in range by small differences in altitude and soil condition.
© **Haroldo Castro**

affinity with the Cape Floristic Region, to the point that some have argued convincingly for the region's inclusion as part of a greater Cape Flora (Jürgens 1991; J. Born, P. Linder, and P. Desmet, unpubl.)

The typical vegetation of the Succulent Karoo is a dwarf shrubland dominated almost entirely by leaf succulents in the Mesembryanthemaceae, Crassulaceae, Asteraceae and Liliaceae families (Milton et al. 1997). Some 1 700 out of a total of 1 843 estimated succulents are leaf succulents in the Succulent Karoo, and this dominance is unique among the deserts of the world (Jürgens 1986). The recent and explosive diversification of the Mesembryanthemaceae, the largest group, has been described as an event unrivaled among flowering plants (Ihlenfeldt 1994; Desmet et al. 1998; Klak et al. 2004). Indeed, the exceptionally high vascular plant diversity and endemism (2 539 species, or 40%, and 80, or 8% of genera) of the Succulent Karoo is associated with massive speciation within the predominantly succulent and bulbous genera. Stem succulents, comprising some 130 species, include species of *Euphorbia, Tylecodon, Othonna, Pelargonium*, and numerous stapeliads. Seasonal bulbs (1 143 species) and annuals (390 species), which appear in the open spaces between the shrubs, provide magnificent spring displays, especially in Namaqualand.

The quartz gravels of the Knersvlakte, as well as similar habitats elsewhere in Namaqualand and in the Little Karoo, support a unique vegetation type characterized by an extremely sparse cover of locally endemic Mesembryanthemaceae and other succulents. Nearly all of these are stemless, embedded forms (stone plants). The Succulent Karoo is home to about 700 such species belonging to the genera *Argyroderma, Bulbine, Conophytum, Crassula, Haworthia*, and *Lithops*. Another unusual feature of much of the Succulent Karoo is the presence of *heuweltjies* or mima-like mounds (Dean and Milton 1999). The mounds are of zoogenic origin, originally created by termites (*Microhodotermes viator*) and often colonized by a wide variety of burrowing animals. As a result, nutrient-enriched subsoil is brought to the surface, creating a substratum physically and chemically very different from the intervening matrix. Thus, *heuweltjies* support a flora that is markedly distinct in appearance and composition from that of the surrounding vegetation.

Among the most famous of all the attractive succulent species found in the Succulent Karoo is the *halfmens* ("half human") (*Pachypodium namaquanum*), a stem succulent endemic to the Richtersveld and that grows to a height of up to 4 m. The stems of these plants are inclined to the north, thus creating an uncanny resemblance to humans peering northwards to the distant plains of southern Namibia. Khoi-khoi folklore has it that the plants are the remnants of an ancient tribe, banished by warfare from their original home in Namibia, which gaze nostalgically across the Orange River to their homeland. The scientific explanation for this unusual orientation is equally engaging (Rundel et al. 1995). Growing on shaded slopes, the plants lean northwards in order to ensure that their leaves and developing flowerheads, pro-

duced during the cool, foggy winter months, are maximally exposed to the sun's warming rays.

The fauna of the Succulent Karoo is rich in endemic species, especially among arachnids, hopliniid beetles, aculeate Hymenoptera, and reptiles (Vernon 1999). Estimates from available data suggest that endemism in insects is especially high (>50%) for groups examined (Hymenoptera [Apoidea] and Isoptera) (Driver et al. 2003). The predictable rainfall appears to have resulted in many resident forms of invertebrates and small vertebrates, which has led to isolation and speciation. Several invertebrate groups are particularly well represented, especially those that reach high levels of diversity in arid regions, such as scorpions (with 18 of the 70 scorpions in the Succulent Karoo endemic; Driver et al. 2003). Monkey beetles (Rutelinae: Hoplini), a group largely endemic to southern Africa, are concentrated in the Succulent Karoo, where some genera are important pollinators of daisies and mesembs.

Among the vertebrates, there are, at present, 74 mammals recorded from the Succulent Karoo, of which two are endemic: De Winton's golden mole (*Cryptochloris wintoni*, VU) and the Namaqua dune mole-rat (*Bathyergus janetta*). Birds are represented by 227 regularly occurring species, including one endemic, the recently described Barlow's lark (*Certhilauda barlowi*). In addition, the black harrier (*Circus maurus*, VU), with its distinctive black-and-white plumage, has the most restricted range of the world's 13 harrier species (Harrison et al. 1997) and is frequently observed hunting over the Namaqualand plains. Amphibians are poorly represented, with only 29 species of frogs, one of which, the desert rain frog (*Breviceps macrops*, VU) is endemic, occurring on the Namaqualand coast of South Africa north to Luderitz in coastal southwestern Namibia. Reptiles are very diverse, with 94 species, of which 15 are endemic. These include 58 lizard and gecko species with 15 endemics (the genera *Cordylus* and *Pachydactylus* are especially rich, with eight and 12 species and six and two endemics, respectively) and 29 snakes, of which none is endemic. The freshwater fish fauna includes 26 indigenous species, though none are endemic (modified from D. Impson et al., unpubl.).

Considering this wealth of unique plant species, and high endemism, it is encouraging that the Succulent Karoo is one of the more intact hotspot systems. Over 90% of the region is used for natural grazing, a form of land use that is, theoretically, compatible with maintenance of biodiversity and ecosystem processes. It is difficult to make accurate estimates of the amount of intact vegetation. It is known that at least 5% of the biome has been irreversibly lost to mining (3%) and cropping agriculture (2%), and about 0.1% to urbanization (Driver et al. 2003). The amount transformed or degraded by overgrazing is unknown, although one estimate states that approximately 70 000 km² , especially the communally owned parts of Namaqualand, have been seriously overgrazed (Davis et al. 1994). Thus, optimistically, only some 30 000 km² of the Succulent Karoo, or about 29%, exist in a relatively pristine state, although this figure is probably much lower.

On the opposite page, another aloe plant from Little Karoo, Oudtshoorn region, South Africa.
© Gerald Cubitt

Above, a Cape sugarbird (Promerops cafer) perched on a Protea flower. One of only two members of the subfamily Promeropinae, this species is endemic to the Cape Region of South Africa.
© M. Watson/Ardea

A number of threats are likely to take on greater importance in this region in the future. The rise of the ostrich farming industry has resulted in the degradation of thousands of hectares of veld in the Little Karoo (Driver et al. 2003). Also, the expected increase in the extent of communal land in Namaqualand and elsewhere in the region will undoubtedly accelerate desertification, too (Hoffman et al. 1999), while dryland farming in Namaqualand is practiced where the annual rainfall is as low as 150 mm per year. And, of course, diamond mining has had a major impact on the Namaqualand coastline and alluvial terraces of the lower Orange River Valley (Davis et al. 1994). Approximately 65% of the South African, and almost all Namibian Atlantic coastline of the Succulent Karoo, has been mined for diamonds. The extraction of heavy minerals, an equally destructive process, continues to develop as a major industry on the coast of southern Namaqualand.

Remarkably, for a country like South Africa renowned for its well-established game parks and reserves, protected area coverage in this hotspot is poor. According to the World Database on Protected Areas, only 2.5% of the area has some form of protection (with only 1.8% in IUCN categories I to IV). Regional information proves the situation is not much better, with only 3.5% of the Succulent Karoo formally protected in category I reserves; these are statutory reserves managed primarily for biodiversity conservation, and include National Parks and Provincial Nature Reserves (Driver et al. 2003). An additional 2.3% of the biome is protected in category II reserves. These are statutory and non-statutory reserves managed for biodiversity conservation and/or other land uses. A statutory reserve managed for biodiversity conservation and other land uses would be classified as a category II reserve rather than a category I reserve. This is the case with the Richtersveld National Park, a contractual national park in which both conservation and other land uses occur. Other category II reserves include municipal reserves and conservancies (voluntary agreements among private landowners). Considering that the region has more than 936 Red Data Listed plant species (Driver et al. 2003), the reserve system for the Succulent Karoo is grossly inadequate for conserving the region's biodiversity. It is estimated that 59% of the region's quarter-degree grid cells would be required in a reserve system to represent each plant species at least once (Lombard et al. 1999).

Recently, there have been two positive developments regarding the conservation status of the Succulent Karoo. First, the reserve system is being expanded, although at the current rate of expansion it will take 130 years to achieve the reservation targets set by the Succulent Karoo Ecosystem Program (SKEP) project (P. Desmet, unpubl.). The creation of the Namaqua National Park (*ca.* 600 km²) in the central uplands of Namaqualand is a positive development. This park is set to expand westwards to encompass Sandveld habitats on the coastal plain as well as the marine zone. Secondly, the SKEP project has created much awareness in the region, as

well as interest in conserving biodiversity, and fortunately funds have become available recently to fuel this awareness and interest. The Critical Ecosystem Partnership Fund (CEPF) has allocated $8 million for this hotspot over five years. Already action is taking place in numerous geographic priority areas, with technical assistance in project design and proposal preparation provided to numerous civil society groups, and grant funds being disbursed in support of conservation initiatives throughout the region. Fortunately, the situation in the Succulent Karoo is such that timely action can still ensure that a strong, representative cross section of its rich and diverse desert landscapes will survive into the future.

MADAGASCAR AND THE INDIAN OCEAN ISLANDS

RUSSELL A. MITTERMEIER[1] • OLIVIER LANGRAND[1]
PORTER P. LOWRY II[26] • GEORGE SCHATZ[27] • JUSTIN GERLACH[47, 48]
STEVEN GOODMAN[49, 50] • MARC STEININGER[2] • FRANK HAWKINS[52]
NORO RAMINOSOA[51] • OLGA RAMILIJAONA[51]
LUCIANO ANDRIAMARO[52] • HARISON RANDRIANASOLO[52]
HARISON RABARISON[52] • ZO LALAINA RAKOTOBE[52]

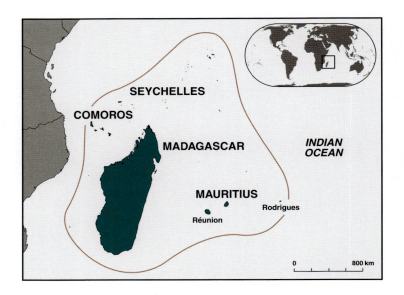

The island of Madagascar, at approximately 590 000 km² the fourth largest on Earth, has long been recognized as one of the world's highest priority hotspots and one of the top megadiversity countries. Although located only about 400 km from the east coast of Africa, the island, another chip off the supercontinent Gondwana, has been isolated from other landmasses for more than 160 million years. Consequently, most of the plant and animal species occurring there have evolved in long isolation, and are unique and found nowhere else. Levels of endemism in most groups of organisms are exceptionally high, not just at the species level, but often at the generic and even the family levels as well.

In addition to Madagascar itself, we include in this hotspot the neighboring western Indian Ocean Islands which, although much smaller, are also very important biologically. These include the independent nations of Seychelles (454 km²; including Aldabra), the Comoros

(1 862 km²), Mauritius (2 040 km²; including Rodrigues), and the French overseas departments of Réunion (2 535 km²) and Mayotte (371 km²; one of the Comoros), which is a departmental collectivity of France. Also included are the Iles Esparses, all of which belong to France: Europa (30 km²), Les Glorieuses (7 km²), Juan de Nova (5 km²), Bassas da India, and Tromelin (1 km²). These Indian Ocean islands add considerably to the overall importance of the hotspot, and bring its total land area to 600 461 km².

The natural vegetation of this hotspot is quite diverse. Madagascar is characterized by tropical rainforest on the eastern side, dry deciduous forests on the western side, and spiny desert in the far south of the country. In the far north, there is a mosaic of dry and moist forest formations, and a series of mountains are found in the north and east (Lowry et al. 1997). The Indian Ocean islands are composed of a range of relatively recent volcanic islands (the Mascarenes and the Comoros), fragments of continental material (the main group of the Seychelles), and the coral cays of the Amirantes and the atolls of the Farquhar, Cosmoledo, and Aldabra groups, as well as the five Iles Eparses. The continental and volcanic islands have high peaks that in the recent past were covered by dense forest; indeed, the Comoros (up to 5 600 mm per year on Grande Comore) and the Mascarenes (up to 6 000 mm per year on Réunion) are sometimes subjected to very high levels of rainfall. The highest peak in the Indian Ocean is the Piton des Neiges on Réunion (3 069 m), which received the heaviest downpour on record (4.9 m of rain in one week in 1980). By contrast, the Seychelles are relatively dry (up to 2 400 mm per year on Mahé).

In terms of its biodiversity, Madagascar's most striking feature is its high levels of endemism, particularly at the generic and family levels. Madagascar also has very high species diversity in certain groups of organisms, especially given its relatively small size. Both of these characteristics are best represented in Madagascar's flora: current plant diversity is estimated to be at least 12 000 species, and possibly as many as 14 000, of which around 90% are endemic (G. Schatz and P. Lowry, unpubl.). In addition, there are seven endemic plant families, which is unmatched by any other country; indeed, only Australia, New Caledonia, and South Africa are comparable in terms of plant endemism at the family level. Madagascar recently made headlines in the botanical world with the rediscovery of *Takhtajania perrieri*, the only Afro-Malagasy member of the primitive family Winteraceae, in the northeast of the country. It is fitting that Madagascar's signature endemic plant, the traveler's tree (*Ravenala madagascariensis*), is pollinated by the island's flagship vertebrate species, the lemurs.

Among vertebrates, some 283 avian species have been recorded, of which 209 breed on the island, and 109 of these are endemic (Hawkins and Goodman 2003); and, not surprisingly, no fewer than five Endemic Bird Areas have been recognized in the country (Stattersfield et al. 1998). At the higher level, 34 out of 148 resident genera are endemic, and there is also high

family-level endemism, with five bird families restricted to the island. There are some extraordinary ancient relict bird species on Madagascar, such as the ground-rollers, cuckoo-rollers, and mesites.

Mammals are represented by 131 species, of which 30 are bats; all but 12 species are endemic (Goodman et al. 2003; Eger and Mitchell 2003). No other country or hotspot comes close in terms of primate family-level endemism, with some five families and 15 genera endemic, and a total of 72 taxa in all (with more still to be described). This incredible primate radiation constitutes the best known of the region's charismatic species, including the aye-aye (*Daubentonia madagascariensis*, EN), the indri (*Indri indri*, EN), and Madame Berthe's mouse lemur (*Microcebus berthae*), at 30 g the world's smallest primate.

Although there is only one endemic amphibian family (Mantellidae) and one endemic reptile family (Opluridae), the reptiles and amphibians exhibit very high levels of endemism. Indeed, of the 340 reptile species, 314 are endemic (Raxworthy 2003), as are an amazing 215 of the 217 described amphibian species. Apart from being extremely rich in these groups, Madagascar may even be the place of origin for some; for example, it has been proposed recently that all the world's chameleons originated here. Among the flagship amphibians and reptiles are the beautiful frogs of the genera *Mantella* and *Scaphiophryne*, the tomato frog (*Dyscophus antongilii*), a bright red, bull-frog-sized animal found only in a tiny area in northeastern Madagascar and, of course, the chameleons.

It is noteworthy that many new species have been discovered on Madagascar in the last decade or so, and, indeed, since the publication of the last *Hotspots* book in 1999. For example, no fewer than 22 new mammal species and subspecies have been described from Madagascar in the last 15 years (including seven full lemur species between 1997 and 2003). Furthermore, many new species remain to be discovered and described; for example, C. Raxworthy (pers. comm.) notes that at least 100 reptile species and about 100 amphibian species await formal description.

Most of the other fauna on Madagascar is poorly known. However, some of the non-marine invertebrate groups that are reasonably well known are: terrestrial snails (651 species, all endemic); scorpions (40 species, all endemic); spiders (459 species, 390 endemics); dragonflies and damselflies (181 species, 132 endemics); lacewings (163 species, 119 endemics); tiger beetles (211 species, 209 endemics [D. Pearson, pers. comm.]); scarab beetles (148 species, all endemic); true butterflies (300 species, 211 endemics); freshwater crayfish (six species, all endemic); and freshwater shrimp of the family Atyidae (26 species, 20 endemics). Overall, total species richness for macroinvertebrate groups covered in a recent review of the natural history of Madagascar is slightly more than 5 800 species, of which 86% are endemic to the island, although several speciose groups of invertebrates are not covered in the volume (e.g., the vast majority of beetle families) (Goodman and Benstead, pers. comm.).

The smaller neighboring Indian Ocean islands are biologically closely linked to Madagascar, are under heavy

On the opposite page, the leaf-tailed geckos of the genus Uroplatus *are endemic to Madagascar and rank among the most cryptically shaped and colored lizards in the world. This species, the aptly-named* U. phantasticus, *is from the region of Ranomafana National Park.*
© Piotr Naskrecki

Above, the Vulnerable helmet vanga (Euryceros prevostii) *is endemic to the northern portion of the eastern rainforests of Madagascar. It is a member of the endemic monophyletic family Vangidae —famous for its amazing variation in bill shape and diversity of ecological niches.*
© Pete Oxford/naturepl.com

141

pressure, and add important endemic biodiversity without adding significantly to the land area covered by this hotspot. For example, in terms of plant diversity and endemism, the flowering plants are represented by about 2 200 to 2 400 species (*ca.* 1 300 in the Mascarenes, 1 000 in the Comoros, and 310 in the Seychelles, several hundred of which are shared among two or more of the island groups); around 810 (34%-37%) of these are endemic (about 585 in the Mascarenes, 150 in the Comoros and 75 in the Seychelles), along with one family endemic to the Seychelles (Medusagynaceae).

Space does not permit detailed discussion of the vertebrate diversity of all the islands, although much research has been conducted on Seychelles recently, and these islands are mentioned briefly here. The Seychelles add a further 104 native breeding vertebrates, with endemics comprising one fish, 11 amphibian, 27 reptile, 14 bird, and four mammal species. In addition, the Seychelles have one endemic amphibian family —the Sooglossidae, an ancient group endemic to this area with its closest relative in the Western Ghats of India— and six endemic amphibian genera. The presence of seven species of caecilian amphibians is bizarre, as these are entirely absent from Madagascar and the other western Indian Ocean islands.

The invertebrate fauna of the Seychelles comprises 3 555 recorded species, with an estimated total of perhaps 5 100 species; of these, approximately 80% are endemic. One truly unique and amazing invertebrate flagship is the endemic giant tenebrionid beetle (*Polposipus herculeanus*, CR), restricted to one small island in the Seychelles, and one of the largest terrestrial invertebrates in the world. The region also supports the largest millipede (*Sechelleptus seychellarum*) and the only secure population of the world's largest terrestrial invertebrate, the coconut or robber crab (*Birgus latro*).

The hotspot includes two distinctive components of freshwater fishes. The smaller islands have depauperate faunas dominated by species that have wide marine distributions and that enter brackish and freshwater habitats to some degree. The few endemics on these islands include a cyprinodont, a chandid, and gobies. Madagascar differs in having a freshwater fauna that includes fishes of continental origin. These groups have undergone radiation on the island, resulting in 93 endemic species (of the hotspot's 97 species), and these also account for all of the hotspot's 14 endemic genera and two endemic families.

Overall, the Madagascar and the Indian Ocean Islands Hotspot (i.e., including not only Madagascar and the Seychelles, but also the remaining Indian Ocean Islands) has a total of at least 155 mammals, 144 of which are endemic; about 313 regularly occurring birds, 183 of them endemic; 381 reptiles, 367 endemic; and at least 228 amphibians, of which 226 are endemic. Plants total at least 13 000 species, and probably as many as 15 000, with a staggering 11 600 (and perhaps 13 500) endemics, and at least 310 endemic genera. The number of endemic families in this hotspot is truly exceptional, totaling 24 in all (16 for vertebrates, including fishes, and eight for plants), and far surpasses that of any other hotspot. This

once again attests to the great global importance of Madagascar and its neighboring islands, and highlights its role as one of the highest priority hotspots on Earth.

The threats to Madagascar and the Indian Ocean islands are well documented, with forest destruction through slash-and-burn agriculture, mining, and logging being among the main causes of habitat loss. In Madagascar, it is estimated that around 90 000 km^2 of closed-canopy primary forest and woodland remained as of 2000, with an average annual rate of loss during the 1990s of 0.9% per year (Steininger et al., unpubl.). Assuming that 90% of Madagascar was once forested (Perrier de la Bathie 1936), this equates to roughly 17% of original primary vegetation remaining. The most heavily impacted habitats are lowland rainforest, dry deciduous forests, and spiny forest. Wetlands, including lakes, rivers, and marshes, are under threat from transformation to rice fields, siltation resulting from soil erosion, and introduced species. The latter have accounted for several extinctions recently. Lemurs, some birds, and smaller mammals are very susceptible to hunting. The pet trade has also had a serious impact on endemic plants and animals of Madagascar, especially amphibians, reptiles, and succulent plants. The proliferation of exotic plant species is also recognized as a major threat affecting the biodiversity of Madagascar and the western Indian Ocean islands, and freshwater ecosystems, in particular, have been seriously impacted by alien plants such as *Eichhornia crassipes* (Langrand and Goodman 1995).

In the Comoros, at least 80% of the native vegetation has been destroyed since human colonization first began over 1 000 years ago. During the period 1990-1995, deforestation reached 5.8% per annum, the fourth highest rate of any country (Jolly and Fukuda-Parr 2000). Today, plantations dominate the land. Mayotte Island also was once forested, with dry, humid, and transitional types recognized. Most of this was destroyed before 1900, leaving fragments of native forest that covered only 3% of the island in 1999 (Pascal 2002), most of which (6.7 km^2) is humid forest. A further 14.8 km^2 of the island's vegetation has been classified as secondary forest up to 300 m. Hunting is a major problem for the avifauna, and species such as the Comoro olive pigeon (*Columba polleni*) are becoming rare as a result.

Réunion was permanently colonized in 1646. Since then, humans have brought about the loss of 75% of the native vegetation area (around 650 km^2 remain) and 50% of the native vertebrate fauna (including 55% of the birds). As is often the case on recent volcanic islands, the introduction of exotic species of fauna and flora is having a huge impact on the survival of endemic species. On the Seychelles, much of the original lowland vegetation was cleared for timber production or agriculture, particularly for coconut plantations and cinnamon exploitation in the granitic islands, although significant reservoirs of biodiversity have survived thanks to the steep terrain of the high islands. The Amirantes, and Cosmoledo and Astove atolls, have also been greatly impacted by coconut plantations.

Given the importance of the hotspot, it is not surpris-

Aerial view of deforested landscape in the central plateau region of Madagascar.
© **Haroldo Castro**

On the opposite page, forest destruction for slash-and-burn agriculture, or tavy as it is known in Madagascar, in spiny desert near Ifaty.
© **Nick Garbutt**/naturepl.com

The El Hierro giant lizard (Gallotia simonyi machadoi) *is considered the most threatened reptile in Europe, as well as one of the five most threatened reptiles in the world. It is currently the flagship species for El Hierro Island (Canary Islands, Spain), and an example of the recovery and conservation of a species that is unique. Today its population is estimated at between 1 000 and 1 600 individuals, in the Tibataje Special Natural Reserve.*
© **Francisco Márquez**

On the opposite page, the Cabrera Archipelago, south of Mallorca Island, Spain, is one of the few sites where Mediterranean-type forests have found refuge, thanks to which this area was declared a national park and, above all, because for many years a military base operated there, hindering the development of this zone, which now has different endemic flora species.
© **Patricio Robles Gil**/*Sierra Madre*

ing that there have been major efforts in biodiversity conservation, and the hotspot, in particular Madagascar, may be entering a new era in terms of biodiversity protection. In Madagascar, the government is about to embark on the third phase of the National Environmental Action Plan, with a five-year program of conservation and sustainable management actions. There are many conservation organizations involved in this effort, both international and local, and the World Bank, Global Environmental Facility (GEF), United Nations Development Program, and French, U.S., German, and Swiss bilateral aid is all being deployed specifically for biodiversity conservation.

In the Comoros, political instability has meant that conservation action has been rather piecemeal until recently, with only limited GEF and IUCN support for the establishment of a marine national park and some work on Livingstone's fruit bat (*Pteropus livingstonii*, CR) by local and international NGOs. The climate for collaboration is set to change, however, and further investment in establishing threatened species conservation programs, through CI and other partners, is under way; and there is a plan to establish a terrestrial national park in Mount Karthala. The Seychelles, by contrast, have several very active conservation NGOs that have had a dramatic impact on the conservation status of many of their threatened species recently. A notable example is the Seychelles magpie robin (*Copsychus sechallarum*, CR), rescued from the edge of extinction over the last ten years by Nature Seychelles and partners. A similar situation applies in the Mascarenes; while there are many species on the verge of extinction, considerable effort has been devoted to captive-breeding and release programs. This is particularly evident in Mauritius, where the Mauritian Wildlife Foundation, Durrell Wildlife Conservation Trust, and other partners have been prominent in rescuing species such as the pink pigeon (*Columba mayeri*, EN) and the echo parakeet (*Psittacula eques*, CR) from extinction.

As of mid-2002, the protected area network of Madagascar included 46 legally protected areas (national parks, strict nature reserves, and special reserves) covering 16 131 km² or 2.7% of the country (Randrianandianina et al. 2003). However, on September 17, 2003, at the World Parks Congress in Durban, South Africa, Madagascar's President, Marc Ravalomanana, made history when he declared his intention to triple protected area coverage over the next five years and to seek assistance from the international community for a $50-million trust fund to make this a reality. Demonstrating once again the interest of the international community, fully $24 million in commitments were made to this trust fund in the first six months following this announcement. The Global Conservation Fund (GCF) at Conservation International is assisting in the design and capitalization of the trust fund. The GCF and the Critical Ecosystem Partnership Fund (CEPF) are also actively supporting the efforts of local partners to identify priority areas for conservation, as well as to plan and create new protected areas in irreplaceable forests in the Menabe region of Western Madagascar, the extensive

rainforests of Makira in northeastern Madagascar, and the Daraina region in the extreme northeast. CEPF's contribution of $4.25 million for conservation in Madagascar has played a major role in helping local partners, such as Association Fanamby, engage in biodiversity conservation at multiple levels. The partnership's support to local groups is set to further expand under a new, three-year small grants program to help Malagasy organizations undertake conservation efforts at a local scale.

A number of the Indian Ocean Islands also have at least some protected area coverage. For example, Réunion has 21 protected areas, all in IUCN category IV and totaling 231 km², while in the Seychelles, 208 km² (46% of the land area) is designated as national parks, with a further 228 km² of marine national parks. These include two World Heritage Sites: the Vallée de Mai and Aldabra. Overall, an analysis of the World Database on Protected Areas shows that there are around 100 protected areas in the hotspot, the majority in IUCN categories I to IV, covering 3% of the surface area.

Although this extremely important hotspot still faces many threats and challenges, recent developments, particularly in Madagascar, give cause for more optimism than ever before. Indeed, the major new commitments being made for Madagascar could mean that this wonderful island, once considered almost a lost cause for conservation, could quickly be transformed into a global model. This renewed interest in the region as a whole will hopefully have a significant impact in the neighboring islands as well.

MEDITERRANEAN BASIN

FRÉDÉRIC MÉDAIL[61] • NORMAN MYERS[8]

The Mediterranean Basin Hotspot covers some 2 085 292 km² and stretches from Portugal to Jordan and from Morocco to northern Italy. It encompasses over 90% of Greece, Lebanon, and Portugal, but less than 10% of France, Algeria, and Libya. In Spain, 6 000 of the country's 7 500 plant species occur within the Mediterranean climate zone; in Israel, 1 500 out of 2 200; and in Morocco, 3 800 out of 4 200 (Quézel 1985; Greuter 1991). The hotspot also includes the Canary Islands, Madeira, and the Selvages (Selvagens) Islands and, in contrast to the former definition of this hotspot

(Myers and Cowling 1999), the region is here considered to also include the Azores and Cape Verde Islands, even though the floristic affinities of these two Macaronesian island groups lie more closely with Europe and Africa, respectively.

Of overwhelming importance in understanding the origins and diversity of the Mediterranean Basin biota is the region's location at the intersection of two major landmasses, Eurasia and Africa. Indeed, the collision between these two continental plates during the mid-Tertiary is responsible for the Basin's spectacular scenery. The Basin's violent geological history has produced an unusual geographical and topographical diversity, with high mountain ranges (more than 4 500 m in elevation), peninsulas, and one of the largest archipelagos in the world (the Mediterranean Sea includes several hundred islands and islets). The physiographic diversity of the region has resulted in a wide range of local climates, with mean annual rainfall ranging from 100 mm up to 3 000 mm (Blondel and Aronson 1999).

The typical and most widespread vegetation type is maquis or matorral, a hard-leaved shrubland dominated by *Cistus*, *Erica*, *Genista*, *Juniperus*, *Myrtus*, *Phillyrea*, *Pistacia*, and other evergreens, and similar in appearance to the chaparral of California and the matorral of Chile (Di Castri and Mooney 1973). Although maquis now covers more than half of the region, much of it has been derived from forest formations created by human-induced disturbances. Frequent burning of maquis results in depauperate vegetation dominated by Kermes oak (*Quercus coccifera*), *Cistus* spp. or *Sarcopoterium spinosum*, all of which regenerate rapidly after fire by sprouting or mass germination.

Shrublands, including maquis and the aromatic, soft-leaved and drought phrygana of *Rosmarinus*, *Salvia*, and *Thymus*, persist in the semiarid, lowland, and coastal regions of the Basin. However, prior to the onset of significant human impact, which started some 8 000 years ago, most of the Mediterranean Basin was covered by some form of forests (Quézel and Médail 2003), including: evergreen oak forests (*Quercus ilex*, *Q. suber*, and *Q. coccifera* ssp. *calliprinos*); deciduous forests (*Quercus canariensis*, *Q. faginea*, *Q. frainetto*, *Q. ithaburensis*, *Q. petraea*, *Q. pubescens*, *Q. pyrenaica*, and *Fagus sylvatica*); and conifer forests (*Abies* spp., *Cedrus* spp., *Juniperus* spp., and *Pinus* spp.).

The flora of the Mediterranean Basin is comprised of around 25 000 species of vascular plants, 13 000 of which are endemic (Quézel 1985; Greuter 1991). These figures include taxonomically doubtful taxa (6% to 9%) and naturalized exotics (less than 3%). As we are considering here only confirmed native species, we subtract 10% for a figure of 22 500 (and 11 700 endemics). The plant species endemic to the Mediterranean Basin are not a random assemblage in terms of their taxonomic affinities, biology, habitat requirements, and geographical distribution. Rather, the flora comprises a complex admixture of Mediterranean woody plants belonging to pre-Mediterranean lineages (start of the Tertiary) (Verdú et al. 2003) and localized neoendemics composed predominantly of herbs and subshrubs in the families Asteraceae, Brassicaceae, Caryophyllaceae, Cistaceae, Fabaceae, Lamiaceae, Poaceae, Ranunculaceae, and so on. Endemics are mainly concentrated on some Tertiary and Pleistocene refugia on islands, peninsulas, rocky cliffs, and mountain peaks (Médail and Verlaque 1997). Nevertheless, endemism at the higher level is very reduced, with only two endemic families (Aphyllanthaceae and Drosophyllaceae), both represented by single species, *Aphyllanthes monspeliensis* and *Drosophyllum lusitanicum*. The Mediterranean Region also harbors a high degree of tree richness and endemism (290 indigenous tree species with 201 endemics) (Quézel and Médail 2003). A number of trees are important flagships, including the cedars (such as the famous cedar of Lebanon, *Cedrus libani*); the argan tree (*Argania spinosa*), a species in the Souss region of southwest Morocco; oriental sweet gum (*Liquidambar orientalis*); and Cretan date palm (*Phoenix theophrasti*) in Greece and western Turkey.

The principal foci in the Mediterranean are 10 regional mini-hotspots within the larger hotspot, characterized by areas of high plant richness and narrow endemism of more than 10% (Médail and Quézel 1997, 1999): the Atlas Mountains in North Africa; the Rif-Betique range in southern Spain and two coastal strips of Morocco and Algeria; Maritime and Ligurian Alps of the French-Italian border; Tyrrhenian Islands; southern and central Greece; Crete; southern Turkey/Cyprus; Israel and Lebanon; Cyrenaica in Libya; and the Canary/Madeira Islands. These 10 areas cover about 22% of the Basin's total area, yet account for almost 5 500 endemic plants, i.e., about 47% of total Mediterranean endemics (Médail and Quézel 1999). Considering the redefinition of the hotspot boundary, the inclusion of the Cape Verde Islands (4 071 km^2) and the Azores (2 407 km^2) with the Canary/Madeira Islands to form an expanded Macaronesian mini-hotspot appears warranted. Clearly, these are priority sites for conservation of these plant components of Mediterranean-Macaronesian biodiversity.

As with the other Mediterranean-climate hotspots, diversity and endemism among vertebrates is much lower than for plants (Blondel and Aronson 1999). The mammal and bird faunas are largely derived from extra-Mediterranean biogeographical zones, with Eurasian and African elements dominating the mammal fauna, whereas Eurasian and semiarid southern elements dominate the avifauna. The North African mammal fauna has closer affinities with tropical Africa than with the Mediterranean Basin. On the other hand, the reptile and amphibian faunas comprise mainly Mediterranean species, and have higher levels of endemism. Many endemic species and genera are archaic lineages, which have probably remained unchanged since their differentiation before the Late Tertiary onset of Mediterranean climate conditions.

The present number of land mammals in the region is about 224, of which 25 are endemic, including several standouts like the Barbary deer (*Cervus elaphus barbarus*); Barbary macaque (*Macaca sylvanus*, VU);

The silhouette of a large conifer on the Sierra de Cazorla in southern Spain.
© **Patricio Robles Gil**/*Sierra Madre*

Moluccas. There are also at least 12 endemic genera in the region, seven on Sulawesi, three in the Lesser Sundas, and two in the Moluccas.

In terms of vertebrate diversity, Wallacea has a total of 223 native mammal species, 126 of which are endemic. If the 124 bat species are excluded, 87 of the 99 non-flying mammals, or 88%, are endemic. Sulawesi has the highest number of mammals (136), of which 82 species and about one-quarter of the genera are endemic. The list of Sulawesi endemic mammals includes flagship species such as the anoa (*Bubalus depressicornis*, EN) —a dwarf buffalo— and babirusa (*Babyrousa babyrussa*, VU), an enigmatic pig with long, recurved upper tusks that penetrate through the skin of the upper lip. In addition, the primates of Sulawesi are all important flagship species, with at least seven species of macaques (*Macaca* spp.) unique to the island and at least five species of tarsier (*Tarsius* spp.).

There are 650 bird species in Wallacea, of which 265 species are endemic, again very high numbers given the land area of the region. Of the 235 genera represented, 26 are endemic, with 16 genera (15 of them monotypic) restricted to Sulawesi and its satellite islands. Sulawesi has the largest bird fauna, with 356 species, including 96 endemics, among them the maleo (*Macrocephalon maleo*, EN), a distinctive megapode currently thought to number between 4 000 and 7 000 breeding pairs. Ten Endemic Bird Areas (identified by BirdLife International) are found entirely within Wallacea (Stattersfield et al. 1998), and BirdLife Indonesia has recently identified 112 Important Bird Areas (IBAs) —priority areas for avian conservation throughout the region— including 33 on Sulawesi, 36 in the Moluccas, and 43 in the Lesser Sundas (Rombang et al. 2002, in prep.).

Reptile diversity is also quite high, with 222 species, 99 of which are endemic. These include 118 lizards, with 60 endemics; 98 snakes, of which 37 are endemic; five turtles, two of them endemic; and one crocodilian, the wide-ranging saltwater or Indo-Pacific crocodile (*Crocodylus porosus*). There are also three endemic genera (all snakes): *Calamorhabdium*, with two species; and *Rabdion* and *Cyclotyphlops*, both monotypic. The best known reptile in Wallacea, and one of Indonesia's most famous species, is the Komodo dragon or *ora* (*Varanus komodoensis*, VU), the heaviest lizard in the world (males can reach about 2.8 m in length and weigh about 50 kg), known from only the tiny islands of Komodo, Padar, and Rinca, and the western end of Flores. Amphibians are represented by 58 native species, all of them frogs; of these, 32 are endemic. The frog fauna is a fascinating combination of Indo-Malayan and Australasian elements, with several local radiations as well.

With freshwater fishes, most of the 310 species recorded from the rivers and lakes of Wallacea are tolerant of both fresh and salt water to some extent.

Around 75 species are endemic. In the Moluccas and Lesser Sundas, the fish fauna is poorly known, but there appear to be around six island endemics. On Sulawesi, however, there are 69 known species, of which 53 (77%) are endemic. The complex of deep lakes, rapids, and rivers which makes up the Malili Lakes in South Sulawesi has at least 15 endemic and quite beautiful telmatherinid fishes, two of them representing endemic genera, three endemic *Oryzias*, two endemic halfbeaks, and seven endemic gobies, as well as about 50 endemic mollusks, three endemic crabs, and a number of endemic shrimps.

The invertebrate fauna of Wallacea remains poorly known, except for groups such as the enormous birdwing butterflies (members of the swallowtail butterfly family). The birdwings are represented by 82 species in Wallacea, 44 of which are endemic. There are also 109 tiger beetle species recorded from this hotspot, 79 of which are endemic (D. Pearson, pers. comm.). Wallacea also has the world's largest bee (*Chalocodoma pluto*) in the northern Moluccas, a creature in which the females can grow to four centimeters in length. This bee is also remarkable because it nests communally in inhabited termite nests in lowland forest trees.

As elsewhere, things have changed dramatically in Wallacea during the course of the past century. The human population has nearly quadrupled, and the Indonesian economy has grown tremendously. In the last decade, one of the world's newest countries, Timor Leste, was created in the hotspot, and many parts of Wallacea have seen political turmoil and dramatic changes. The first commercial logging operation in Wallacea began in the early part of the century, and forests have been cleared for agricultural programs, for industrial timber plantations, and for land settlement schemes. Much of the remaining forest is allocated as timber concessions and other areas are threatened by mining developments. Furthermore, as has been so obvious with the El Niño-related fires that have raged through much of Indonesia from mid-1997 to the present, fire continues to be a problem —and is now greatly exacerbated by increased drying because of logging and plantation agriculture, and sometimes by intentional burning as well (Brown 1998). Invasive alien species are a threat that is certainly widespread, but too little understood. Hunting and trapping for the pot, and the exotic pet trade, are widespread. Terrestrial and marine conservation issues can not be separated, as the livelihoods of a huge proportion of the region's human inhabitants come from the sea and are under pressure from overexploitation and pollution.

As a result of the different human impacts on the Sulawesi environment, there has been substantial decline in forest cover, although less than that in most of the other hotspots. What remains is also partly a function of dryness and altitude. Lowland areas have suffered more than the highlands and, while dry forest

On the opposite page, view of the Gamalama Volcano (Halmahera Island) from the Panau Lagoon on Ternate Island, North Moluccas.
© **Gerald Cubitt**

Above, the Malayan pangolin (Manis javanica) is distributed from Burma and Thailand to Java and the Philippines. There is a high demand for pangolin scales for traditional medicines in many parts of the world, and particularly so in Southeast Asia, and the meat is also eaten by indigenous peoples.
© **Michael Pitts**/naturepl.com

types in general have only about 10%-20% remaining, moist and wet forest types have substantially more. The Lesser Sundas are thought to have only about 7% forest cover remaining, while Sulawesi is still about 42% covered in original forest (FWI/GFW 2002). Overall, about 45% of Wallacea still has some forest cover; however, if one considers forest that is still in more or less pristine condition, the percentage drops to only 15%. This loss of forest habitat, particularly in the lowlands, has caused dramatic and severe declines in the populations of numerous forest species (many as much as 90%); as an example, Wallacea holds around 5% of the world's threatened birds.

At this point in time, forest protection in Wallacea is inadequate. For the hotspot as a whole, protected area coverage is around 24 387 km², or 7% of its original extent. Around 6% of the protected areas coverage is represented by reserves in IUCN categories I to IV. As an example of the poor representation of biodiversity in protected areas, only 35 of the 112 IBAs that have been identified are protected. Of course, establishment of protected areas is only a beginning. Once created, they need management and the cooperation of local people, the government, and the private sector in order to be successful in conserving biodiversity.

Although little known outside the region, Wallacea does have a number of interesting conservation stories. One of these is in the 3 000-km² Bogani Nani Wartabone (previously Dumoga Bone) National Park in northern Sulawesi, one of the most important conservation areas on the entire island. In the 1980s, the World Bank helped WWF to encourage establishment of this park for the purpose of protecting the upper watershed of the Dumoga River, which was to be used to irrigate 110 km² of rice fields. The park had support from provincial and district officials for many years, but recently has suffered from large numbers of small-scale gold miners, who have poisoned the river with mercury and have cleared forest. Agricultural encroachment and illegal logging, hunting, and rattan collection are also on the increase. Recently, the government of Gorontalo Province on Sulawesi increased the size of the Paguyaman Forest, the stronghold of the babirusa.

On Sulawesi, over the last nine years, Conservation International has been engaged in community-based conservation in the Togean Islands. The Togeans occupy the central portion of Tomini Bay, stretching over a distance of about 90 km. The main threats are overfishing and destructive fishing, as well as illegal logging and small plantation developments. Recently, the local government has declared its intention to proclaim the Togeans as a marine park for tourism, covering 4 000 km² of marine and terrestrial habitats.

The Wildlife Conservation Society (WCS) carried out a three-year island-wide biodiversity survey, covering eighteen forests, to understand the status of key wildlife species, their habitats, and the factors contributing to their distribution and abundance. Based on their findings, recommendations for conservation priorities will be made to governments at the national, provincial, and regional levels. WCS also assists the government in managing several protected areas throughout northern Sulawesi by providing technical assistance through wildlife monitoring, joint forest patrols, GIS analyses, helping to establish a formal collaborative management scheme, monitoring and increasing breeding success of maleo birds, and through the Wildlife Crimes Units, a collaborative program established to strengthen conservation law enforcement.

The Nature Conservancy is active in Komodo National Park, which covers 1 730 km², including 1 320 km² of coral reefs and sea at the eastern tip of Flores. Conservation activities have included awareness programs, the formation of a dive club and lodge which incorporates ecotourism training facilities, reaching agreement on how to allocate tourism revenues, capacity-building for communities and the conservation agency, and alternative livelihood programs to draw people away from overfishing, fuelwood collection, setting fires to promote grazing, and dynamiting reefs to catch fish.

On the Sangihe-Talaud Islands, between northern Sulawesi and the Phillipines, seven endemic bird species depend on two forest areas that are shrinking even though they are protected. BirdLife Indonesia and the World Bank-GEF have successfully promoted a process to resolve community-government conflicts that had prevented progress in forest conservation, and are now working with all parties concerned. BirdLife International and BirdLife Indonesia have worked together on Sumba Island in the Lesser Sundas for the past eight years. Two National Parks have been declared to protect the most important remaining forests on the island, disputes over community land inside the park have been resolved, and communities have started to take action to stop illegal logging and trapping inside the area. The program is working to formalize the role of local communities in management and protection of the park, and to set up a sustainable management system that involves all local stakeholders. BirdLife Indonesia has also undertaken surveys and identified priorities for action throughout the Lesser Sundas and the Moluccas. On Tanimbar Island in the southeast Moluccas, this has been followed up with a project to help local government and communities plan the management of their still-extensive forests (which are home to eight endemic bird species). On Halmahera, development of conservation action to protect the critical forests on the island was suspended with the violence in 1999 and has been revived in 2004.

Although Wallacea is still in relatively good shape compared to most other hotspots, much needs to be done to ensure that its large number of endemic species and unique ecosystems are maintained.

A spectral tarsier (Tarsius spectrum) *in a fig tree in the Tangkoko-Batuangus-Dua Saudara National Park in northern Sulawesi. This is one of at least five species endemic to the Wallacea Hotspot.*
© **Tui De Roy**/Auscape

On the opposite page, knobbed hornbill (Aceros cassidix), a large hornbill species endemic to Sulawesi.
© **Tim Laman**/National Geographic Image Collection

176

PHILIPPINES

LAWRENCE HEANEY [50] • PERRY ONG [53] • ROMEO TRONO [54]
LEONARD CO [54] • THOMAS BROOKS [2]

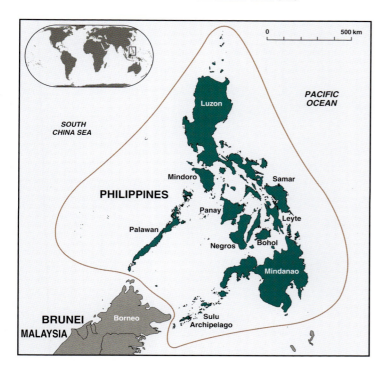

The Philippines is one of the few nations that is, in its entirety, both a hotspot and a megadiversity country. The Philippines is made up of more than 7 100 islands (of which 700 are inhabited by humans), covers 297 179 km², and lies entirely in the tropics, between 5°N and 21°N. The archipelago stretches over 1 810 km from north to south, and measures 1 104 km at its widest point. Northern Luzon is only 241 km from Taiwan (with which it shares some floristic affinities), and the islands off southwestern Palawan are only 40 km from Malaysian Borneo. Palawan, which is separated from Borneo by a channel some 145 m deep, has floristic affinities with both the Philippines and Borneo in the Sundaland Hotspot, and strong faunal affinities with the Sunda Shelf (Esselstyn et al., in press), but is here included within the Philippines Hotspot.

The archipelago is formed from a series of isolated fragments that have long and complex geological histories, some dating back 30-50 million years. With at least 17 active volcanoes, these islands are part of the "Ring of Fire" of the Pacific Basin, extending from Indonesia to Japan and eastern Russia, and around the western edge of both American continents.

Until fairly recently, almost the entire area of the Philippines (94%) was covered by some form of rainforest. Trees of the family Dipterocarpaceae were diverse (at least 45 species), with this dipterocarp-dominated forest covering most of the islands from sea level to about 1 000 m. Above these elevations, lowland forest grades into montane forest, dominated by oaks, laurels, and ericaceous plants. Above 1 000 m, the forest undergoes a dramatic change, with a rise in rainfall (to as high as 12 000 mm per year), cooler temperatures, an increase in steepness of the terrain and, at the highest elevations, a dense moss cover and a

number of distinct taxa. It is in this habitat that levels of endemism are the highest, at least proportionately; all 16 of the bird species endemic to Mindanao are present in mossy forest on Mt. Kitanglad. The montane forests (which originally covered only about 10%-12% of the country), have limited economic value and so have not been as heavily exploited as the lowland forest; the montane forests now represent about half of the primary forest remaining in the Philippines.

The patchwork of isolated islands, the tropical location of the country, and the formerly extensive areas of rainforest have resulted in high species diversity in certain groups of organisms and a very high level of endemism. There are five major and at least five minor centers of endemism, ranging in size from Luzon, the largest island at 103 000 km² which, for example, has at least 31 endemic species of mammals, to Sibuyan Island (445 km²) with four endemic mammals, to tiny Camiguin Island, a 265-km² speck of land north of Mindanao, which has at least two species of endemic mammals.

There is some uncertainty as to the number of seed plant species in the Philippines. The "classic" compilation (Merrill 1923-1926) recognized 7 620 indigenous species in 1 308 genera and 194 families, and 5 832 species (76.5%) as endemic. By way of synonymy and the addition of newly described taxa through the Flora Malesiana Project (1948-present), a revised estimate is in the order of around 8 000 species of flowering plants or angiosperms, 33 species of gymnosperms, and 1 100 species of ferns and allies (see Fernando et al. 2003) This approximates the estimate of plant diversity made earlier by Ashton (1997). Endemic species total a minimum of 6 091, comprising 5 800 angiosperms, 6 gymnosperms, and 285 ferns and allies. No families are endemic, although certain families (such as the Orchidaceae, the largest family of flowering plants in the hotspot) reach very high levels of species endemism, and only 26 genera are endemic (22 of them represented by single species; Fernando et al. 2003), indicating that endemism in this hotspot is mainly at the species level.

There are at least 167 native terrestrial mammal species in the Philippines, of which at least 102 are endemic, one of the highest levels of mammal endemism in any hotspot. The largest and most impressive of the mammal species in the Philippines, and indeed a flagship for the hotspot, is the tamaraw (*Bubalus mindorensis*, CR), the dwarf water buffalo of Mindoro Island now thought to number only a few hundred. Other flagship Philippine endemics include the Visayan spotted deer (*Rusa alfredi*, EN), now reduced to only a few hundred individuals on the islands of Masbate, Negros, and Panay (and thought to be extinct on Cebu and Guimaras); the golden-capped fruit bat (*Acerodon jubatus*, EN), probably the heaviest bat in the world, weighing up to 1.2 kg; and the rodents, of which 15 new species have been discovered in the last ten years, and including

On the opposite page, Mala Palao Island in Bacuit Bay, off Palawan in the Philippines.
© **Jean-Paul Ferrero**/*Auscape*

Above, the elusive Luzon bleeding-heart pigeon (Gallicolumba luzonica) *is endemic to Luzon in the Philippines, occurring mainly in lowland forest.*
© **Konstantin Mikhailov**/*naturepl.com*

179

the spectacular adaptive radiation of giant cloud rats. Importantly, at least one species of mammal thought to be extinct in the Philippines, the Negros naked-backed fruit bat (*Dobsonia chapmani*), has recently been rediscovered on Cebu and Negros islands. Mammal endemism is also very high at the generic level; of the 85 genera of mammals in the Philippines, 23 are endemic.

Bird diversity is moderate at 535 regularly occurring species, but endemism is very high at 185; among individual islands, Luzon has the largest numbers of single-island endemics, and is one of seven Endemic Bird Areas recognized by BirdLife International that fall within the Philippines Hotspot (Stattersfield et al. 1998). The most famous of all bird species is the Philippine eagle (*Pithecophaga jeffreyi*, CR), the second largest eagle in the world, and which has been severely affected by habitat loss such that it only survives on Luzon, Mindanao, and Samar, where the largest tracts of forest remain. Other particularly endemic-rich taxa include pigeons, kingfishers, hornbills, babblers, sunbirds, and flowerpeckers. The only endemic family in the Philippines is the Rhabdornithidae, represented by the Philippine creepers (*Rhabdornis* spp.).

Reptile diversity is quite high at 235 species, with some 160 species and six genera endemic; one of these (*Myersophis*) has a single species of snake (*M. alpestris*) from Luzon. Among these, an important flagship is the Philippine crocodile (*Crocodylus mindorensis*, CR), considered to be the most threatened of all crocodiles, having been reduced to only 100 animals in 1993. Amphibians are moderately diverse with 99 species, of which 74 are endemic. These totals are increasing rapidly with the continuing description of the Philippine herpetofauna (Brown et al. 2001).

The hotspot has a moderate-sized inland fish fauna, with 281 native species in 49 families. Although lakes are usually uncommon on islands, the high level of geological activity in the Philippines has produced a large number of lakes, many of which are landlocked. The development of lacustrine environments is associated with endemism and, apparently, with the evolution of several notable species flocks. The hotspot has nine endemic genera of inland fishes and at least 67 endemic species, many of which are restricted to single lakes. One such species is *Sardinella tawilis*, a freshwater sardine found only in Taal Lake.

Among invertebrates, insects are the most speciose group, with a current count of 20 942 species and an overall endemicity of 69.8%, in 6 185 genera and 499 families (Gapud 2002). There are 132 species of tiger beetles in the Philippines, of which 113 species occur nowhere else (D. Pearson, pers. comm.), while butterflies are estimated to number some 915 species, of which 362 are endemic (Treadaway 1995; Danielsen and Treadaway 2004).

Besides its remarkable endemism, the Philippines,

unfortunately, is also the world leader in terms of threat, with about 6%-7% of the original old-growth, closed-canopy forest remaining, and far less than that, probably on the order of 3%, estimated to remain in the lowland regions (Environmental Science for Social Change 1999). Thus, lowland rainforests are the most threatened forest type. A further 14% of the country remains as second-growth forest in various stages of degradation, but still capable of regeneration if left alone. Unquestionably, the most damaging practice has been the extensive commercial logging (both legal and illegal) that has taken place in the past. As late as 1945, as much as 60%-65% of the Philippines was covered by old-growth forest, but the rate of logging accelerated quickly after World War II, with old-growth forest cover dropping to 55% in 1950, 30% by about 1975, and 20% by 1988. Recently, lumber exports have declined drastically (by 90% in the last 20 years), but this is principally because there is virtually nothing left to export. However, the prospect of a major increase in mining is now an imminent threat. In 1997, regions where mining applications took place covered over 25% of the land area of the country, and included over 50% of the remaining primary forest.

Currently, around 11% of the total land area of the Philippines is under some form of protection; however, when one considers only protected areas in IUCN categories I to IV, this figure drops to 6%. Indeed, in the late 1980s, the Haribon Foundation, the country's foremost conservation NGO, stated that none of the protected areas currently in existence met international standards for protection and management. An IUCN report from 1988 estimated that two-thirds of the parks contained human settlements, and 27% of their cumulative area was covered by disturbed habitat or agriculture. In 1992, the government established a National Integrated Protected Areas System (NIPAS) throughout the country. To assist in the implementation of this law, a U.S. $20-million grant was provided by the Global Environment Facility/World Bank for the Conservation of Priority Protected Areas Project (CPPAP), which focused on improving management and protection in 10 top priority protected areas. One of the ten sites selected was the Palanan Wilderness Area on the island of Luzon. At 3 500 km^2, the national park that has been established there is by far the largest in the country, and covers perhaps 7% of the remaining primary rainforest of the Philippines.

A strong focus on creating effective national protected areas is the best hope for those few remaining extensive tracts of forest in the Philippines, for example, in the Northern Sierra Madre mountains and Central Cordillera of northern Luzon, on Palawan, and in the Kitanglad Range of Mindanao, and on some smaller, but endemic-rich islands such as Sibuyan and Camiguin. Meanwhile, local and community protected area mechanisms are desperately needed to conserve the

The greater mouse deer (Tragulus napa) *is widespread in Southeast Asia. This Endangered subspecies* (T. n. nigricans) *is found only on the island of Balabac in the Philippines.*
© **Jean-Paul Ferrero**/*Auscape*

On the opposite page,
Idea leuconoe, *commonly called the tree nymph, has an endemic subspecies* (I. l. princesa) *on Palawan, Philippines.*
© **Haroldo Castro**

last fragments of habitat in the endemic-rich, but heavily populated, Visayan Islands (Cebu, Negros, and Panay), Mindoro, and Tawi-Tawi. In addition, biodiversity research studies, steps to halt all commercial logging in remaining natural forest (and to allow secondary forest to regenerate into mature native forest), effective cooperation with local communities, and programs that prevent subsistence farmers from moving into forest, whether primary or partially logged, are crucial.

In 2000, a national conservation priority setting exercise was undertaken that involved more than 300 natural and social scientists from more than 100 local and international institutions representing major stakeholders spanning academia, government, civil society, the donor community, and the private sector. This exercise led to the identification of 206 conservation priority areas, of which 170 are terrestrial and inland waters and 36 are marine areas (Ong et al. 2002). Of these, only 53 priority areas have some form of protection because of their inclusion under the NIPAS, another 57 priority areas are being processed for inclusion under NIPAS, and 96 priority areas have no legal protection as they are outside the NIPAS. Of the 53 priority areas that are under NIPAS, their boundaries need to be redrawn as most of them include highly degraded areas and exclude areas of high biodiversity importance (Ong 2002). The Critical Ecosystem Partnership Fund (CEPF) is investing $7 million in three key conservation corridors identified in the priority-setting process, as well as in key sites for threatened species that fall outside those corridors. The corridor conservation effort in the Sierra Madre region on Luzon has led to a significant extension of one protected area and the formation of another, both of which will contribute to connecting the series of protected areas that run from the island's northeastern tip to the watershed of Metro Manila.

In conclusion, since the Philippines has one of the densest and most rapidly expanding human populations in Asia, its need for economic and social reform that will alleviate the causes of poverty is even more closely tied to biodiversity conservation than is usually the case. If ever there was a time and place for immediate and effective conservation action, it is now in the Philippines. There is still time to stave off disaster, but rapid action in this unique and troubled hotspot is needed now. As an offshoot of the 2000 priority-setting exercise and the lessons learned from conservation initiatives of the 1990s, new trends of working together emerged, some of which include the Network for Nature concept that aims to bring together stakeholders at the local, regional, and national levels from a wide spectrum of society so as to conserve the biodiversity of the hottest of the hotspots. Indeed, there is still hope to save the Philippines Hotspot from being the first country in the world to experience mass species extinction spasms and environmental collapse.

SOUTHWEST AUSTRALIA

JOHN S. BEARD [43]

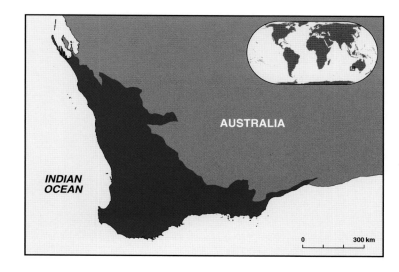

The Southwest Australia Hotspot is located in the enormous State of Western Australia, between latitudes 26° and 36°S, and longitudes 114° and 126°E, and originally covered 356 717 km² in extent. The climate is Mediterranean in character, with most of the rain falling in winter. The total average winter rainfall varies from over 1 400 mm in the extreme southwest to 300 mm in the interior, the number of dry months increasing from 3-4 to 7-8 as rainfall declines. Inland, the boundary of the hotspot closely approximates the 300-mm isohyet.

As defined here, the Southwest Australia Hotspot comprises the Southwest Botanical Province of Beard (1980, 1990; Davis et al. 1995), but excludes the neighboring Southwestern Interzone. The vegetation of the Southwest Botanical Province has been mapped in detail to show original natural vegetation before the arrival of Europeans. The vegetation is almost entirely woody, forming forest, woodland, shrubland, and heath, and there are no grasslands. Among the principal vegetation types in this region are *Eucalyptus* woodlands (formerly covering 25.9% of the Province, but of which 89% has been cleared), and the *Eucalyptus*-dominated "mallee" shrubland (which formerly covered 22% of the Province, but has now been 50% cleared). *Kwongan* is a term adapted from the Aboriginal Nyungar language to cover the various Western Australian types of Mediterranean shrubland, comparable with the maquis, chaparral, and fynbos of other countries with such systems (Pate and Beard 1984). The principal structural types of kwongan are thicket, scrub-heath, and heath, which together comprise about 30% of the original vegetation. These formations have also been cleared to a large degree: 59% of the once extensive kwongan heath formations have been cleared.

Many of the vegetation units in this Province are of an endemic character. While *Eucalyptus*-dominated forests, woodlands, and mallee occur in eastern Australia, the dominant species and a majority of the associated species in the west are endemic. Kwongan is a

On the opposite page, heathland vegetation at Toolbrunup Peak and Mt. Hassell in the Sterling Ranges National Park in southwestern Australia.
© **Marianne F. Porteners**/*Auscape*

formation unique to Western Australia. Although analogous "heaths" occur in the east, certain structural forms of kwongan such as the *Acacia-Casuarina-Melaleuca* thickets are endemic. The majority of species in the kwongan flora are also endemic.

In terms of plant diversity and endemism, the Southwest Botanical Province has a total of 5 571 species, of which 2 948 (52.9%) species are entirely confined to this Province; a further 1 462 species (26.2% of species present) extend slightly beyond its borders into the Southwestern Interzone or Eremaea and can still be considered endemic to a more broadly defined concept of southwestern Australia (Beard et al. 2000). The flora of the Southwest Botanical Province comprises 139 families, of which four are endemic: the Ecdeiocoleaceae, Cephalotaceae (represented by the pitcher plant *Cephalotus follicularis*, VU), Emblingiaceae, and Eremosynaceae. In addition, 87 (12.5%) of 697 genera are endemic. The ten largest families (including the Myrtaceae with 785 species, of which 92% are endemic, and Proteaceae with 684 species, 96% endemic) comprise 61% of the flora, while the number of species per genus averages eight, although the ten largest genera (including *Acacia* with 397 species, 51% endemic, and *Eucalyptus* with 246 species, 52% endemic) far exceed this figure (Beard et al. 2000).

Foremost among a wealth of flagship plant species in this region are the *Banksias* of the family Proteaceae (which are 100% endemic), the "blackboys" of the family Xanthorrhoeaceae (so named because these plants with their tall inflorescences reminded early settlers of aborigines with spears), and the giant *Eucalyptus* characteristic of the southern portion of this region, including the *jarrah* (*E. marginata*), the *marri* (*E. calophylla*), and the *karri* (*E. diversicolor*), the latter forming a canopy at about 70 m, with some individuals attaining 80 m or more, ranking this southwestern Australian endemic as one of the tallest trees on Earth.

Vertebrate diversity in this hotspot is not nearly as high as that of plants. Mammals number 57 species, of which 12 are naturally endemic to this hotspot. Although overall diversity is low, there are some very interesting higher-level endemics. The honey possum (*Tarsipes rostratus*), among the few truly nectivorous mammals, is the only living representative of the family Tarsipedidae, and the numbat (*Myrmecobius fasciatus*, VU) is the only member of the marsupial family Myrmecobiidae. Another appealing flagship marsupial, this time an endemic genus from the kangaroo family, Macropodidae, is the quokka (*Setonix brachyurus*, VU), a small wallaby confined to the mainland, where it has been declining in numbers, and two small offshore islands (Rottnest Island and Bald Island).

Bird diversity is relatively low, but endemism is a little higher than for most of the other Mediterranean-type systems. Some 285 species are regularly recorded from this region, and 10 of these are endemic. BirdLife International also lists Southwest Australia as one of their Endemic Bird Areas (Stattersfield et al. 1998). Among the birds, flagship species include the black swan (*Cygnus atratus*), the principal state emblem of Western Australia, and the noisy scrub bird (*Atrichornis clamosus*, VU), so called because the male is particularly vociferous.

Reptile diversity is quite high, not surprisingly, since Australia, as a country, is considered the world leader in reptile diversity (Mittermeier et al. 1997). A total of at least 177 species are found in the Southwest Australia Hotspot, of which 27 are endemic. The most interesting of these is the western swamp tortoise (*Pseudemydura umbrina*, CR), a monotypic genus endemic to the region and now found only in one or two small swamps at Bullsbrook, near Perth. Another endemic genus is the short-nosed snake (*Elapognathus minor*), which is confined to the humid coastal plains of the hotspot. Amphibians are somewhat less diverse, as is usually the case for a dry region, but the 33 species include 19 endemics, four of which represent endemic genera: *Myobatrachus gouldii*, *Metacrinia nichollsi*, *Arenophryne rotunda*, and *Spicospina flammocaerulea*.

The Southwest Australia Hotspot has a very small amount of freshwater habitat and a correspondingly small fish fauna with only 20 native species. It is, however, one of the most distinctive faunas, 10 (50%) of its species and three of its genera being endemic. Most remarkable is the salamanderfish (*Lepidogalaxias salamandroides*), which constitutes the one endemic family (Lepidogalaxiidae) that is entirely restricted to this small hotspot, surviving in the harsh conditions of its ephemeral pools and highly acidic peat habitats. Located near the southern limits of the freshwater world, the hotspot's fish fauna is dominated by remnants of ancient Gondwanan groups including the southern lampreys and galaxiids (Allen et al. 2002).

The biggest threat to the unique biota of Southwest Australia has been land clearing for agriculture, as the entire Southwest Botanical Province falls within the Intensive Land-use Zone. This has left a legacy of substantial habitat loss and probably species loss as well. Nearly all the land that can be farmed economically has been now utilized, and expansion of farms into virgin areas has stopped. Clearing of remaining vegetation on existing farms still takes place, though restrictions have been placed on certain areas for environmental purposes such as protection of water supplies. It is estimated that 30% of the native vegetation in this hotspot remains in the Intensive Land-use Zone, which is more or less synonymous with the Southwest Botanical Province; the Swan Coastal Plain, wheatbelt, and mallee regions have been largely cleared, and only patches of original native vegetation remain (Shepherd et al. 2002).

Currently, the most serious threat is the spread of root disease ("jarrah dieback") caused by the root fungus *Phytophthora cinnamomi*. This disease was first noticed in the jarrah forests around 1940. Unfortunately,

The Vulnerable numbat (Myrmecobius fasciatus) *is the only representative of an endemic family, the Myrmecobiidae, now restricted to the Southwest Australia Hotspot. The species is unique in that it is the only marsupial adapted to a diet of termites; it lacks effective teeth and has a long, sticky tongue used to lick up those insects.*
© **Jean-Paul Ferrero**/*Auscape*

On the opposite page, giant eucalyptus trees, including karri (Eucalyptus diversicolor) *and* jarrah (E. marginata)*, in Shannon National Park in southwestern Australia.*
© **Jaime Plaza van Roon**/*Auscape*

the pathogen responsible was not identified until 1965, by which time thousands of hectares of forest, both trees and associated flora, were affected. By 1974, it was estimated that 2 820 km² had been affected and that the disease was spreading at the rate of 200 km² per year, which turned out to be an overestimate. The disease can be severe on sites where soil drainage is obstructed; most of these have now been impacted so that only isolated trees continue to be attacked by "jarrah dieback." However, new concern has arisen as *Phytophthora* has been found attacking kwongan habitats outside the forests, in particular the Stirling Range National Park, where it has caused mortality among susceptible plants like the grass trees (*Xanthorrhoea* spp.) and members of the Proteaceae, especially *Banksias*. As indicated above, these are particularly important flagship species and their loss would be tragic.

Conservation in Western Australia is vested in the hands of the State Department of Conservation and Land Management (CALM), which maintains a series of national and state protected areas. Some 10.8% of the hotspot is under some form of official protection, a figure that remains unchanged when one includes only reserves classified in IUCN categories I to IV. An important issue, however, is that of the representativeness of existing protected areas. Biodiversity surveys were never used to determine appropriate sites for protected areas, meaning that there is an uneven representation of different ecosystem types in this region. Many existing reserves are small, and are isolated "islands" of natural vegetation within vast areas of farmlands. Furthermore, many species endemic to the Southwest Province have very restricted ranges and a number of rare species are found only on private land, meaning that the cooperation of landowners has to be sought to ensure their protection.

All things considered, the Southwest Australia Hotspot is one of the least threatened of the hotspots, and has one of the best opportunities to achieve representation of all the region's biodiversity in protected areas. Maintaining the integrity of the existing protected area coverage is clearly one step, but much vacant land that is not good for either farming or pastureland, and unlikely to be disturbed in the near future, could also be conserved. And finally, and perhaps most important, is an increasing desire on the part of the government to look into the possibility of creating new reserves in key pieces of privately owned land in under-represented vegetation types —in order to increase restricted-range species and ecosystem coverage in the region's protected area network. A variety of approaches to creating such private reserves through tax and other fiscal incentives already exist, and could very well be put to use here. If these steps can be taken and succesfully implemented over the long term, the Southwest Australia Hotspot could indeed become one the best-protected hotspots on Earth.

NEW ZEALAND

DAVID R. GIVEN [38] • ALAN SAUNDERS [39] • DAVE TOWNS [40]
ALAN TENNYSON [41] • KERI NIELSON [42]

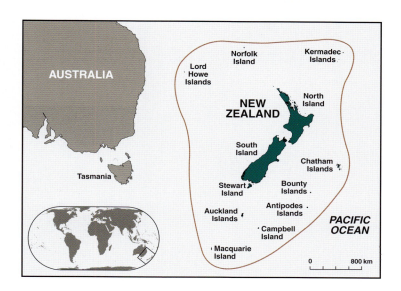

New Zealand (Aoteraroa) is the only hotspot that encompasses the entire land area of a developed nation. A piece of Gondwanaland that separated from Australia about 82 million years ago (Sutherland 1999), it now forms an isolated archipelago located some 2 000 km to the southeast of Australia in the southern Pacific Ocean. It covers 270 197 km², with the three main islands, North Island, South Island, and Stewart Island, making up 90% of the land area. Smaller outliers are the Chatham Islands (963 km²) 800 km east of South Island, the Kermadec Islands (34 km²) to the north, and the Subantarctic Islands to the south (including the Bounty Islands, Antipodes Islands, Campbell Island, Snares Islands, Auckland Islands, and Macquarie Island). Also included here are Lord Howe (14.6 km²) and Norfolk (36.8 km²) islands, both Australian territories.

Climate is an important determinant of biotic patterns in New Zealand. The country is strongly influenced by its mid-temperate location, northeast-southwest orientation, and hilly to mountainous topography, with about 75% of the land area above 200-m altitude and reaching a maximum altitude of 3 700 m on Aoraki (Mount Cook). The mountains form a barrier to westerly airflow, resulting in 12 000 mm or more annual rainfall on the western flank of the Southern Alps, one of the highest on Earth, and heavy falls of winter snow. In striking contrast, rain-shadow areas east of the Southern Alps can experience as little as 300 mm annually. The Kermadec Islands have a subtropical climate, with warm, moist conditions throughout the year, while the Chatham Islands have a cloudy, humid climate, with cool, wet winters and warm, often dry summers. The southern Subantarctic Islands have a generally windy, cool, temperate-montane climate and relatively low levels of sunshine.

New Zealand's forest ecosystems are greatly depleted, but perhaps the most impressive of those remaining are the forests of giant New Zealand kauri (*Agathis australis*), which are restricted to the far north of New Zealand, being replaced further south by forests dominated by

On the opposite page, the New Zealand pigeon (Hemiphaga novaeseelandiae) is a large and impressive forest pigeon endemic to New Zealand. There are reports that this pigeon, which may actually represent two distinct species, is declining in parts of its range.
© **Patricio Robles Gil**/*Sierra Madre*

angiosperms. In the southern part of North Island and on South Island, extensive areas of forest are dominated by Gondwanan gymnosperms of the family Podocarpaceae, by southern beech (*Nothofagus*), and by various combinations of these with broad-leaved angiosperms. The podocarp and beech-podocarp forests on the western flanks of the Southern Alps are among the most extensive temperate rainforests on Earth. Scrub and shrublands are of widespread occurrence in drier parts of eastern South Island and North Island; they are often floristically rich, with numerous endemic species. With its many offshore islands, New Zealand has a diverse coastal flora with a significant number of coprophilous plants associated with nesting seabirds, penguin rookeries, and sea mammal colonies. Above the timberline, snow grasses (*Chionochloa* spp.) often dominate, with floristically rich alpine herbfields in wetter sites and on areas of late snow-lie. At higher altitudes, the nival zone is characterized by cushion plants, many of them endemic and including the peculiar and distinctive "vegetable sheep" (*Raoulia* and *Hastia* spp.), which are highly compacted shrubs of the family Asteraceae.

New Zealand has relatively low plant species diversity, with 3 400 species (including 2 300 vascular species and 1 100 liverworts and mosses), but high endemism. At least 1 865 vascular plants are endemic (81%) and an additional 220-440 liverworts and mosses (20%-40%), the exact number for the latter not yet having been determined. In addition, of the estimated 390 plant genera, there are about 35 endemic genera. Some of the more interesting plant species on New Zealand include the endemic fern *Loxoma cunninghamii*, whose closest living relatives are three species of the genus *Loxomopsis* from Central America, and the pingao sand sedge, belonging to the endemic monotypic genus *Desmoschoenus*. There is also a single endemic family, the Ixerbaceae, represented by a single species (*I. brexiodes*).

Vertebrate diversity in New Zealand is low overall, but again, there is high endemism. The number of regularly occurring bird species in New Zealand totals 198, of which 89 are endemic. New Zealand is thought to have the most diverse seabird community in the world, with no fewer than 84 species known to breed there; for example, it is estimated that at least three-quarters of the world's penguins breed in the New Zealand region (D. Towns, unpubl.). A recent staggering development has been the rediscovery of the New Zealand storm petrel (*Oceanites maorianus*), in waters just off New Zealand's North Island. Birds were seen in January and November of 2003, the first records of this supposedly Extinct species, previously known only from fossil material and three nineteenth-century specimens. New Zealand also has 15 endemic bird genera (of a total of 71) and three endemic extant bird families (Acanthisittidae, Callaeidae, and Apterygidae), a very high number for a country of this size. Among the surviving avian fauna, the flightless, nocturnal kiwis, of which there are three species (*Apteryx* spp.), are the most famous New Zealand endemics. In addition, three very large parrots are endemic to New

Zealand, including the kakapo (*Strigops habroptilus*, CR), the most unusual of all psittacine birds, and the kea (*Nestor notabilis*, VU), a large, inquisitive, long-beaked mountain parrot restricted to the mountainous areas of South Island. Indicative of New Zealand's importance for bird conservation is the fact that BirdLife International recognizes five Endemic Bird Areas (EBAs) for this hotspot: North Island; South Island; the subantarctic Auckland Islands; the Chatham Islands to the east of South Island; and Norfolk Island (Stattersfield et al. 1998).

Reptiles are represented by 37 species on New Zealand, and all native species are endemic and, remarkably, five of the six genera represented are endemic. The largest terrestrial reptile in this hotspot is the tuatara (*Sphenodon* spp.), a member of an endemic order (Sphenodontida), and the only case in which an entire reptilian order is endemic to a single country. It was previously thought that only one species, *S. punctatus*, existed, but a second species, *S. guntheri*, has now been recognized. These reptiles, superficially resembling iguana lizards, are the last survivors of a group that lived side by side with the dinosaurs and whose heyday was the Triassic Period some 200 million years ago (May 1990).

Amphibians and mammals are the two groups of terrestrial vertebrates that are poorly represented. There are only four native frog species, all highly primitive and members of an endemic family, Leiopelmatidae, and genus, *Leiopelma*, found only on New Zealand. Native mammals on New Zealand number only two, both of them endemic bats, but one, the New Zealand lesser short-tailed bat (*Mystacina tuberculata*, VU), is the only living representative of an endemic family, Mystacinidae.

The hotspot harbors one of the smallest but most distinctive inland fish faunas of any hotspot, with 39 species in 15 genera, and 25 endemic species. This fauna is dominated by members of the family Galaxiidae, a group of coolwater trout-like fishes restricted to the southern tips of South America, Africa, Australia, New Zealand, and a few small islands such as Lord Howe and the Campbell Islands. Of the 51 galaxiid species known worldwide, 19 occur in the hotspot and 16 are restricted to it. A related family, the Retropinnidae or New Zealand smelts, is represented in the hotspot by three endemic species including the only member of the endemic genus *Stokellia*.

A distinctive element of the New Zealand biota is the widespread occurrence of gigantism (Daugherty et al. 1993). Some of the giant forms include the now extinct flightless moas and Haast's eagle among the birds, and also giant insects, myriapods, flatworms, land snails, centipedes, slugs, earthworms, and some plants. The world's heaviest insect, the *weta* or wingless cricket of Little Barrier Island (Hauturu) weighs up to 70 g and is one of 12 species of *Deinacrida*, the ancestors of which roamed the Jurassic forests.

However, this biodiversity represents only a small percentage of what existed prior to human settlement on these islands. As is the case with many oceanic islands, humans arrived fairly late on New Zealand, with the Maoris first arriving perhaps 700-800 years ago (Ministry

On pp. 188-189, lush tree-fern forest on North Island, New Zealand.
© **Patricio Robles Gil**/*Sierra Madre*

Above, the Endangered brown kiwi (Apteryx mantelli) *from Westland, South Island, New Zealand. This particular form, the Okarito brown kiwi, may require recognition as a distinct species.*
© **Tui De Roy**/*Minden Pictures*

for the Environment 1997) and the Europeans in the early part of the nineteenth century. Since then, remarkable species like the giant moas (which reached nearly 3 m in height) and the immense Haast's eagle that preyed on the moas, have gone extinct. Human impact on the pristine ecosystems of New Zealand can be divided into three main categories: predation through hunting, fishing, and gathering; habitat destruction through deforestation, wetland drainage, and ecosystem degradation of various kinds; and, particularly, introduction of alien species, both plant and animal. Since European settlement alone, some 16 land birds, one native bat species, one fish, at least a dozen invertebrates and 10 plants are believed to have gone extinct, while other species such as the tuataras, the stitchbird (*Notiomystis cincta*, VU), and the North Island saddleback (*Philesturnus carunculatus rufusater*) survive only on offshore islands.

Furthermore, prior to the arrival of humans in New Zealand, indigenous forest covered some 230 000 km², or about 85% of the country, with the remainder being native grasslands, duneland ecosystems, and wetlands. Today, the forest has been reduced to 62 000 km², or about 23% of the country, and only about 35 000 km² (13%) of this is still in more or less pristine condition. Grasslands, on the other hand, have now increased from 10 000-20 000 km² to more than 140 000 km², or 52% of the country; however, most of this is grazed or overgrown with introduced grasses, leaving only about 15 000 km² in more or less pristine condition. Duneland ecosystems, one of the most threatened ecosystem types in the country, are now down to no more than 250 km². Wetland systems have been especially heavily impacted; once covering perhaps as much as 10 000 km², or almost 4% of the country, they have now been substantially reduced in extent, with only about 4 000 km² still remaining in good condition. In terms of natural habitat, then, it is estimated that remaining indigenous habitat in more or less primary condition amounts to 35 000 km² of forest, 15 000 km² of native grassland-scrub, 4 000 km² of wetlands and other aquatic systems, 2 600 km² of smaller island ecosystems, 1 800 km² of alpine systems, and about 1 000 km² of coastal systems, for a total of 59 400 km² (or 22% of the land surface of the country).

The protected area network of the New Zealand Hotspot includes 3 345 protected areas in IUCN categories I to IV, covering around 22% of the hotspot. The additional protected areas in IUCN categories V and VI bring the total surface area of the hotspot under a reasonable level of protection to 27%, a very high percentage by international standards. Comparing this figure with the 59 400 km² estimated above to remain in more or less pristine condition, it is likely that much of what is left intact in New Zealand is already under some form of protection. In part, this is because a lot of New Zealand is mountainous, and areas like the Southern Alps are protected because the land can't be used for anything else; lowlands, on the other hand, are not nearly as well protected. At least 60 protected areas have been set aside as Nature Reserves or Wildlife Sanctuaries specifically to protect threatened species. These include many of the offshore and outlying islands ranging from the large subantarctic Auckland and Campbell Island groups, Little Barrier (Hauturu), and Kapiti, to the warm temperate Kermadec Islands.

To deal with the incomplete coverage of the country's native ecosystems in the protected area network, several initiatives have been undertaken. For example, one important initiative has been the subdivision of New Zealand into a network of Ecological Regions and Ecological Districts, with subsequent development of rapid survey techniques to assess them. Under the Protected Natural Areas Program (PNAP), these methods aim to identify sites of conservation value which are representative of the study area. The Department of Conservation (which is the main government agency that administers protected areas in New Zealand), local government, and other agencies then begin landowner discussions, with a view to protection. Many landowners are coming to value habitat remnants and rare species, and this opens up an array of possibilities for innovative conservation practices, where the energy and interest of individuals can be combined with the resources of the government and other agencies. Recently, the New Zealand Government has encouraged development of "mainland islands" that are intensively managed, predator-free areas where threatened species can be re-established.

Finally, no discussion on New Zealand would be complete without a word on invasive species, which have contributed to the decline and extinction of many native species in this country. While formal habitat protection is important, active pest management is required if further extinctions are to be avoided. Conservation practitioners in New Zealand have earned an international reputation for their achievements in eradicating invasive mammals from islands and, more recently, controlling animal and plant pests at "mainland" sites. Twelve species of pest mammals and one predatory bird have been successfully eradicated from offshore and oceanic islands in the New Zealand region (Veitch and Bell 1990). Significant recent advances have involved a new capability to eradicate rodents from much larger islands using aerial bait application techniques, and the use of more effective quarantine and contingency procedures to reduce the risks of further invasions. For example, Norway rats (*Rattus norvegicus*) were recently eradicated from Campbell Island (112 km²), opening the way for important species recovery and ecological restoration objectives. The Department of Conservation is applying a strategy to develop capacity to eradicate different suites of invasive species from further islands and to refine procedures to minimize invasion risks (Cromarty et al. 2002). Important recent progress has also been made in controlling invasive species on the New Zealand "mainland" —sites not surrounded by water, where terrestrial pest invasion rates are higher than on remote islands. Better planned and more consistently supported pest animal and weed control programs have resulted in significant conservation outcomes being recorded (Saunders 2000).

The Vulnerable Brother's Island tuatara (Sphenodon guntheri) is one of two species of the order Rhynchocephalia, the only living representatives of one of the six major groups of reptiles. Although these unique creatures date back to the time of the dinosaurs, they are now restricted to a handful of small islands in the Cook Strait, which separates New Zealand's North and South Islands. The New Zealand Hotspot is the only biodiversity hotspot with an endemic order of terrestrial vertebrates.
© Russell A. Mittermeier

NEW CALEDONIA

Porter P. Lowry II [26] • Jérôme Munzinger [33]
Philippe Bouchet [34] • Hubert Géraux [35] • Aaron Bauer [36]
Olivier Langrand [1] • Russell A. Mittermeier [1]

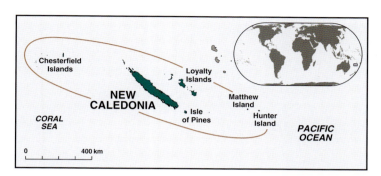

New Caledonia is one of the smallest of the hotspots, and has some of the highest levels of endemism, especially in plants. It lies at the southern extremity of the Melanesian Region, some 1 200 km east of Queensland, Australia and 1 700 km northeast of New Zealand. Until recently, New Caledonia was classified as a French Overseas Territory, but is now in the process of becoming an Overseas Country ("Pays d'Outre-Mer") with substantial political autonomy that stops short of full independence.

Unlike the nearby island nations of the East Melanesian Islands Hotspot, which are of volcanic origin, the main island of New Caledonia, Grande Terre (16 595 km²), was once part of the great ancient continent of Gondwana, from which it became separated 65-80 million years ago. Of more recent origin are the 1 600-km long reef (second in the world) that encircles Grande Terre and the raised limestone Loyalty Islands to the east (Ouvéa, Lifou, Tiga, and Maré, plus a few uninhabited islands). The hotspot includes the Belep Islands to the north of Grande Terre, and the Isle of Pines, immediately south. The Chesterfield Islands further to the west, and the uninhabited volcanic islands of Matthew and Hunter to the east, are politically dependent on New Caledonia and also included here, although their value for terrestrial biodiversity conservation is limited. The total land area of New Caledonia, therefore, comes to 18 972 km².

Despite its small size, New Caledonia is biologically very diverse and, like the other hotspots that are also pieces of Gondwana (Madagascar and New Zealand), has very high levels of endemism, both at species and higher levels, especially among plants and invertebrates. Plant diversity and endemism are truly outstanding in global terms, with 3 270 vascular plant species, of which 2 432 species (74.4%) are endemic. These are in 808 genera, of which 108 (13.4%) are endemic (updated from Jaffré et al. 2001). Furthermore, there are five endemic families —Amborellaceae, Paracryphiaceae, Strasburgeriaceae, Oncothecaceae, and Phellinaceae (Morat 1993; Jaffré et al. 2001)—, a truly amazing number for such a small area and exceeded only by Madagascar and the Cape Floristic Region of South Africa. Conservative estimates suggest that as much as 5% of the vascular plants in New Caledonia remain undescribed, which would bring the total to more than 3 400 species (Lowry 1998).

The flora occurs in four main natural vegetation types, namely humid evergreen forest, sclerophyllous forest, low- to mid-altitude maquis and high-altitude maquis formations. Grassland and *niaouli* (*Melaleuca quinquenervia*) savanna today occupy more than 6 000 km² or 32% of the area, and are often mistaken by visitors and residents as the typical landscape of New Caledonia. These are, in fact, highly disturbed anthropogenic formations that are maintained by repeated fire and grazing by cattle and introduced deer; the *niaouli*, an invasive, non-endemic (and possibly even non-native) eucalypt, has a thick, papery bark that makes it resistant to fire.

Humid evergreen forest once covered some 70% of the territory, or more than 13 000 km², but has now been reduced to only about 4 000 km². Around 2 012 plant species are found in the rainforest, of which 82.2% are endemic, making it the richest of New Caledonia's vegetation types (Jaffré et al. 1998, 2001). Sclerophyll forest once covered about 23% of New Caledonia, or more than 4 400 km²; however, it has now been drastically reduced to just 45 km² (Bouchet et al. 1995; Jaffré et al. 1998; H. Géraux, unpubl.), making sclerophyll forest the most threatened vegetation type in the territory. Even what little remains is generally very degraded and fragmented into small patches of 20-30 ha or less (though there are a few blocks that exceed 100 ha), surrounded by agricultural land. A recent study suggests that New Caledonia's sclerophyll forest is the most threatened tropical dry forest in the world (Gillespie and Jaffré 2003). Sclerophyll forest is not as rich as humid evergreen forest or maquis, but nonetheless contains numerous endemic species; some 456 plant species have been recorded from this forest type (57.5% endemic) (Jaffré et al. 1998, 2001).

New Caledonia's unusual maquis is a specialized edaphic formation that is now the most extensive vegetation type in the territory. High-altitude maquis is very limited, but still occupies almost all of its original extent of 100 km². Some 200 plant species occur in high-altitude maquis, of which 91% are endemic to New Caledonia. In contrast, low- to mid-altitude maquis is now the most extensive natural formation in the country. It once occupied only about 5% of the country, but has now expanded, largely as a result of fire disturbance, to cover some 4 400 km², or 23% of New Caledonia. Some 1 144 plant species occur in this kind of maquis (89% endemic) (Jaffré et al. 1998).

Certain plant groups in New Caledonia are particularly exceptional: of 44 gymnosperm species, 43 are endemic, including 13 endemic species of *Araucaria*, an ancient group of Gondwanaland gymnosperms, of which there are only 19 worldwide (Setoguchi et al. 1998) and the world's only parasitic gymnosperm, *Parasitaxus ustus*. The territory also has 31 endemic species of palms, representing 15 endemic genera out of a total of 16 (Hodel and Pintaud 1998). Furthermore, New Caledonia is home to the endemic, monotypic family Amborellaceae, which comprises a single species, *Amborella trichopoda*, recently shown to represent the basal-most branch in the evolutionary tree of the flowering plants (see, for example,

On the opposite page, pines (Neocallitropsis pancheri) in Madeleine Falls Botanic Reserve, Southern Province, New Caledonia.
© Jean-Paul Ferrero/*Auscape*

193

MAPUTALAND-PONDOLAND-ALBANY

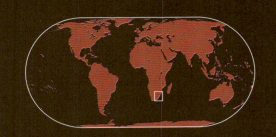

The Maputaland-Pondoland-Albany region lies along the east coast of southern Africa below the Great Escarpment. It extends from the extreme southern parts of Mozambique (Limpopo River) and Mpumalanga (Olifants River) in the north, through Swaziland and KwaZulu-Natal, to the Eastern Cape Province in South Africa in the south. The Maputaland-Pondoland-Albany region is very diverse and complex floristically, climatologically, and geologically. There are at least three clear foci of high endemism and high diversity in the area, the names of which have been amalgamated as the name of this hotspot. These foci are Maputaland (= Tongaland) in the north, Pondoland further south, and Albany in the southwest. The Maputaland-Pondoland-Albany region is not only a center of endemism, but also a marked center of diversity across the taxonomic spectrum.

The Maputaland-Pondoland-Albany Hotspot is about 274 316 km^2 in size, and its boundaries correspond broadly to White's (1983) delimitation of the Tongaland-Pondoland Regional Mosaic. However, as defined here, it is a bit larger than this region as it extends further inland to include areas of temperate grassland and forest lying below 1 800 m along the Great Escarpment in KwaZulu-Natal and the Eastern Cape, and below 1 200 m further north in Swaziland, Mpumalanga, and Limpopo (see Davis et al. 1994; Van Wyk and Smith 2001). Following Van Wyk and Smith (2001), it also extends further west in the south to include the Albany center of plant endemism. The Maputaland area has strong floristic and faunistic connections with the Coastal Forests of Eastern Africa Hotspot to the north, whereas the Pondoland region shows some floristic links with the Cape Floristic Region further south.

The Maputaland-Pondoland-Albany Hotspot borders several important areas of plant diversity and endemism, including the Cape Floristic Region Hotspot, and the Barberton, Wolkberg, and Drakensberg Alpine Centers of Plant Endemism (Van Wyk and Smith 2001), which are considered as outliers of the broader Eastern Afromontane Hotspot.

The topography of the Maputaland-Pondoland-Al-

bany region is very diverse, ranging from ancient and young sand dunes and low-lying plains in the north to a series of rugged terraces deeply incised by river valleys in the central and southern parts. Several mountain ranges, including the Sneeuberg (highest peak in the region: Kompasberg in Sneeuberg, 2 502 m), Winterberg (2 369 m), Amatola Mountains (1 937 m), Ngeli Range (2 268 m), Lebombo Mountains (699 m), and Ngoye Range (486 m), also occur within the Maputaland-Pondoland-Albany region, while the Great Escarpment borders it to the west. The break-up of Gondwana, and subsequent cycles of uplift and erosion shaped the landscape of the Maputaland-Pondoland-Albany region. These processes formed the Great Escarpment, which receded from the coast after the break-up event and the establishment of an effective drainage system. Today, the Great Escarpment separates the elevated interior plateau of southern Africa from the coastal lowlands. Regional geology consists of basement granites, gneisses and schists, various sedimentary deposits, lavas (basalt and dolerite intrusions), and marine sediments of various ages. The climate of the

On the opposite page, Strandloper Falls in the Mkambati Nature Reserve, Pondoland.
© **Patricio Robles Gil**/*Sierra Madre*

219

Maputaland-Pondoland-Albany region ranges from subtropical-tropical in the low-lying, northern coastal areas to more temperate with frost in winter on higher ground away from the coast.

Six of South Africa's eight biomes enter into the hotspot, and 27 of the 68 vegetation types that occur within South Africa, Lesotho, and Swaziland, according to Low and Rebelo (1998), as well as one that they do not recognize, are represented within the region. One type of forest (namely Licuáti forest, previously called sand forest), three types of thicket, six types of bushveld, and five types of grassland, including the coastal plateau sourveld grasslands of Pondoland, the short mistbelt grasslands, and the woody grasslands of Maputaland, are endemic to the Maputaland-Pondoland-Albany Hotspot.

The forests of the Maputaland-Pondoland-Albany region, despite their naturally fragmented distribution, are of special interest. Forest vegetation covers less than 30 000 km² in South Africa (of which approximately 80% falls within the hotspot); these warm temperate forests have by far the highest tree richness of any of the world's other temperate forests, with some 598 tree species occurring (Silander 2001). This richness in tree species is exceeded only in the evergreen forests of East Asia, where 876 species grow in a much larger area. South African forests are also between three and seven times richer in tree species than other forested areas of the Southern Hemisphere, even though the other Southern Hemispheric forests cover a much larger area (Silander 2001).

The thicket biome of southern Africa, the largest part of which occurs within the Maputaland-Pondoland-Albany region, is thought to be the most species-rich formation of woody plants within South Africa. It has been suggested that thickets are extremely ancient and include many elements basal to the Cape and Succulent Karoo flora (Vlok et al. 2003). In addition to forest and thicket, grassland is also of particular importance in this hotspot, especially as it is the most threatened and least protected of all the biome types in southern Africa.

This hotspot also has a remarkable succulent flora that is mainly concentrated in the Albany region. The succulent riches of southern Africa are well known (especially that of the Succulent Karoo Hotspot), with over 46% (4 674 taxa in 58 families) of the world's succulents growing naturally in southern Africa (Smith et al. 1997). This is perhaps not surprising, as large parts of the southern African landscape are prone to regular droughts, to which numerous plant species have adapted by developing succulent leaves, stems, and roots. However, whereas leaf succulents predominate in the western, mainly winter-rainfall parts of southern Africa, the succulents of the Maputaland-Pondoland-Albany region are predominantly stem succulents.

The Maputaland-Pondoland-Albany region is not exceptionally diverse as a region of cultural diversity when compared with other parts of southern and central Africa. However, the region is very densely populated (over 20 million people), with extensive informal township and urban development, especially along the coastline. In some parts the human population reaches densities of up to 1 900 people per km² (Durban and surroundings). Other parts are less densely populated; the Pietermaritzburg and Port Elizabeth areas, for example, have population densities of around 500 people per km², while Umtata and East London population densities are up to 100 people per km². Most of the region is subjected to high population densities, with only a third of the land surface area having population densities of below 50 people per km².

Nevertheless, the hotspot remains a significant pluricultural, multilingual, and multi-ethnic region. Its oldest known inhabitants were various tribes of Bushmen (Saan) and Khoekhoe. Sadly, these cultures are now essentially gone from the region, although limited assimilation of the original Khoesaan languages is still reflected by the presence of so-called click sounds in widely spoken Nguni languages. Modern-day cultural groups centered in the Maputaland-Pondoland-Albany region include the Zulu, Xhosa, Swazi, Ronga, and Shangaan. Other cultures, mainly centered in and around urban areas, include the English and Afrikaners (speakers of Afrikaans —the only Germanic language to have developed outside Europe), as well as Indians. As a former Portuguese colony, Portuguese is one of the official languages in Mozambique and is widely spoken and understood in the Mozambican part of the hotspot.

Biodiversity

Based on species numbers, the Maputaland-Pondoland-Albany region is the second richest floristic region in Africa, after the Cape Floristic Region. An estimated 8 100 species from 243 families occur within the Maputaland-Pondoland-Albany region, and at least 1 900 (23%) species are endemic to the region. Plant families rich in endemics are (approximate number of species endemic to the Maputaland-Pondoland-Albany region in parentheses): Asteraceae (266), Apocynaceae (203; including Asclepiadaceae and Periplocaceae), Fabaceae (200), Asphodelaceae (155), Iridaceae (110), Euphorbiaceae (96), Scrophulariaceae (81), Lamiaceae (77), and Mesembryanthemaceae (76). One endemic family occurs within the Maputaland-Pondoland-Albany Hotspot, the monotypic Rhynchocalycaceae. In all, there are 1 524 vascular plant genera in the hotspot, of which 39 are endemic, including: *Acharia* (Achariaceae), *Bergeranthus* (Mesembryanthemaceae), *Dahlgrenodendron* (Lauraceae), *Dermatobotrys* (Scrophulariaceae), *Emicocarpus* (Asclepiadaceae), *Helichrysopsis* (Asteraceae), *Heywoodia* (Euphorbiaceae), *Pseudosalacia* (Celastraceae), *Rhynchocalyx* (Rhynchocalycaceae), *Stangeria* (Stangeriaceae), and *Umtiza* (Caesalpiniaceae).

Vertebrate diversity and endemism are low relative to most other hotspots. Birds are the most diverse group

The blood lily or snake lily (Scadoxus puniceus) is one of South Africa's most striking bulbous plant species. As with other closely related species, the bulb of this species is poisonous and deaths have been reported following its ingestion (as the species is widely used in traditional medicine to treat coughs and gastrointestinal problems).
© **Cristina G. Mittermeier**

On the opposite page, historically, nyalas (Tragelaphus angasii) were widespread in thicket and forest habitats in Mozambique, occurring as far south as the Hluhluwe River in KwaZulu-Natal, South Africa. Their current distribution is more widespread, due largely to introductions outside their former range.
© **Patricio Robles Gil**/*Sierra Madre*

of vertebrates in the hotspot, with 541 regularly occurring species. The hotspot forms part of the Southeast African Coast Endemic Bird Area recognized by Bird-Life International (Stattersfield et al. 1998), with four restricted-range species: Rudd's apalis (*Apalis ruddi*), pink-throated twinspot (*Hypargos margaritatus*), Neergaard's sunbird (*Cinnyris neergaardi*), and lemon-breasted canary (*Serinus citrinipectus*).

The reptiles are the second most diverse vertebrate group in the hotspot. Of the 205 species occurring, 36 are endemic. At least seven species of dwarf chameleon (*Bradypodion* spp.) occur in the hotspot: the Transkei dwarf chameleon (*B. caffrum*), the Kentani dwarf chameleon (*B. kentanicum*), the black-headed dwarf chameleon (*B. melanocephalum*), the Zululand dwarf chameleon (*B. nemorale*), Setaro's dwarf chameleon (*B. setaroi*), the Natal Midlands dwarf chameleon (*B. thamnobates*), and the southern dwarf chameleon (*B. ventrale*). All have very restricted distributions within the region. There is one endemic genus (*Macrelaps*), represented by a single species, the Natal black snake (*M. microlepidotus*).

There are a total of 193 species of mammals, and at least five species are endemic, including two species of golden mole, Marley's golden mole (*Amblysomus marleyi*) and the giant golden mole (*Chrysospalax trevelyani*, EN), and the four-toed elephant shrew (*Petrodromus tetradactylus*).

The frogs of the Maputaland-Pondoland-Albany hotspot number 80 species, of which 12 are endemic. Two genera are endemic, both represented by single species: Boneberg's frog (*Natalobatrachus bonebergi*, EN) and Rattray's or hogsback frog (*Anhydrophryne rattrayi*, EN).

Of the 73 indigenous species of freshwater fishes occurring within the Maputaland-Pondoland-Albany region, 20 are endemic, including four species of barb (*Barbus* spp.) (Skelton 2001). The Maputaland-Pondoland-Albany Hotspot also harbors an exceptionally rich and diverse invertebrate fauna. Charismatic insect groups such as butterflies and moths are well represented in the hotspot, with several rare and localized species. Among the more spectacular butterflies are *Charaxes pondoensis*, a species confined to a small area of coastal forest in the vicinity of Port St. Johns. The Lycaenidae is the largest family of butterflies in southern Africa, and several rare species are endemic to the hotspot. The pale yellow Bashee River buff (*Deloneura immaculata*) is known from only three specimens collected from Fort Bowker on the Bashee River in 1863. The species has not been recorded since, despite an extensive search by numerous collectors over the years, and is considered Extinct.

The phylum Onychophora comprises a fascinating group of ancient, caterpillar-like animals whose fossil record shows that they have not changed substantially in 400 million years. They are the most primitive group of animals to walk with the body raised upon legs (Hamer et al. 1997). There are two genera endemic to the larger southern African region, *Opisthopatus* and

Peripatopsis. Of the nine described species of Onychophora in South Africa, the genus *Opisthopatus* is largely confined to the Maputaland-Pondoland-Albany Hotspot; *O. roseus* (CR), one of two species in the genus, is extremely rare and only known from Ngeli Forest near Kokstad (Hamer et al. 1997). *Peripatopsis* is represented in this region by the endemic *P. moseley*.

Finally, the family Microchaetidae (Oligochaeta) contains four genera and over 100 described species of truly amazing earthworms. The family is endemic to southern Africa, with the Maputaland-Pondoland-Albany Hotspot a major center of diversity for the group. Moreover, the monotypic genus *Michalakus* is endemic to the region, as are perhaps the majority of species in the genus *Tritogenia* (Plisko 1998). Many microchaetids in the Maputaland-Pondoland-Albany region are gigantic and inhabit moist, undisturbed, primary grassland or forest. Perhaps the most remarkable is *Microchaetus vernoni*, with adults known to reach a length of 2.6 m and a diameter of about 10 mm. It is only known from grassland in Vernon Crookes Nature Reserve, southern KwaZulu-Natal, a relatively small (2 189 ha) conservation area to which another two species, *M. zaloumisi* and *M. ambitus*, are endemic.

Flagship Species

The Maputaland-Pondoland-Albany Hotspot is a source of numerous plants that have been developed successfully as horticultural subjects across the globe, including *Tecomaria capensis*, *Plumbago auriculata*, *Crassula ovata*, *Carissa macrocarpa*, and many of the flagship species discussed here. One such flagship, the bitter aloe (*Aloe ferox*), is one of the best known and most conspicuous floristic elements in the southern parts of the hotspot. This medium to large, single-stemmed aloe is arguably the most important medicinal plant in South Africa. The yellowish brown leaf exudate has been used for several hundred years as the primary ingredient of a purgative drug known commercially as Cape Aloes.

The bird-of-paradise flower (*Strelitzia reginae*) is a hotspot endemic that grows up to 2 m high in its natural habitat in the Eastern Cape coastal bush. Today, it is a popular horticultural subject in many parts of the world and has even been adopted as the civic emblem of Los Angeles. This species hybridizes readily with the sword-leaved crane flower (*S. juncea*), another hotspot endemic. A tree member of the genus, Natal wild banana (*S. nicolai*), is also endemic and distributed along nearly the whole of the eastern seaboard of the region.

Commonly known as Christmas bells, *Sandersonia aurantiaca* is a monotypic genus endemic to this hotspot, which has beautiful orange-yellow flowers and lily-like growth. In past times, this flower was so plentiful in the region that it was common to see Zulu women walking with huge bunches that they collected

On the opposite page, the Cercopithecus mitis *group of guenons is represented in the Maputaland-Pondoland-Albany Hotspot by the distinctive endemic Samango monkey subspecies,* C. m. labiatus.
© **Patricio Robles Gil**/*Sierra Madre*

*Above, poor man's cycad (*Encephalartos villosus*) in the St. Lucia World Heritage Site in KwaZulu-Natal, South Africa.*
© **Patricio Robles Gil**/*Sierra Madre*

in the field, selling them from door-to-door as cut flowers. Recently, however, it seems that this species is getting increasingly rare.

About 40 species of red-hot poker (*Kniphofia* spp.) occur within the Maputaland-Pondoland-Albany Hotspot. Of these 40 species, at least half are endemic. The chosen flagship species, *Kniphofia rooperi*, is a large and sturdy plant that flowers about mid-September. Unlike the typical expectation of red-hot pokers having bright red flowers, this species' flowers are orange-yellow in color. Already many cultivars of *Kniphofia* have been produced by horticulturists, including the use in some cases of *K. rooperi* as one of the parents.

An important avian flagship is the southern race of Cape parrot (*Poicephalus robustus robustus*), which can be distinguished from the northern race by its brownish head. It is dependent on the yellowwoods (*Podocarpus* spp.) for both nesting sites and food, although illegal harvesting of yellowwood timber for the furniture market severely threatens the existence of this subspecies. Another striking flagship is Woodward's barbet (*Stactolaema olivacea woodwardi*) which, in southern Africa, is restricted to the Ngoye Forest between Eshowe and Empangeni in KwaZulu-Natal. The species also occurs on the Rondo Plateau in Tanzania; however, the precise taxonomic status of these disjunct populations is not clear. The pink-throated twinspot and Neergaard's sunbird are both endemics of the northern parts of the hotspot. The pink-throated twinspot is mostly confined to low-lying coastal areas, but in Zululand is also found at the top of the Lebombo Mountains, inhabiting the edge of the forested slopes. Neergaard's sunbird is confined to the coastal plains north of Lake St. Lucia. Other bird flagship species include Gurney's sugarbird (*Promerops gurneyi*), the spectacular Knysna turaco or Knysna lourie (*Tauraco corythaix*), and the southern subspecies of Delegorgue's pigeon (*Columba delegorguei delegorguei*).

Reptilian flagship species include the seven species of the dwarf chameleons (genus *Bradypodion*) and three endemics: the Natal hinged tortoise (*Kinixys natalensis*), the Albany adder (*Bitis albanica*), and Tasman's girdled lizard (*Cordylus tasmani*). The Natal hinged tortoise occurs throughout the Lebombo Mountain range; the Albany adder is a very rare snake confined entirely to the Algoa Bay area of the Eastern Cape; and the Tasman's girdled lizard is endemic to the Algoa Bay area, where it lives under the "apron" of dead leaves on tall aloes, or on dead aloe stems lying on rocky slopes.

One of the most notable mammal flagships, and arguably among the most important for the hotspot, is the southern subspecies of the white rhinoceros (*Ceratotherium simum simum*). This species was once common and widely distributed throughout southern and East Africa. The reduction in its range in recent times is largely due to hunting for its prized horn. The southern race narrowly survived extinction in the KwaZulu-Natal's Hluhluwe-Umfolozi Park, which acted as a refuge during the times when the southern white rhino was at its most vulnerable, being reduced to a few dozen in number. In one of the greatest conservation success stories in African conservation, the southern white rhino has since increased in number to more than 12 000, with many having been relocated to other areas.

Two dainty antelope species also serve as important flagships. The blue duiker (*Philantomba monticola*) has a disjunct distribution in southern Africa, the southern population being confined to the hotspot. The southern form of the blue duiker favors forest, thicket, and dense coastal bush, and appears to be unaffected by the availability of drinking water. Blue duikers are severely threatened by habitat destruction and fragmentation of populations, and are heavily poached with dogs and by snaring. The southern race of the suni (*Neotragus moschatus zuluensis*) is endemic to the hotspot. It is a secretive, little antelope that is very habitat-specific, relying on forest with high stem density and low ground cover. The Zululand suni's distribution is currently quite restricted due to the destruction of its habitat. It is both sensitive to, and dependent on, the modification of its habitat by factors such as the feeding behavior of cattle, nyalas, and elephants, harvesting activities by humans, and the impact of fire on forest margins and understory. Three small mammals deserve mention as flagships, namely the red bush squirrel (*Paraxerus palliatus*, VU), and the two golden mole species.

Frog flagships of the Maputaland-Pondoland-Albany region include the aforementioned Boneberg's frog and Rattray's frog. The former is restricted to forests along the coasts where recent housing developments and sugarcane plantations have destroyed much of its habitat. The latter is known from the Amatola and Katberg Mountains in the Eastern Cape Province, where it occurs along streams in thick vegetation; commercial timber plantations are the main threat to this frog's continued existence. Other notable species include the golden spiny reed frog (*Afrixalus aureus*), Pickersgill's reed frog (*Hyperolius pickersgilli*, EN), and the soprano or whistling rain frog (*Breviceps sopranus*), a recently described species so called because it utters a long, high-pitched whistle. The golden spiny reed frog, with its gold-colored back, is endemic to the hotspot (where it occurs in low-altitude grasslands), while Pickersgill's reed frog is also endemic and is found in the coastal lowlands of KwaZulu-Natal.

Among the flagship freshwater fishes are the Sibayi goby (*Silhouettea sibayi*), which occurs in a variety of freshwater and brackish habitats, and the border barb (*Barbus trevelyani*, CR), which is restricted to the Keiskamma and Buffalo river systems in the Eastern Cape, and inhabits pools and riffles of clear rocky streams, where it feeds on insects, seeds, and algae. The Eastern Cape rocky (*Sandelia bainsii*, EN) is restricted to the Buffalo, Keiskamma, Great Fish, and Kowie river systems in the Eastern Cape; interestingly,

Girl and infant in the Maputo Elephant Reserve, Mozambique.
© Cristina G. Mittermeier

On the opposite page, in addition to the irreversible loss of habitat in the Maputaland-Pondoland-Albany Hotspot to cultivation, urbanization, and plantations, localized mining activities —specifically titanium extraction from coastal sand dunes— have also led to loss of natural vegetation.
© Patricio Robles Gil/*Sierra Madre*

the only other species in the genus is endemic to streams in the Cape Floristic Region.

The hotspot also has a very rich and varied scarab or dung beetle (Scarabaeidae: Scarabaeinae) fauna. One rare species, the flightless dung beetle (*Circellium bacchus*), has a very restricted present-day distribution and has captured the imagination of visitors to the Addo Elephant Park in the Eastern Cape. The only member of its genus, it is named after the god of wine, probably because of its somewhat erratic, stumbling behavior! This must be one of the few insect species in the world for which special road signs have been erected, alerting motorists not to drive the wheels of their vehicles over elephant and buffalo dung pads in roads.

Threats

Having one of the highest human densities in sub-Saharan Africa (Esterhuysen 1998a, b), the Maputaland-Pondoland-Albany Hotspot is threatened by a number of human activities. Land cover information derived from satellite data indicates that permanent and complete transformation of habitat has affected 19% of the region. This has been caused mainly by cultivation (12.7%), plantation forestry (3.4%), and urbanization (1.7%). A further 30% of the natural vegetation has been severely damaged and permanently degraded so that it now exists only in a secondary state, while about 27% is in a poor, in-between, non-pristine state. This degradation has mainly been caused by harvesting of indigenous woodlands, soil erosion, overgrazing and shifting cultivation, and invasive species. A maximum of 24.5% of the hotspot can be considered close to the pristine state.

Degradation of the thicket and grassland biomes has been particularly severe. By 1981, more than 50% of the thicket biome in South Africa was seriously overgrazed and 9% has been permanently transformed (Le Roux 2002). Since then, these figures have probably increased significantly, all the more worrying since only 5% of the thicket biome is formally protected in South Africa. Between 60% and 80% of the grasslands of South Africa are irreversibly transformed, while only 2% are formally conserved (Le Roux 2002). Many of these are (were) primary grasslands that took hundreds of thousands of years to develop their present diversity, and which do not recover their original floristic composition after destruction. The same holds true for those parts of the grassland biome that enter into the Maputaland-Pondoland-Albany region. For example, the endemic grassland type "Pondoland coastal plateau sourveld" is the smallest veld type recognized by Acocks (1953), and is seriously threatened by overgrazing, sugarcane production, and commercial timber plantations.

Cultivation practices that threaten and degrade habitats in the hotspot include both large-scale commercial agriculture and subsistence farming. Subsistence farming occurs mainly in communal areas, and consists mostly of shifting cultivation which, while not expanding in the region at the moment, does affect entire landscapes covering hundreds of square kilometers. In many of these areas it is impossible to find even a small portion of the landscape that has not been affected by cultivation. When such areas do exist, they are often under severe grazing pressure from domestic livestock. The subtropical areas of this region are also particularly well-suited to sugarcane production, and South Africa's large sugar industry is based entirely within this hotspot. Consequently, commercial sugarcane farming has completely transformed large tracts of land, especially in the coastal regions north and south of Durban. Cultivation in South Africa increased by 122% in area between 1987 and 1994 (Le Roux 2002) and, as human population numbers increase and the pressure to produce food continues, this trend is likely to continue into the future, resulting in more habitat loss.

Industrial timber production is the second largest cause of habitat loss in the region. Plantations form very large continuous stands of alien trees along escarpment slopes, coastal plains, and midland mist belts, and are a particularly serious threat to grassland habitats. Several hundred thousand hectares of species-rich primary grassland in the hotspot have already been destroyed by commercial afforestation, and plans are under way to establish more alien tree monocultures, especially in parts of the Eastern Cape. The effects of these commercial tree plantations on biodiversity and water runoff have been devastating. Besides transforming habitats, the alien trees alter the natural hydrological regime by using much more groundwater than the indigenous vegetation and affect the chemical and physical status of soils. Pine trees (*Pinus* spp.), eucalypts (*Eucalyptus* spp.), and Australian wattles in the drier northern areas (*Acacia* spp.) are the three groups of plantation trees that have the largest negative impact on the grasslands of the region.

Urbanization is the third largest threat to natural habitats and vegetation in the region. There are three major urban centers in the region, namely Maputo in southern Mozambique, and Durban and Port Elizabeth in South Africa. The growth of cities appears to be an unstoppable phenomenon of the modern era, which almost always leads to the formation of unplanned sprawling slums on the outskirts of the cities. The Durban-Pietermaritzburg area in KwaZulu-Natal is one of the three largest urban centers in South Africa, and has a population of around three million people. Recently, an industrial development zone was designated at Coega, adjacent to Port Elizabeth and, with strong political backing, this is likely to promote urban and industrial spread.

Almost half of the region is communally owned and supports livestock numbers far in excess of what is considered ecologically sustainable. These high livestock numbers have caused extensive degradation of

On the opposite page, among a number of important protected areas in the Maputaland-Pondoland-Albany Hotspot is the Tembe Elephant Reserve in the north of KwaZulu-Natal Province in South Africa. Plans are underfoot to try to link this protected area with the Maputo Elephant Reserve in neighboring southern Mozambique.
© **Patricio Robles Gil**/*Sierra Madre*

Above, the southern white rhino (Ceratotherium simum simum) was near extinction at the beginning of the twentieth century, but was brought back from the brink by what was then called the Natal Parks Board. It is now by far the most abundant rhino species in the world —to the point that several dozen are sold every year to restock other parks and private ranches in South Africa and elsewhere in the region.
© **Russell A. Mittermeier**

the natural rangelands. Vegetation that has not (yet) been permanently degraded is seriously threatened by overgrazing. In the combined areas of communal and commercially owned rangelands, overgrazing has degraded 25% of the total area covered by the hotspot to the point that the vegetation is in a very poor condition, with altered species composition and reduced vegetation cover. Extensive invasion by alien plant species and localized mining activities (specifically titanium extraction from coastal sands) are two other threats to natural vegetation in the region.

In southern Mozambique, specifically, one of the major threats is the large-scale conversion of trees into charcoal to supply the growing demand for firewood for the larger Maputo Metropolis. Important timber species such as chamfuta (*Afzelia quanzensis*) are also being harvested extensively from natural vegetation, in many cases illegally.

Conservation

An analysis of the World Database on Protected Areas reveals that 8.4% of the Maputaland-Pondoland-Albany Hotspot is conserved in various forms of protected areas. This figure drops only slightly when one considers only protected areas classified in IUCN categories I to IV (7.4%). The South African National Parks, a statutory body within the Department of Environmental Affairs and Tourism, manages several national parks within the area, including the Greater Addo Park (24 000 ha) and the Mountain Zebra National Park (6 536 ha); however, management of most protected areas in KwaZulu-Natal falls under the jurisdiction of Ezemvelo KwaZulu-Natal Wildlife. In Mozambique, the management of conservation areas falls under the Direcção Nacional de Florestas e Fauna Bravia (DNFFB) of the Ministério da Agricultura e Pescas. The Greater St. Lucia Wetland Park (256 644 ha) was declared a World Heritage Site under the World Heritage Convention of UNESCO, and efforts are under way to establish a transfrontier conservation area that would link nature reserves in Swaziland, southern Mozambique, and northeastern KwaZulu-Natal. Numerous other conservation areas —managed by provincial or local governments or private individuals— of varying sizes occur within the hotspot.

Current conservation initiatives include the establishment of the Baviaanskloof Megareserve, the expansion of the Greater Addo Park and the Mountain Zebra Reserve, the wild coast initiative, and the Subtropical Thicket Ecosystem Planning (STEP) project. The Licuáti Forest Reserve (established in 1943 with the purpose of protecting woody plant species, particularly chamfuta) and the Maputo Elephant Reserve are the primary conservation areas in southern Mozambique. However, law enforcement in these areas is very poor, and they are not very well protected (Izidine 2003).

The existing protected area system does not represent the biodiversity of the hotspot, in terms of both species and the processes required to sustain them. This is especially true of the Pondoland area, where only a few small conservation areas are present. Grasslands, woody grasslands, and coastal forests and thickets are just some of the habitats that are inadequately protected. A major problem is that the conservation areas of the hotspot have mostly been established with the protection of big game in mind, and a number of floristically interesting and often unique areas, for example the Noorsveld in the southern parts, therefore still go unprotected.

One of the more important private initiatives in the region is the conservancy program. The conservancy concept originated in KwaZulu-Natal in 1978, and involves the establishment of committees of landowners who pledge to protect the natural environment, or certain aspects thereof (they may choose, for example, to focus on a specific species to look out for and protect) on the land they own. There are currently about 218 conservancies in KwaZulu-Natal alone, covering about 1.5 million ha, including 167 rural, 38 urban and suburban, 4 township, 4 industrial, and 5 marine conservancies. Members of the conservancy program (currently numbering 2 761 members of the public and 372 game rangers) attend lectures and participate in various conservation programs.

YOLANDE STEENKAMP [16, 134]
BRAAM VAN WYK [134]
JANINE VICTOR [13]
DAVID HOARE [17]
GIDEON SMITH [13, 134]
TONY DOLD [132]
RICHARD COWLING [133]

Grass crinum (Crinum acaule) *is found in northern KwaZulu-Natal, mainly on the Maputaland coastal plain. Much of the habitat of this species has undergone extensive afforestation with exotics and also degradation in some densely settled areas.*
© **Patricio Robles Gil**/*Sierra Madre*

On the opposite page, satellite data has shown that around 20% of the original vegetation of the Maputaland-Pondoland-Albany Hotspot has been irreversibly transformed through cultivation, plantations, and urbanization. In addition, more than half of what remains has been degraded through the loss of indigenous woodlands, soil erosion, overgrazing, and invasive species.
© **Patricio Robles Gil**/*Sierra Madre*

228

COASTAL FORESTS OF EASTERN AFRICA

Scattered along the coastal margins of eastern Africa are a chain of relict forest and thicket patches set within savanna woodlands, wetlands, and increasing areas of farmlands and fallow. These forested areas are typically tiny and fragmented, but contain remarkable levels of biodiversity, which often varies dramatically between forests. During the past twenty years, studies of the Coastal Forests of Eastern Africa have resulted in this forest mosaic being recognized as a globally important conservation priority in a number of major analyses completed for this region (Stattersfield et al. 1998; Olson and Dinerstein 1998; Myers et al. 2000; Burgess et al., in press).

The northern boundary of this hotspot, as defined here, is located in the remaining small patches of coastal (riverine) forest along the Jubba and Shabelle rivers in southern Somalia (Madgwick 1988; Clarke 2000a). In Kenya, the hotspot is confined to a relatively narrow (up to 40 km) coastal strip, except along the Tana River, where it extends some 120 km inland to include the forests of the Lower Tana River. In Tanzania, the hotspot runs along the coast with coastal forest patches such as Rondo up to 80 km from the sea. There are also some outliers located up to 300 km inland at the base of the Udzungwa Mountains of the Eastern Arc mountain chain (Burgess et al. 1998), and minute patches up to 325 km inland in northern Mozambique (Timberlake et al. 2004).

The southern boundary of the Coastal Forests of Eastern Africa is more problematic. White (1983) previously mapped the vegetation of coastal Somalia, Kenya, Tanzania, and Mozambique as far south as Inhambane within his Zanzibar-Inhambane Regional Mosaic. The World Wildlife Fund (WWF) divided the Zanzibar-Inhambane Regional Mosaic of White (1983) into the Northern and Southern Zanzibar-Inhambane Coastal Forest Mosaic ecoregions, with the boundary between the Northern and Southern ecoregions in southern Tanzania and the Southern ecoregion extending to Maputo in southern Mozambique (Olson et al. 2001; Burgess et al., in press). Clarke (1998b) defined an entirely new phytogeographical region, the Swahilian Regional Center of Plant Endemism from Somalia to northern Mozambique, and a Swahilian-Maputaland Regional Transition Zone from northern Mozambique to just north of Maputo. For the

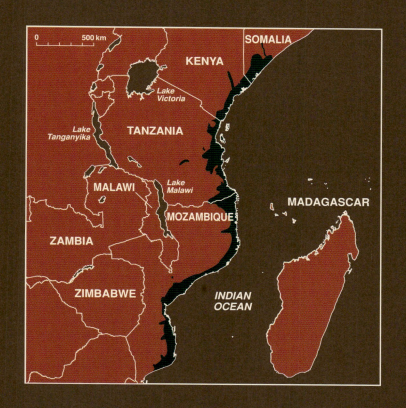

purposes of this chapter, the Coastal Forests of Eastern Africa Hotspot includes the Northern and Southern Zanzibar-Inhambane Coastal Forest Mosaic ecoregions, and the Zambezian Coastal Flooded Savanna as defined by WWF (Burgess et al., in press), such that the Limpopo River forms the southern boundary of the hotspot. This corresponds, roughly, to the Swahilian Regional Center of Plant Endemism and the Swahilian-Maputaland Regional Transition Zone of Clarke (1998b). The hotspot also includes all islands lying immediately offshore, including Zanzibar, Pemba, Mafia, and the Bazarruto Archipelago off Mozambique, such that the total land area covered by this hotspot is around 291 250 km².

Much of the region covered by this hotspot was formed from the deposition of marine sediments since the break-up of Pangea (Clarke and Burgess 2000), with younger sediments closer to the coast. Over the past 30 million years, tectonic activity has resulted in the formation of low ridges and swells, which has caused the shoreline to move in and out from its present position, with the subsequent uplifting and erosion of sediments. Faulting associated with the development of the Great Rift Valley also affected the region, with one such fault isolating Pemba Island through the formation of a deep-water marine trench.

On the opposite page, the strikingly beautiful and Endangered Zanzibar red colobus (Procolobus kirkii) is confined entirely to the island of Zanzibar, with its stronghold in and around the Jozani Forest.
© **Anup Shah**/naturepl.com

Climatically, the hotspot is largely tropical, although it is almost subtropical in the southern reaches. The climate is characterized by high temperatures (23°C or more north of the Limpopo River) and high humidity, by incidental sunlight with little seasonal or annual variation, and variable rainfall. There are two rainy seasons (long, April-June; short, November-December) in the north, merging into one (November-April) in the south. Rainfall ranges from 2 000 mm/year (Pemba and Mafia) down to 500 mm/year in northern Kenya and 800 mm/year in parts of southern Tanzania/northern Mozambique, although average rainfall in most of the coastal forests is between 900 and 1 400 mm/year. Dry seasons can be severe and El Niño effects dramatic. Current daily, monthly, and annual rainfall fluctuations are thought to be more significant than those of the Quaternary Period, which apparently were less severe along the eastern African coast than elsewhere on the continent (Clarke 2000b).

The vegetation of this hotspot is characterized by a complex mix of moist forests (for example, at the base of the Eastern Arc Mountains) and drier forests with coastal thicket, fire-climax savanna woodlands, seasonal and permanent swamps, and littoral habitats. The littoral vegetation includes mangrove vegetation along some parts of the coast, especially in sheltered bays and along river mouths. This complexity is partly natural, although the influence of anthropogenic activities over thousands of years is believed to have been vital in shaping the "natural" vegetation now found in the area. Trees dominate the coastal forest flora, with some of the more abundant species being *Afzelia quanzensis*, *Albizia* spp., *Bombax rhodognaphalon*, *Combretum schumannii*, *Croton* spp., *Cussonia zimmermannii*, *Cynometra* spp., *Dialium* spp., *Diospyros* spp., *Grewia* spp., *Hymenaea verrucosa*, *Manilkara* spp., *Millettia stuhlmanni*, *Nesogordonia holtzii*, *Ricinodendron heudelotii*, *Scorodophloeus fischeri*, *Sterculia appendiculata*, *Sorindeia madagascariensis*, *Xylia africana*, and *Zanthoxylum* spp. Lianas are also common as, too, are shrubs, herbs, grasses, sedges, ferns, and various epiphytes. Most coastal forests are found up to 500 m above sea level, although in Tanzania they occur up to 1 030 m on Handeni Hill, but this is highly unusual (Burgess and Clarke 2000).

The distinction between the coastal forests and the Eastern Arc Mountains has been a matter of some debate (e.g., Lovett et al. 2000), and J. Lovett (pers. comm.) has argued that the boundary between the two forest types is continuous and can not be resolved. A gradation between the two forest formations is found at the eastern base of the East Usambara, Uluguru, Udzungwa, and Nguru ranges. The altitudinal separation is generally placed between 500 and 800 m (e.g., White 1983). Other coastal forests are not contiguous with mountain forest habitats and are often separated from the mountains further inland by hundreds of kilometers of drier Zambezian woodlands. Furthermore, the flora has affinities with that of West Africa, suggesting an ancient connection with the Guineo-Congolian lowland forests (Lovett and Wasser 1993; Clarke et al. 2000).

The Endangered golden-rumped elephant shrew or sengi (Rhynchocyon chrysopygus) is endemic to the coastal forests of Kenya north of Mombasa. During the day, these animals forage on the forest floor for invertebrates and spend the night in leaf-litter nests on the ground. The size of these animals is about 50 cm long.
© Galen Rathbun

On the opposite page, the crested guineafowl (Guttera pucherani) is a wide-ranging species. It is not globally threatened, but its population may be affected by habitat loss and hunting.
© Cristina G. Mittermeier

Biodiversity

Studies generally indicate that, for all taxonomic groups, the region of highest endemism within this hotspot stretches from northern Kenya to southern Tanzania (probably extending into northernmost Mozambique), with other parts being somewhat impoverished biologically, although additional survey work in Mozambique may yet reveal an unknown wealth of biodiversity. At a finer scale, two important subcenters of endemism can also be recognized. The first straddles the border between Kenya and Tanzania —the "Kwale-Usambara" local center of endemism—, while the second is found in southern Tanzania —the "Lindi" local center of endemism (Burgess et al. 1998; Clarke 2001). Narrow ranges and disjunct distributions typify the endemic species. There is also a huge turnover of species between forest patches, especially in the less mobile species. For example, forests that are only 100 km apart can differ in 80% of their plants (Clarke et al. 2000), and 70% of their millipedes (Hoffman 2000).

The entire Coastal Forests of Eastern Africa Hotspot contains an estimated 4 050 plant species within around 1 050 plant genera, of which 1 750 plant species and 28 genera are endemic; most of the endemic genera are monotypic. Around 70% of all endemics (1 225 species) and 90% of the endemic genera have been recorded from forest habitats; 92% of all Swahilian endemic species are recorded from closed canopy vegetation types (forest, woodland, bushland, and thicket). Indeed, the lowland forest habitat is the most biologically valuable, with at least 554 endemic plant species and 18 of the 28 described endemic genera confined entirely to it (Clarke et al. 2000; G.P. Clarke, unpubl.). The forested habitats probably contain no more than 750 plant genera, given that their endemic species are distributed among 495 genera. The non-forested vegetation of the coastal strip of eastern Africa (i.e., swamp, wooded grassland, coastal margins) is also important, with at least 812 endemic plants and members of 10 endemic genera recorded from it. Some 47% of the region's endemic species have been recorded from non-forest vegetation, which covers at least 275 000 km^2 of land (0.3 endemic plants per 100 km^2 of habitat), whereas the coastal forests cover a total of 6 259 km^2 (8.8 endemics per 100 km^2 of habitat) (Burgess et al. 2003b). Clearly, it is the forest patches that have the highest biodiversity importance per unit area. In addition, approximately 40% of the endemic plants are confined to a single forest (for example, the Rondo Forest area in southern Tanzania, has 60 endemic species and two endemic genera, and the Shimba Hills, Kenya, have 12 endemic species) (Clarke et al. 2000; Clarke 2001).

Similarly, these forest patches are important in terms of vertebrate diversity and endemism. Birds are represented by 636 species, of which 12 species are endemic. Pemba Island, which is considered an Endemic Bird Area (EBA) by BirdLife International (Stattersfield et al. 1998) contains four endemic bird species: the Pemba white-eye (*Zosterops vaughani*), Pemba green-pigeon

more endemic species than any other site in the Albertine Rift, and is the top priority for conservation in this hotspot at present.

About 14% of Africa's reptiles, and 19% of the continent's amphibians, occur in the Albertine Rift. As with other groups, it is likely that these numbers will increase with additional survey work. Sixteen reptile species (of a total of 175 recorded) and 31 amphibians (of 146 species) are endemic to the region, with the Virunga National Park having the highest numbers of endemic species for both groups. Three amphibian genera are endemic to the Albertine Rift, all represented by single species: Parker's tree toad (*Laurentophryne parkeri*), the Itombwe golden frog (*Chrysobatrachus cupreonitens*), and African painted frog (*Callixalus pictus*, VU). The former two species are confined to the Itombwe Massif, although the African painted frog is known from both the Itombwe Massif and western Rwanda.

The lakes of the Albertine Rift (Albert, George, Edward, Kivu, and Tanganyika) contain large numbers of endemic fish species. Although not strictly thought of as Albertine Rift habitats, these lakes do show a history of interconnection with one another and also with Lake Victoria (Snoeks 2000). Lake Tanganyika is home to over 300 fish species, and about 75% of them are endemic. However, only 10% of Lake Tanganyika's shore has been explored and over 1 200 species (vertebrates and invertebrates) have been recorded, making it the second highest recorded diversity for any lake on Earth (Patterson and Makin 1998). Lakes George and Edward have 56 fish species endemic to these two lakes, while Kivu and Albert have 15 and 6 endemic fishes, respectively. A conservative estimate of freshwater fish diversity indicates that, together with their surrounding drainages, the lakes Kivu, Edward, George, Albert, and Tanganyika harbor over 400 fish species, 274 of which are endemic. Most of the endemic fishes are cichlids, with 226 endemic species and 47 endemic genera. However, a more recent assessment suggests that these numbers are a clear underestimate, and that the number of endemics could be at least 366 species, with around 350 of these being cichlids (Snoeks 2000). These colorful fish are very popular with aquarists, and there are many new species awaiting discovery and scientific description. Other families that have high levels of endemism include bagrid catfishes (with two endemic genera), spiny eels (11 endemic species), and snooks (five endemic species). The Nile perch (*Lates niloticus*) is the most infamous snook of the six Tanganyika *Lates* species. Able to reach a length of two meters, this species is associated with the extinction of about 200 endemic cichlids following its introduction to Lake Victoria in 1954 (Ogutu-Ohwayo 1990). The snooks, together with two small pelagic herrings —*Limnothrissa miodon* and *Stolothrissa tanganicae*—, comprise the bulk of the commercial fisheries' catch in Lake Tanganyika (FAO 2001).

While invertebrate taxa have been poorly studied, this region is known to have a large number of endemic butterflies. The total number of butterfly species found in the Albertine Rift is unknown, but in Uganda, inventories of the forests in the Albertine Rift show that at least 581 species of butterflies (16% of the estimated 3 630 species in Africa) occur in this part of the hotspot alone (Howard and Davenport 1996). Given the numbers from Uganda and Tanzania, it is possible that up to 1 300 butterflies might occur in the Rift, about 36% of Africa's total. Currently, 117 endemic species from 49 genera are known from the Albertine Rift (Plumptre et al. 2003a). A single genus is restricted to the Albertine Rift, namely *Kumothales*, while the Ufipa swallowtail (*Papilio ufipa*) is found only in Mbizi Forest on the Ufipa Plateau.

The Albertine Rift is important not only for its biodiversity, but also for its ecological processes. The savannas of the Murchison Falls, Virunga, and Queen Elizabeth National Parks, used to contain the highest biomasses of large mammals on Earth, at least until the 1960s (Laws et al. 1975; Plumptre and Harris 1995). War and poaching led to major decreases in the numbers of large mammals in these parks, but most of these species are still present and have the potential to recover to their former levels if afforded good protection. The volcanoes in the Virungas influence the ecology of a large portion of the Virunga National Park and its surroundings; there are probably unique species associated with these volcanoes, but few surveys of their fauna and flora have been conducted.

Flagship Species

The Albertine Rift is steeped in flagship species, but the mountain gorilla (*Gorilla beringei beringei*, CR) and Grauer's gorilla (*G. b. graueri*, EN) are the best known. Made famous through the pioneering work of George Schaller and Dian Fossey, the mountain gorilla has been the focus of many wildlife films and Hollywood movies. Loss of habitat and hunting led to a decline in the population of mountain gorillas to a low of about 250 in the Virungas (Sholley 1991), and about 300 gorillas in Bwindi Impenetrable National Park by the late 1980s (Butynski and Kalina 1998; Butynski 2001). Since then, better protection has led to increases in both populations, with the current estimate at about 380 in the Virungas and 320 in Bwindi. Grauer's gorilla has not fared as well over the same time period. As recently as 1996, it was estimated that there were 16 900 Grauer's gorillas in eastern DRC (Hall et al. 1998), but the civil war that has raged since 1998 has resulted in major declines in some areas (for example, in parts of their range in the Kahuzi-Biega National Park). Much of the decline is due to hunting for bushmeat by rebel groups and by people mining for gold, diamonds, and coltan (columbo-tantalite), a substance used in computer chips and cellular phones.

Chimpanzees are found in many of the Albertine Rift forests, yet quite a number of their populations are small and unlikely to be viable in the long term unless corridors among protected areas are maintained. They

On the opposite page, Afroalpine flora on Mt. Mikeno in the Virunga Volcanoes, Democratic Republic of the Congo.
© **Gerry Ellis**/*Minden Pictures*

Above, the possibility of expanding Mahale Mountains National Park on the shore of Lake Tanganyika to include other areas of importance along Lake Tanganyika and to the east is currently being investigated. This area is thought to be particularly rich in endemic plants, and is also the site of one of the longest-running research programs on chimpanzee ecology and behavior.
© **Ferrero-Labat**/*Auscape*

are probably one of the most important seed dispersers in a forest and, as such, their loss could seriously affect forest composition. In addition to chimps, the Albertine Rift is rich in other primate species, including at least 27 recorded thus far. Fortunately, primate hunting is rare in Uganda, Rwanda, Burundi, and Tanzania, meaning that these animals are not as threatened here as in the DRC and West Africa, and are, therefore, usually easy to see where they occur. As such, they provide great potential for tourism in the region. Mountain gorilla and to some extent chimpanzee tourism have become popular, but the marketing of primate tourism for other monkeys should be given more emphasis. Both l'Hoest's (*Cercopithecus lhoesti*) and owl-faced guenons (*C. hamlyni*) are charismatic species, as is the golden monkey, (*C. mitis kandti*, EN), a beautiful guenon with a soot-black coat and golden-orange mantle across its back and head, and which is now confined to the Virunga Volcanoes and part of Nyungwe Park.

The Ruwenzori duiker (*Cephalophus rubidus*, EN), sometimes considered a subspecies of the black-fronted duiker (*C. nigrifrons*), is restricted to the mountains after which it takes its name, where it occurs at high elevations, commonly in Hagenia woodland. At the other end of the size scale is the Ruwenzori otter shrew (*Micropotamogale ruwenzorii*, EN), one of only three representatives of the family Tenrecidae found on the African mainland, a family that is otherwise restricted entirely to Madagascar. The Ruwenzori otter shrew is an aquatic species, frequenting montane and lowland streams. Its closest relative, the Mount Nimba otter shrew (*M. lamottei*), is found in similar habitats in the vicinity of Mt. Nimba in the Guinean Forests of West Africa Hotspot.

Of the birds present in the Albertine Rift, the Rwenzori turaco (*Musophaga johnstoni*) is probably the most stunning of the endemic species, with its mantle of iridescent green, orange-yellow cheeks, blue back and tail, and bright red primary feathers. Found in 10 forest islands of the Albertine Rift, this species is a good flagship for the montane forests. The beautiful, bright green African green broadbill (*Pseudocalyptomena graueri*, VU), with its grey-blue throat, is the sole representative of an endemic genus, and is confined to only three sites within the Rift. Grauer's rush warbler (*Bradypterus graueri*, EN), while not the most visually exciting, is a good flagship species for isolated mountain swamps. This species is confined to small patches of swamp above 2 000 m and occurs in small populations separated from each other by large distances. There are several endemic sunbird species —the regal sunbird (*Cinnyris regia*), Rockefeller's sunbird (*Nectarinia rockefelleri*, VU), Rwenzori double-collared sunbird or Stuhlmann's sunbird (*Cinnyris stuhlmanni*), blue-headed sunbird (*Cyanomitra alinae*), and purple-breasted sunbird (*Nectarinia purpureiventris*)—, and all serve as excellent flagship species, with their brilliant coloration and presence in most of the Albertine Rift forests.

Of the reptiles, the chameleons are the best flagship species. Five species are endemic to the Albertine Rift,

including the Rwenzori three-horned chameleon (*Chamaeleo johnstoni*), which reaches a length of 30 cm and is found in many of the montane forests of the Albertine Rift. The three horns on its head make it look like a miniature Triceratops, and are used by males to fight over females. The strange-horned chameleon (*Bradypodion xenorhinus*) is similar in size, but has a circular protuberence on the end of its nose. This species is confined to the Rwenzori Mountains, where it is very rare, having been overcollected for the wildlife trade.

With a wingspan of 24 cm, the African giant swallowtail (*Papilio antimachus*) is the continent's largest butterfly and is found at many sites in the Albertine Rift. Three large, conspicuous, yet rare swallowtail butterflies (*P. leucotaenia*, *P. ufipa*, and *Graphium gudenusi*) serve as important invertebrate flagships, particularly because they can help bring attention to those protected areas where there are fewer of the larger vertebrate flagships.

Finally, the plant genus *Impatiens*, with 18 endemic species, comprises important flagships, as species from this genus have prominent flowers of various shades of white, pink, and red, and are found in the forest understory. The genus is widespread and is much favored by duikers for food.

Threats

The Albertine Rift has some of the highest human population densities on the African Continent, with up to 750 people per square kilometer in Rwanda and southwest Uganda. Much of the land in this region has been converted to agriculture, and the average family size is 6-10 people. As a result, the pressures on the remaining natural vegetation in this region are enormous, since the further subdivision of land by families for their children is impossible and the demand for more land is intense. Many of the protected areas are fragments or islands in a sea of humanity, with marked borders between forest and cultivation. These islands suffer from edge effects due to the abrupt changes in microclimate and from human use of the forest edges. People in this region are also among the poorest in Africa and rely to a great extent on the environment for their livelihoods. Forests provide these people with necessary materials such as rope, bean stakes, firewood, timber, medicines, fruit, bushmeat, and honey. Fire is also a threat in some regions, such as on the Ufipa Plateau, where the last remnant of Congolian forest, Mbizi, is under serious threat from fire. The peculiar nature of this type of forest-grassland mosaic and the geographic relief on which it sits, mean that there are exposed hill ridges and radiating peninsular extensions of forest that stretch along the valleys. These rapidly become isolated by fire and thus more accessible to human disturbance (Davenport 2002).

A crude estimate can be made of the amount of natural habitat remaining based on the area remaining as protected habitat (11.8%; see below) and the authors' knowledge of zones outside these protected areas.

In the transboundary region of Uganda, Rwanda, and the Democratic Republic of Congo, the volcanic highlands of the Virungas and Uganda's Bwindi Impenetrable National Park shelter the last 670 Critically Endangered mountain gorillas (Gorilla beringei beringei) *in the world. Chimpanzees, golden monkeys, forest elephants, giant forest hogs, African buffaloes, and a rich variety of avifauna, reptiles, and amphibians share this heartland of incredible biodiversity.*
© **Gerry Ellis**/*Minden Pictures*

Based on this, it is likely that no more than 20% of the habitat can be described as "intact," while a further 25%-30% is degraded but still relatively natural. An analysis of forest change over the past 15 years using satellite images shows that over 1 500 km² has been lost to agricultural production in the forested areas of the Albertine Rift (Plumptre et al. 2003a). This is 0.5% of the area of the Albertine Rift and 2.2% of its forested area. Much of this loss has occurred outside protected areas. In spite of the fact that there is little support for protection, many forests survive simply because they have some protected status. However, the remaining protected areas are experiencing a degradation of the habitat, and forest use within protected areas has often increased during times of insecurity. For instance, the mahogany trees that had been managed relatively carefully in Uganda since the 1930s have been felled in the past 20 years because of corrupt practices and the inability of the forestry staff to control illegal activities. As a result, many species that require undisturbed habitat are now confined to a few small patches within the forest reserves and parks.

The trade in bushmeat is not as developed as in the Congo Basin, but is probably increasing. There is some indirect evidence that soldiers are returning from the Congo to Rwanda and Uganda with a taste for bushmeat. Poaching in the savanna parks in Uganda and the DRC is high at present with hippos, buffalos, and the larger antelope species being targeted. Snares are also set in forests and lead to death or injury of many species. For example, in the forests of Uganda, 25% of all chimpanzees have maimed limbs or are missing hands or feet as a result of snare injuries (Plumptre et al. 2003b). Hunters are mainly after duikers and bushpigs in the forests. Primates tend to be targeted in the DRC and around Rwenzori Mountains National Park. Most hunting in Uganda, Rwanda, and Burundi is through the use of snares or by driving prey into nets with dogs. In the DRC there is more reliance on the use of guns, especially with the proliferation of AK-47 assault rifles during the civil war there.

Insecurity and civil strife in the Great Lakes region has led to the degradation and loss of protected areas. Militia groups have hidden in protected areas and used them to launch attacks on the nearby inhabitants. Thus, protected areas have not been viewed favorably by the local communities living adjacent to them. On the other hand, forests have been places to which the local people could flee during conflict, so attitudes vary across the region depending on how protected areas were used. Several protected areas have been lost or reduced in size as a result of the wars, particularly in Rwanda and Uganda. However, where conservation groups maintained some support or presence on the ground, protected areas have generally survived intact. The greatest losses from these wars have been trained protected-area staff. More than 100 staff members were killed in the protected areas in eastern DRC in the last six years. Similarly, about a third of the staff working with the gorillas in Rwanda were killed between 1990 and 1999. These losses have rarely been documented, and little support has been provided to their families because it has always happened at a time when funding was limited and needs were great. Sometimes civil wars or insecurity can help protected areas because they prevent people from entering these areas to carry out illegal activities. It has been clear that the forests in Uganda suffered most as the economy started to grow after the wars and the demand for timber for reconstruction grew with it.

Conservation

Currently, about 37 000 km² of the Albertine Rift is protected in parks, wildlife-game reserves and forest reserves, representing about 11.8% of the total area of the Albertine Rift. Many of the protected areas are concentrated in the north of the region, while fewer in number and also in total area occur in southeastern DRC and southwest Tanzania. The largest protected area in the region is Virunga National Park (8 000 km²), which was established in 1925; it links the Volcanoes National Park in Rwanda with Queen Elizabeth, Rwenzori Mountains, and Semuliki National Parks in Uganda to form a much larger landscape of protected areas, the Greater Virunga Landscape, which totals 12 800 km². A priority-setting exercise evaluating sites in the Albertine Rift based upon total species richness and number of endemic and threatened species identified Virunga National Park, Itombwe Massif (unprotected as yet), and Kahuzi-Biega National Park (6 000 km²), in the DRC; Semuliki (219 km²), Kibale (766 km²), and Bwindi Impenetrable (331 km²) National Parks in Uganda; and Nyungwe National Park (980 km²) in Rwanda as the most important of the terrestrial sites for conservation. Lake Tanganyika was also identified for freshwater conservation. Additional areas with many endemic and threatened species but fewer total species were Rwenzori Mountains National Park (996 km²) and Echuya (34 km²) and Kasyoha-kitomi (399 km²) Forest Reserves in Uganda; Kibira National Park (379 km²) in Burundi; Mt. Kabobo in the DRC (unprotected as yet); and Lakes Edward and George (Plumptre et al. 2003a).

Several protected areas are World Heritage Sites —Virunga, Rwenzori Mountains, Bwindi Impenetrable, Kahuzi-Biega National Parks— or Biosphere Reserves —Queen Elizabeth National Park (2 230 km²), with proposals currently to expand Virunga Park to include all the Virunga Volcanoes region, namely Mgahinga Gorilla Park (42 km²) in Uganda and Volcanoes National Park (150 km²) in Rwanda and their mountain gorillas under the World Heritage Site listing.

The Albertine Rift has recently become a focus of several conservation NGOs, in large part because of its high vertebrate diversity. Since 2001, a process, supported by the John D. and Catherine T. MacArthur Foundation, to develop a strategic framework for conservation and

Gorilla populations in the Rift have plummeted due to hunting and habitat loss. The Critically Endangered mountain gorillas plummeted to a low of 250 animals in the Virungas in the late 1980s (but have recovered slightly to 380 animals). Reliable estimates for the Endangered Grauer's gorilla (Gorilla beringei graueri) are not available, but it is known that there have been major declines in some areas.
© **Bruce Davidson**/naturepl.com

The red-hot pokers of the genus Kniphofia *are a distinctive feature of the vegetation above 3 000 m. This one has attracted a Tacazze sunbird* (Nectarinia tacazze) *to feed on the nectar.*
© Patricia Rojo

On the opposite page, the Endangered mountain nyala or gedemsa (Tragelaphus buxtoni) *is the last large animal to be discovered in Africa, having been described in 1910. Endemic to Ethiopia, it is likely that only 800 to 1 200 mountain nyalas survive throughout their restricted range.*
© Patricio Robles Gil/*Sierra Madre*

joint planning for protected areas has been implemented to bring together NGOs, protected area authorities, and government ministries in each country. Within this framework, there is a strong emphasis on involving local communities in the management of protected areas. Uganda, in particular, has been pioneering approaches to conservation that involve the communities adjacent to protected areas. Each park or wildlife reserve has a community conservation warden who holds regular meetings with the local villagers. There is a process of sharing revenue from tourists with these communities, and currently 20% of all gate receipts are put in a fund for community use (provided it is compatible with conservation).

Several protected areas in Uganda and the DRC are contiguous with one another or linked across international boundaries, thus increasing their conservation significance. The International Gorilla Conservation Programme, a coalition formed in 1991 comprising the African Wildlife Foundation, Fauna and Flora International, and the World Wide Fund for Nature (WWF), has been very successful in encouraging coordination and joint management among Uganda, Rwanda, and the DRC in the Virunga Volcanoes and Bwindi Impenetrable National Parks, even when these countries were at war. Their model has been replicated by the Wildlife Conservation Society (WCS) further north, to include all the contiguous protected areas linked to the Virunga National Park. This "Greater Virunga Landscape" contains more vertebrates than any other single set of contiguous protected areas in Africa (Plumptre et al. 2003a). While many protected areas are islands, the natural habitat in eastern DRC (forest and woodland) and in western Tanzania (woodland) is more intact, and it is still feasible to manage natural habitat as corridors to link protected areas. There are possibilities of expanding Mahale Mountains National Park to include other areas of importance along Lake Tanganyika and to the east. Similarly, it may be possible to set up linkages between Kahuzi-Biega National Park and Maiko to the north and Itombwe to the south, provided land uses in between are compatible with nature conservation. Conservation International, WWF, the Dian Fossey Gorilla Fund (International and Europe), WCS and the German Agency for Technical Cooperation (GTZ) are all working in this region to conserve biodiversity and to maintain linkages that exist. Much of the work in this region is supported by the Congo Basin Forest Partnership, which was launched in September of 2002, and is an association of 29 governmental agencies and NGOs working to promote sustainable management of Congo Basin Forest ecosystems and wildlife, as well as to improve the lives of people living there. In Uganda and Tanzania, the World Bank and UNDP-GEF and the European Union are supporting much of the conservation of Rift sites. Managing these areas as larger landscapes will increase the likelihood of their long-term survival, whereas leaving them as islands means accepting the loss of certain species, particularly large mammals.

As peace comes to the DRC, the pressures on the natural habitat will multiply. Logging and mining companies are already lining up to obtain concessions. There is a real need to identify which remaining sites deserve to be protected before they are lost to logging, mining or agriculture. Itombwe Massif is a clear leading contender for protected area status while, further south, additional survey work could yet reveal that Mt. Kabobo and the Marungu Massif require protection. The Tayna Community Reserve to the west of Lake Edward is also partially established, but needs biological surveys to determine its richness.

What we know already of the Albertine Rift indicates that it is very important in terms of vertebrate conservation, and yet much of it is still poorly known. Botanically, it may not be as rich as other sites in the world, but again there is a great need for more survey work, particularly of herbaceous plants and ferns. Conservation efforts in this region have to try to balance the pressing human requirements and poverty with the needs of the wildlife in the ever-shrinking natural habitat of this region. Many protected areas alone are just too small to conserve viable populations of the megafauna that still survive here. There is a need to maintain the linkages between protected areas where they still exist if the larger vertebrates are to survive in the long term. It will be harder to lobby for the conservation of these protected areas if these charismatic megafauna are lost in a region where human population density and poverty are so high, and their conservation is a top priority.

Andrew Plumptre [66]
Tim Davenport [73]
Mathias Behangana [74]
Robert Kityo [74]
Gerald Eilu [74]
Paul Ssegawa [74]
Corneille Ewango [66]
Charles Kahindo [74]

ETHIOPIAN HIGHLANDS

The Ethiopian Highlands are distinguished from the rest of Africa by their vast extent of high ground. They cover an area of some 519 278 km², almost 95% of which falls within the political borders of modern Ethiopia, although also to a lesser degree in neighboring Eritrea. There are also isolated montane outliers, including, for example, Jebel Elba and Jebel Hadai Aweb, parts of which are politically in Egypt but are administered by Sudan, and Jebel Ower near Port Sudan. The geographic and cultural heartland of this region is a vast plateau, averaging 2 200 m and split into two halves by the Great Rift Valley. The Ethiopian Highlands have a lower altitudinal limit of around 1 100 m, but in many areas the biogeographical boundary between the Highlands and the neighboring arid zone of

the Horn of Africa is higher, and averages around 1 500 m (Yalden et al. 1996). The cutoff is affected by local conditions and variation occurs throughout its length, although at the northern end of the Highlands it is lower than at the southern end. The boundary is somewhat artificial in that there are species that transgress it in both directions, but there is still a clear-cut separation between highland (Afromontane) flora and lowland (Somalia-Masai) flora (Friis et al., in press).

The Ethiopian Highlands are thought to have begun to rise some 75 million years ago. As the Earth's crust began to diverge in three plates, volcanoes erupted on the surface and resulted in an intrusion of trap lavas that were deposited on the underlying marine Cretaceous rock. Between about 45 and 35 million years ago, the lava was widespread and built up a thick layer of basalt, up to 3 000 m in some places. During the Oligocene, the lava deposits folded into an arch or dome, probably coinciding with the formation of the Red Sea Rift, and later Oligocene and Miocene lavas overlaid this arch to produce the high plateau. The mighty rift that now splits the Ethiopian dome into the northern and southern massifs began in the Miocene, 13-12 million years ago, and was fully formed by the Pliocene, 5-4.5 million years ago (Davidson and Rex 1980).

The volcanic activity that dominated the Ethiopian dome between 45 and 5 million years ago largely precluded the establishment of a stable fauna and flora. Thus, it is only in the last 4.5-4 million years that the Ethiopian Highlands have become habitable. However, this period of volcanism was followed by severe climatic fluctuations during the Pliocene and Pleistocene; being a highland area, it was affected by periods of glaciation between 120 000 and 20 000 years ago (although the Bale Mountains appear to have been glaciated as little as 14 000 years ago; H. Osmaston and W. Mitchell, pers. comm.). At this time, the surrounding areas were covered with open grassland, dry montane forest, and heath. As the climate warmed, the broad belts of subalpine vegetation contracted, and became restricted to higher altitudes. Vegetation has only somewhat recently colonized these areas, although some remain barren, such as the central peaks area in the Bale Mountains, where the landscape seen today has resulted from the lava outpourings modified through a process of erosion by water, wind, and ice.

Considering this turbulent past, and because the Ethiopian Highlands are geologically relatively young, they remain somewhat impoverished in terms of their fauna and flora. Indeed, for much of their recent history, the highlands have been geographically isolated: the Nile and floodplains of the Sudd, which lie to the west of the area, were impassable for many potential colonists from the west, while the majority of the lowlands that surround the highlands are arid, including the eastern Sahara to the north, the arid areas of northern Kenya to the south, and the Somali arid zone to the

east. On the other hand, the altitude and isolation of the highlands have favored speciation of colonists to the region. These colonists arrived via a number of different routes, the most important being the surrounding dry lowlands, although some tropical species may have arrived from moist areas in the south and southwest, passing through the barriers posed by the Kenyan deserts in the south and the White Nile floodplains in the west (Kingdon 1990).

Although most species in the region are of Afrotropical origin, some Palearctic influences are also evident. During the dry, glacial periods, the jebels and escarpments flanking the Red Sea allowed connectivity with temperate biomes to the north and the Arabian Peninsula, and a number of Palearctic representatives achieve their southernmost limit in the highlands.

The Ethiopian Highlands are extremely rugged and varied, with some regions characterized by steep escarpments and deep valleys. Rising to a height of 4 620 m at the summit of Ras Dashen in the scenic Simien Mountains, the highlands are truly the "Roof of Africa," with the majority of land over 3 000 m in Africa being found in this region (Yalden 1983). Indeed, around 73% of Sub-Saharan Africa's Afroalpine ecosystem (which is defined as being over 3 200 m) is found in Ethiopia.

The altitudinal zonation of the Ethiopian Highlands is pronounced, so much so that highlanders refer to each zone in terms of its habitability and the agriculture that can be practiced (see Threats). The foothills or lower elevations (800-1 500 m) of the Ethiopian Highlands, known as *kolla*, support woodland vegetation which is dominated by *Terminalia*, *Commiphora*, *Boswellia*, and *Acacia* species. At slightly higher elevations (1 500-3 000 m), the vegetation, termed *dega* or *weyna dega*, is dominated by the conifers *Podocarpus falcatus* and *Juniperus procera*. Above 3 000 m, the Afroalpine ecosystem, known locally as *wurch*, consists of grassland and moorland with an abundant herb layer. The Bale Mountains contains the largest patch of Afroalpine ecosystem (2 067 km^2, or 17.5% of all Afroalpine areas on the continent; S.D. Williams and I. May, unpubl. data). The treeline is dominated by *Hagenia abyssinica* and *Hypericum revoltum*. Above this, the heathland scrub is dominated by heathers such as *Erica arborea*. Besides the red-hot pokers of the genus *Kniphofia*, a distinctive feature of the vegetation in this zone is the giant *Lobelia rhynchopetalum*, which is particularly characteristic of Afroalpine vegetation. However, the flora is not sharply delineated from that of the ericaceous belt at slightly lower altitudes (Davis et al. 1994).

At the southern end of the Bale Mountains lies the enigmatic Herenna Forest. The altitudinal cline on which the forest grows has resulted in marked vegetation belts. The uppermost belt is dominated by *Rapanea* and tree heathers, while the moist slopes of the Herenna Forest are typified by a shrubby zone of *Hagenia* and

On the opposite page, the gelada (Theropithecus gelada) *lives in the high-altitude grasslands of Ethiopia and is one of the few primate genera endemic to a single country.*
© Patricia Rojo

Above, another Ethiopian Highlands endemic is the wattled ibis (Bostrychia carunculata)*. This gregarious species has been recorded in flocks of more than a hundred birds in the Bale Mountains.*
© Patricio Robles Gil/*Sierra Madre*

Schefflera growing alongside with the giant lobelias *Lobelia gibberroa*. Dense stands of mountain bamboo (*Arundinaria alpina*) are also found. Below 2 400 m, clouds and localized rain support a dense, moist forest, with trees over 30 m tall, their branches covered with epiphytes. While the Herenna Forest appears to be relatively impoverished, it does harbor endemic species, many of which are at the higher altitudes. These include the Bale monkey (*Cercopithecus djamdjamensis*), a little-known endemic primate, and a rich endemic amphibian fauna (Largen 2001). The very lowest and driest part of Herenna serves as an example of the sort of forest that once covered a much larger part of Ethiopia (Kingdon 1990).

Besides Herenna, the other remaining tract of forest —the largest within the highlands— is in the Welega, Illubabor, and Kefa areas of Ethiopia. These forests share a remarkably small proportion of their species with similar habitats in East and Central Africa (Yalden et al. 1996). As noted earlier, the arid and semiarid belt stretching from southern Sudan to northern Kenya must, therefore, despite its relative narrowness (500 km), be an effective barrier to the forest-dwelling species of the Guineo-Congolian forest block, and this despite the "stepping stone" provided by the Imatong Mountains of southeast Sudan (which contain representatives from the Central African Forests).

The climate of the area is complicated by influences from both the Atlantic and Indian Ocean systems, and at least eight climatic zones are identified (Gamachu 1977). Rainfall varies from 520 mm in the north to 2 370 mm in the southwest of the highlands and occurs in complex uni- or bimodal patterns. Overall, the Ethiopian Highlands play a crucial role in climate control in the entire region of northeast Africa by attracting large amounts of orographic rainfall (Hillman 1988). While within the highlands this has obvious implications for the ecosystems, humans —numbering in the tens of millions— are dependent on the water that originates from the Ethiopian Highlands. Hundreds of streams from the highlands join to form seven major rivers —the Great Abbai (Blue Nile), the Tacazze, the Awash, the Wabe Shebelle, the Juba (in turn, formed from the Web, Genale, Welmel, Dumal, and Dawa rivers), the Ghibie and Omo, and the Sobat (from the Akobo and Baro rivers). The largest of these rivers have carved out deep gorges, most notably the Tacazze, Great Abbai, and Ghibie that split the northern dome, and the Wabe Shebelle of the southern dome.

The Ethiopian Highlands also support a rich and ancient cultural diversity; as an example, modern Ethiopia harbors some 70 languages. The Ethiopian Orthodox Church was founded in Axum in the fourth century; Harar, probably founded in about the eleventh century, is considered as the fourth holiest Muslim city in the world.

On pp. 266-267, the enigmatic Herenna Forest, which lies to the south of the Bale Mountains, shows a marked altitudinal cline in vegetation, including an upper belt dominated by Rapanea *and tree heathers.*
© **Patricio Robles Gil**/*Sierra Madre*

Above, the spot-breasted lapwing (Vanellus melanocephalus) *is endemic to the Ethiopian Highlands; a site of particular conservation importance for this species is the Gudo Plain, just west of Addis Ababa.*
© **Patricio Robles Gil**/*Sierra Madre*

Biodiversity

The Ethiopian Flora Project was initiated in 1980 (Hedberg 1984; Friis and Ryding 2001; and see references in the Horn of Africa chapter) and has documented the majority of plant taxa in the greater Horn of Africa region (the Solanaceae, Lentibulariaceae, Pedaliaceae, and ferns and fern allies have yet to be included). This effort has been complemented by an ongoing compilation, review, and assessment of the threatened endemic flowering plants (the Red List Initiative for Plants of Ethiopia and Eritrea which, to date, has added over 300 taxa to the IUCN Red List; Kelbessa et al. 2003).

The Ethiopian Highlands harbor an estimated 5 200 vascular plant species in an estimated 1 563 genera and 185 families. Of these, 555 species (10.7% of the total) are endemics, with some groups, the majority of them associated with the open grasslands, dry woodlands, and heaths, being very diverse (e.g., the Compositae). The genus *Senecio* is particularly diverse, with 12 of the 24 species being endemic. There is only one endemic, monotypic genus from the area (*Nephrophyllum abyssinicum*, which is found on heavily grazed pastures, open ground, and rocky areas on steep slopes between 1 650 and 2 700 m); no plant families are endemic.

Endemism among vertebrates, particularly at the generic level, is relatively high in this region, especially when one considers the mammals. Thirty-one of the 193 mammal species in the Ethiopian Highlands are endemic to the area. Remarkably, there are six endemic genera of mammals, and four are monotypic (three rodent genera, *Megadendromus*, *Muriculus*, *Nilopegamys*; and one primate genus, *Theropithecus*). The other endemic genera are *Desmomys* and *Stenocephalemys*, represented by two species each. As with the plants, these are associated with high-altitude, open grasslands and dry woodlands.

An estimated 680 species of birds are known to occur regularly in the highlands and of these, 29 are endemic. Most of the bird species that are endemic to the highlands are distributed widely, but five are restricted to tiny pocket areas in the southern highlands. The latter region is considered an Endemic Bird Area (EBA) in the analysis of Stattersfield et al., as is the Central Ethiopian Highlands, with four species confined to it. There are four endemic genera, three of which are widespread (*Cyanochen*, *Rougetius*, and *Parophasma*), while the fourth has a very localized distribution in the south of the area (*Zavattariornis*). The blue-winged goose (*Cyanochen cyanoptera*) is interesting because it seems to have resulted from a chance landfall that has found an amenable environment in the Ethiopian Highlands; the species is closely related to the sheldgeese of the alpine and temperate grasslands of South America. In contrast, the Ethiopian bush-crow (*Zavattariornis stresemanni*, VU), along with the white-tailed swallow (*Hirundo megaensis*, VU) and Prince Ruspoli's turaco (*Tauraco ruspolii*, VU), are thought to be relicts caught at the confluence of four major biogeographic zones at the southern tip of the highlands.

The amphibian fauna includes six endemic genera (*Sylvacaecilia*, *Altiphrynoides*, *Spinophrynoides*, *Balebreviceps*, *Ericabatrachus*, and *Paracassina*), all of which comprise single species, with the exception of *Paracassina*, which is represented by two frog species. There is also a high level of endemism at the species level (23 species, of a total of 59). The reptilian fauna is less interesting, although of the 80 species present, 15 are endemic, including two species of chameleon (*Chamaeleo harennae* and *C. balebicornutus*).

Only 64 fish species occur in Lake Tana and the other rivers draining the Ethiopian Highlands. Lake Tana is the source of the Blue Nile, and with a surface area of over 3 000 km², is the most prominent freshwater feature of the Ethiopian Highlands. Nearly a quarter of fish species are endemic to Lake Tana, including a loach *Nemacheilus abyssinicus* and 14 large cyprinid barbs. *Barbus megastoma* is one of the largest of a number of important food fishes and can grow to more than 80 cm, which is unusually large for this genus (Nagelkerke and Sibbing 1997).

The number of species in all taxa has been steadily rising over the past 20 years, meaning that the totals given here are provisional. The Ethiopian Highlands is an area where little systematic collecting has taken place, and many areas, particularly the forests of the southwest (where expeditions to date have been limited in duration and poorly equipped), are largely unexplored. On the rare occasions that exploratory work is carried out, it is productive: at least five new species of small mammals have been described from the Ethiopian Highlands in the last 15 years. As a further example, the mountain nyala (*Tragelaphus buxtoni*, EN) was one of the last large mammals to be described on the African Continent, in 1910. In conclusion, the final total of both recorded species and endemics will almost certainly turn out to be much greater. In addition, the recognition of the endemic fauna and flora of Ethiopia requires adequate knowledge of areas of similar ecology and history (e.g., the Rwenzori Mountains in the Albertine Rift) to be certain that presumptive Ethiopian endemics are absent elsewhere (Yalden et al. 1996).

Flagship Species

Almost all the flagship species are confined to the Afroalpine ecosystem, the open grasslands or the montane forests. On the high plateau (3 100-4 640 m), the giant *Lobelia rhynchopetalum* is instantly recognizable, reaching a height of nine meters when flowering. Giant lobelias grow to 2-3 m before sending up a single inflorescence of dark blue-purple flowers. Every few years, the lobelias have a "musth" year when, for unknown reasons, the greater proportion of the plants flower. The inflorescence is hollow and has several thousand

flowers. Each flower produces several thousand tiny seeds. One inflorescence can, therefore, produce over seven million seeds! Once the plants have flowered, they die —although the dead plant "skeletons" last for several years and are characteristic of this zone.

At these altitudes, plants face two main challenges: the high levels of solar irradiation, and the extremes in temperature and wind. The young, sensitive leaves of giant lobelias are protected from the strong sunlight by always being vertical. The older leaves, which have a non-photochemical quenching mechanism for protection against ultraviolet irradiation, are horizontal. Young lobelias protect themselves against the extremes in temperatures by forming a "nightbud," tightly closing their leaves at night about the apical meristem. The young, sensitive leaves are also furry, which insulates them. The overall anatomy of the leaves —a circular, rosette form— acts as a parabolic reflector for the apical meristem to warm it and optimize growth. In older plants, the old leaves hang down to protect the stem, which is full of water. Their stems also have thick cork layers, again insulation to prevent water in the stem from freezing. The older leaves, in turn, can withstand temperatures down to –6ºC.

The Ethiopian wolf (*Canis simensis*, CR) is a rare endemic also found in the Afroalpine ecosystem. With fewer than 450 individuals remaining in seven small and isolated populations, the Ethiopian wolf is the rarest canid in the world. Initially considered to be of Afrotropical origin as a specialized derivative of the common jackal (Yalden and Largen 1992), it is now resolved to be of Palearctic origins. Genetic work has shown that it is most closely related to the grey wolf (*Canis lupus*), from which it diverged an estimated 100 000 years ago (Gottelli et al. 1994). Although Ethiopian wolves are solitary hunters, specializing on diurnal rodents, they are social animals, living in packs of up to 13 adults that are dominated by an alpha breeding pair. All pack members actively help to rear the young, despite the uncertainty of paternity that may occur through extra-pack copulations solicited by the alpha female (Sillero-Zubiri and Gottelli 1995a, b; Sillero-Zubiri et al. 1996).

The walia ibex (*Capra walie*, CR) is another Palearctic species which, despite the presence of other, charismatic flagships in the region and its close relationship with the widespread Nubian ibex (*C. nubiana*), has become a symbol for wildlife in Ethiopia —mainly because of the interest of trophy hunters and explorers who arrived first in the Simien Mountains, which are their only remaining refuge.

Three charismatic highland mammal species have Afrotropical origins. The first, the mountain nyala, was once widespread two to three million years ago, but their numbers have declined because of agricultural expansion and killing, and today less than 3 000 individuals remain, the majority of which are found in the Bale Mountains. The giant mole-rat (*Tachyoryctes*

Rouget's rail (Rougetius rougetii) *is an Ethiopian Highlands endemic, and is particularly characteristic of the moorlands of Ethiopia. The species mainly lives at elevations of up to 4 100 m, where it inhabits small pockets of grass and wet hollows with plenty of cover.*
© **Patricio Robles Gil**/*Sierra Madre*

269

macrocephalus) is found only in the Bale Mountains and forms the main prey of the Ethiopian wolf. These mole-rats are solitary, but their wide-ranging burrow systems overlap with those of other individuals. Each burrow system has over 90 m of tunnels, covering an area of up to 400 m^2. In some areas, they reach staggering densities, with about 6 000 mole-rats/km^2 (Sillero-Zubiri et al. 1995).

Unlike the mountain nyala and giant mole-rats, the majority of geladas (*Theropithecus gelada*) are found in the northern highlands. Gelada is the Amharic name for this species, which occupies a unique environmental niche as the only graminivorous primate species. Like other graminivores, they require a relatively large intake of leaves, stems, and rhizomes to fulfill their nutritional requirements and consequently spend long periods of the day grazing. The basic unit of gelada social structure consists of one reproductive male and up to ten reproductive females and their young. These units share a common home range and typically forage together as a "band." In turn, bands often aggregate to form foraging herds that can number as many as 600 individuals, although the composition of these large foraging groups is remarkably flexible.

Prince Ruspoli's turaco stands out as the prominent avian flagship of the highlands: it is attractive, threatened, and associated with a declining habitat. The species is an arboreal frugivore, feeding largely on figs, as well as *Podocarpus* and *Juniperus* fruits, and is usually observed alone or in groups of up to 11 individuals. The melodious song of the Abyssinian catbird (*Parophasma galinieri*) is characteristic of the woodlands throughout much of the Ethiopian Highlands. Pairs of birds call at dusk, particularly during the rainy season. Around wetlands —streams, bogs, and marshes— in the more open habitats and the Afroalpine ecosystems, Rouget's rail (*Rougetius rougetii*) is a common sighting. The rail has a conspicuous white tail, which it flicks frequently when disturbed. In contrast with the above species, which are fairly widely distributed, the charismatic Ethiopian bush-crow, first reported in 1938, has a very confined distribution at the southern end of the highlands. It is a gregarious species, moving in flocks of up to 30 birds, and is thought to be a cooperative breeder, with three birds attending to a nest.

Threats

The threats to the Ethiopian Highlands are underpinned by high human population pressure. Over the past 60 years, the population of Ethiopia has increased ten fold (from seven million in 1940 to an estimated 70 million in 2004). Eighty percent (56 million) of the country's population live in the highlands. This has put land, both for agriculture and for livestock husbandry, at a premium. Of the farmlands in the country, 94% are operated by seven million smallholders cultivating an average of less than one hectare. People are pushing the limits to which agriculture is practiced. In some areas, land is being tilled for barley production on the steepest slopes (sometimes in excess of 45°) at altitudes of up to 4 100 m.

The exploitation of the Ethiopian Highlands by humans is not a modern phenomenon. Indeed, it has been estimated that it has been ongoing for thousands of years, particularly to the west of the Rift Valley, and this has destroyed most of the natural vegetation, including a great part of the forests. Indeed, as mentioned earlier, highlanders even refer to each vegetation zone in terms of its habitability and the agriculture that can be practiced there: *wurch* (Afroalpine; more than 3 000 m; too cold to be habitable; no agriculture); *dega* (temperate; 2 300-3 000 m; barley, wheat, potatoes, pulses); *weyna dega* (warm temperate; 1 500-2 300 m; tef, maize, wheat, pulses); and *kolla* (tropical; 800-1 500 m; sorghum) (and with *bereha* being the hot and dry lower altitudinal areas at less than 800 m; no rainfed cultivation).

A suite of plants, whose maximum productivity lies between 1 800 and 2 100 m, were domesticated historically in the Ethiopian Highlands, which includes their centers of diversity and origin. They include khat (*Catha edulis*), ensete (*Enset ventricosum*), noog (*Guizotia abyssinica*), finger millet (*Eleusine coracana* for beer), tef (*Eragrostis tef*) and coffee (*Coffea arabica*) (Harlan 1992). The exact date and location for the domestication of all these plants are unknown. On the basis of linguistic, historical, geographic and botanical studies, there is no doubt that, with some variation, they are very ancient crops and most authors put the date at between 6 000-3 000 years ago.

Besides agricultural crops, Ethiopia has the largest national herd of domestic livestock, and cattle in particular, in Africa. In part, the number of cattle in the country might result from the absence of wood (which has been previously removed through human exploitation for fuel and construction), as the majority of Ethiopian highlanders use cattle dung as their principal source of fuel. The livestock is increasingly using the more extreme areas to graze. In 2002, the livestock in a discrete area of the Bale Mountains reached an unprecedented density of 314 animals/km^2. Besides the effects of erosion and increasing the abundance of unpalatable or poisonous species, overgrazing also heightens competition between livestock and wildlife species. In addition, livestock and the domestic dogs that often accompany it increase the risk of disease transmission to wildlife species. Two rabies epidemics in the past 14 years have occurred among Ethiopian wolves by transmission from domestic dogs, and this serves as a constant reminder of the seriousness of this threat. Dogs also pose a further, insidious threat to wolves through hybridization.

Finally, humans have hunted and killed birds and mammals, reducing their populations to a fraction of

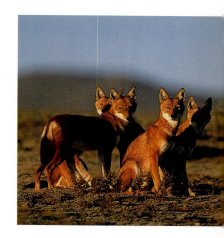

*On the opposite page, this giant lobelia (*Lobelia rhynchopetalum*) is a characteristic species of some Afromontane regions, reaching a height of as much as nine meters when flowering. These plants have special adaptations to help them survive at such high altitudes, with older leaves able to withstand temperatures to –6°C.*
© **Patricio Robles Gil**/*Sierra Madre*

*Above, the rarest canid in the world, the Ethiopian wolf (*Canis simensis*), which is Critically Endangered, now numbers less than 450 animals, and is threatened by loss of habitat to agriculture and grazing, diseases such as rabies, hybridization with domestic dogs, and human persecution.*
© **M. Harvey**/*DRK PHOTO*

what they were 150 years ago. The killing of animals has not just been for subsistence use or potentially as a buffer during famines. During (frequent) political upheavals in the region, the infrastructure of the national parks has been successively used and then destroyed by armed groups, who also kill animals for food. Furthermore, because the national parks and wildlife populations held within them have been largely associated with repressive regimes (particularly the "dergue," the military-Marxist regime of Mengistu Haile Mariam in Ethiopia), the population vented suppressed anger by destroying park infrastructure and slaughtering large mammals (Yalden et al. 1996).

The sum of these factors has resulted in a massive transformation of the environment, and it is estimated that as much as 97% of the original vegetation has been lost. Because human exploitation is linked to it, altitude has also had a profound effect on the extent of the original vegetation that remains. The original vegetation that remains only does so because it is confined to the ecosystems that are extreme and defy human use. These are the steep escarpments of the Rift Valley and the river gorges, the cold Afroalpine plateaus, and a few patches of thick forest. Consequently, several key areas of the remaining original vegetation emerge as being critically important to the biodiversity of the Ethiopian Highlands. These are obviously very limited in size, as they are not only geographic islands above the surrounding lowlands, but also islands in a human-transformed environment.

This local elderly woman in Debre Libanos relies on whatever bits and pieces she can carve off old stumps.
© **Patricio Robles Gil**/*Sierra Madre*

Conservation

The degree to which the natural vegetation and animal populations have been lost means that the region's diversity is acutely threatened. In Ethiopia, despite having a wildlife conservation organization that has been active for just under 40 years, as well as a succession of foreign advisors and periodic injections of donor assistance, there has been remarkably little impact on arresting the decline of many habitats and species.

While modern conservation efforts struggle to be successful, the Ethiopian Highlands contain the oldest records of conservation efforts on the continent. The Emperor Zera Yacob (1434-1468) noted the loss of forest cover on what is now known as Wuchacha Mountain. The forest was replenished at his orders using seeds and seedlings of *Juniperus procera* to create Menagesha Forest, which stands today (Gilbert 1970).

More remarkably, although not quite as old, in the Guassa-Menz area of North Shoa, Ethiopia, local communities implemented a sustainable natural resource management system in the seventeenth century. The system, known as *Qero*, allowed equitable use and distribution of natural resources (thatching grass, fuelwood, and grazing) that were, and still are, important for the livelihood security of the community. By regulating exploitation of the area, the management system has also effectively protected the biodiversity of the Afroalpine ecosystem of the Guassa-Menz area.

When the *Qero* arose, it was supported by the authority of the Ethiopian Orthodox Church, a powerful component of this ancient society. The system declined in 1975 as a result of the Agrarian Reform of 1975, which was introduced under the socialist regime that came to power in the revolution of 1974. People who were previously excluded from resource use gained uncontrolled access through their constituent peasant association. When it became apparent that the resource management system was declining under the land tenure reform, the community responded by establishing the Guassa Committee, known locally as *Idir*. The committee retained significant community representation and was still deemed acceptable to the political and social order of the socialist regime. The remarkable adaptation and subsequent persistence of the system suggests that it is stable and resilient in the face of significant political change (Tefera 2001).

Apart from these noteworthy examples, the realization of the conservation significance of the Ethiopian Highlands has been late in coming; arguably, it has yet to be fully grasped by the leaders of the countries spanned by the highlands. While policies are largely in place (e.g., the National Conservation Strategy, 1994; the Conservation Strategy of Ethiopia, 1997; the Donor Coordination Group on the Environment-Contribution to the Poverty Reduction Strategy Paper (PRSP) Discussion, 2001; the Ethiopian Sustainable Development and Poverty Reduction Program, 2002), the strategies are not being implemented.

In 1909, Ethiopia passed its first wildlife legislation designed to regulate "sport" hunting —particularly of elephants. However, prior to 1944, the fauna and flora of the highlands were still largely viewed as an infinite source of food and other materials, and as a source of "sport" for the upper echelons of society and expatriates in the country. The Preservation of Game Proclamation of 1944 reinforced earlier legislation to regulate hunting and to prevent the overhunting of certain species.

With interest from international conservation organizations, the Ethiopian Wildlife Conservation Organization (EWCO) was established in 1964 (Hillman 1993a). Because of a lack of wildlife management experience (*cf.* the experience that was built in neighboring Kenya and Uganda through their colonial past), the majority of the early work —the production of legislation and the designation of protected areas— was largely carried out by expatriates. It has only been since the first batch of trainees returned from the Mweka Wildlife College in Tanzania in the early 1970s that Ethiopian nationals have started taking senior positions within the EWCO.

The EWCO has been pivotal in the formulation of legislation to protect the fauna and flora, as well as in the designation, establishment, and management of national parks. However, the efforts of the EWCO have been starved for resources and the legislation designed to protect wildlife has proved impossible to enforce.

A system of conservation areas has formed the basis of the wildlife conservation strategy in Ethiopia (Hillman 1993b). When they were proposed, they were based on what was known about the fauna and habitats at the time, and were primarily directed toward the more spectacular assemblages of large mammals and those species considered to be endemic and at risk (Yalden et al. 1996). However, since this network was proposed, only two of the 14 "national parks" and "sanctuaries" have been legally constituted, namely Awash National Park and Simien Mountains National Park, the latter of which is recognized as a World Heritage Site (Hillman 1993b). Even these two have never been adequately secured, staffed or equipped. The numerous "wildlife reserves" and "controlled hunting areas" are little more than nominal, and provide no protection for the fauna and flora. Indeed, only 3% of the Ethiopian Highlands is conserved in protected areas in IUCN categories I to IV.

Since the mid-1970s, difficulties in wildlife conservation have been exacerbated by famines, refugee problems, civil unrest, armed rebellions, and war. This series of events threatens the livelihoods of the present generation of Ethiopians. As long as such events continue and society remains stricken by poverty and food insecurity, it is unlikely that wise conservation measures will be implemented.

However, *if* the region's current and proposed national parks were fully established and administered, they would have the potential to provide some level of protection for many of the region's endemic species. It is notable that the conservation areas were specifically designed to protect the mammalian fauna. Therefore, a re-assessment of the conservation areas of the region is warranted because they may not protect endemic species across other taxa.

The Bale Mountains National Park is the single most important conservation area that has been proposed in the Ethiopian Highlands, harboring the finest and most intact remnant of the highland's original vegetation. The Bale Mountains have 1 321 species of flowering plants, 163 of which are highland endemics, including the 27 Bale endemics (e.g., *Euryops prostratus*, *Gladiolus balensis*, *Maytenus harennensis*, and *Solanecio harennensis*). These mountains also contain more than half the global populations of both the Ethiopian wolf and mountain nyala. Of the mammals that have been recorded there, 26% are Ethiopian endemics (including the Bale monkey, Starck's hare (*Lepus starcki*), and eight species of rodents, including the Bale endemics —the giant mole-rat, unstriped grass rat (*Arvicanthis bli-*

cki), and brush-furred mouse (*Lophuromys melanonyx*). Among several rare endemic amphibians, there are four species found in Bale alone, including one monotypic, endemic genus, the Bale Mountains narrow-mouthed frog (*Balebreviceps hillmani*, EN) (Largen 2001), and there are two chameleons that are Bale endemics (Largen 1995; M. Largen and S. Spawls, pers. comm.). The conclusion is that if conservation efforts in the Bale Mountains are not successful and people continue to exploit the resources in an unsustainable way, more species of mammals (and the analysis remains to be done for other taxa) would go extinct there than in any other area of equivalent size on the globe (J. Malcolm, pers. comm.).

The Ethiopian Wolf Conservation Program (EWCP), which has its base in the Bale Mountains, has demonstrated that working successfully in the difficult climate of Ethiopia is possible. Information on Ethiopian wolves was only first collected during the mid-1970s (Malcolm 1976, 1977, 1988), and through the 1980s and early 1990s (Hillman 1988; Sillero-Zubiri 1994). These studies gave the EWCP (based out of the Wildlife Conservation Research Unit of the University of Oxford) a foundation, which was bolstered by the publication of a conservation action plan (Sillero-Zubiri and Macdonald 1997).

Consequently, the responsibilities of the EWCP have evolved to ensure the conservation of the Ethiopian wolf and its Afroalpine ecosystem. This is achieved by a three-pronged approach: securing the conservation of areas of Afroalpine ecosystem, their biodiversity and ecological processes; assessing, addressing, and counteracting threats to the survival of Ethiopian wolves; and enhancing the focus on and strength of the environmental sector, and particularly biodiversity conservation, within Ethiopia.

Conservation in the Ethiopian Highlands is far from being secure, but there may be room for hope. While its focus has been conspicuously away from natural resource and wildlife conservation, the present Government of Ethiopia has been making progress towards creating a climate in which wildlife conservation could, potentially, play a role. In such a climate, tourism and the revenues generated from it could grow. If this is linked to the unique fauna and flora of the region, then wildlife conservation could receive more attention and political will.

STUART WILLIAMS [67, 68]
JOSÉ LUIS VIVERO POL [81]
STEVEN SPAWLS [82]
ANTENEH SHIMELIS [67]
ENSERMU KELBESSA [83]

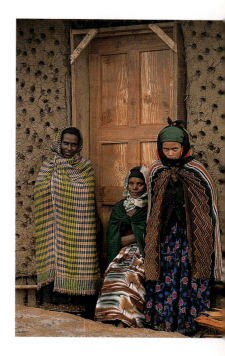

Local women in village near the Herenna Forest, Bale Mountains, Ethiopia.
© **Patricio Robles Gil**/*Sierra Madre*

On pp. 274-275, wood is a scarce commodity in the Ethiopian Highlands, having been previously removed through human exploitation for fuel and construction. Today, the majority of Ethiopian highlanders use cattle dung as their principal source of fuel, possibly one reason why Ethiopia has the largest national herd of domestic livestock in Africa. Here, people coming to market in Dinsho village, near the headquarters of Bale Mountains National Park.
© **Patricio Robles Gil**/*Sierra Madre*

273

HORN OF AFRICA

The Horn of Africa was already a renowned biological hotspot 5 000 years ago, when the ancient Egyptians sent expeditions to the "Land of Punt" to bring back unique natural commodities such as frankincense and myrrh. During the times of the ancient Greeks and Romans, these products were brought to Europe by caravans along the incense route through the Arabian deserts. Even the isolated island of Socotra, with its famous cinnabar (dragon's blood) and aloe, was part of this trading system more than 2 000 years ago.

The Horn of Africa is here defined as the arid Horn and basically covers the area east of the Ethiopian Highlands (although it includes the Rift Valley, which divides the Ethiopian Highlands into two major blocks), also including the xeric bushlands of northeastern Kenya and the southern coastal parts of the Arabian Peninsula. The arid Horn covers most of Somalia (including Somaliland and Puntland), Djibouti, and parts of Ethiopia, Eritrea, Kenya, Yemen, Oman and, very marginally, Sudan. The area covers around 1.65 million km², but a relatively large proportion of the land, such as the Danakil Depression in Ethiopia, has a very depauperate flora, and the approximately 5 000 species of vascular plants known from the region actually occupy only a small percentage of the area. Included in this hotspot is the Socotra Archipelago, with the main Socotra Island and three smaller islands off the coast of northeastern Somalia, covering about 3 636 km², and a few hundred small islands in the Red Sea, of which Dahlak Island is the largest (643 km²).

Phytogeographically, all of the arid Horn as defined here belongs to the Somalia-Masai region of endemism (White 1983; White and Léonard 1991), which also extends further south through the Kenyan lowlands into northern Tanzania. The Horn of Africa in the present sense can be regarded as the core part of the Somalia-Masai region.

The most widespread vegetation type of the arid Horn is *Acacia-Commiphora* bushland (about 30 species of *Acacia* and 50 species of *Commiphora* are endemic to the area), but evergreen bushland, succulent shrubland, dry evergreen forest and woodland, semidesert grassland, and low-growing dune and rock vegetation occupy considerable areas as well. Succulents are common, including numerous endemic species of, for example, *Euphorbia* and *Aloe*. Small areas of mangrove are also found, both on the African and the Arabian sides, as well as riverine

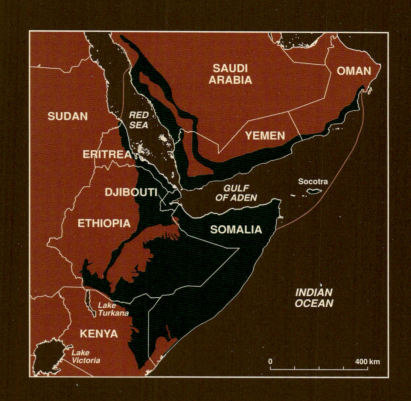

vegetation along the major rivers: Wabe Shabelle, Jubba, and Awash.

The altitude within the arid Horn ranges from 155 m below sea level at Lac Assal in Djibouti to about 2 400 m above sea level in the mountains of northern Somalia, but most of the area is below 500 m. The Haghier Mountains on Socotra reach just above 1 500 m altitude and the highest escarpments in Hadramaut on the Arabian side reach about 2 000 m. An unusual feature of the region is that land plants, such as the doum palm (*Hyphaene thebaica*, Arecaceae), can have an altitudinal range from about 100 m below sea level to about 1 000 m above sea level. The altitudinal delimitation between the arid Horn flora and the highland floras in Ethiopia, Eritrea, and Yemen is not always clearly distinguishable in the field, and also varies between about 1 500 to 2 000 m according to local climate, geology, and topography. Still, there is a clear-cut separation between highland (Afromontane) flora and lowland (Somalia-Masai) flora (Friis et al., in press).

The arid Horn, including the southern Arabian Peninsula and Socotra, appears to have been elevated by about the upper Eocene some 40 million years ago. Geological evidence indicates that the Arabian Peninsula and Africa separated by about 10 million years ago, forming the incipient Red Sea and Gulf of Aden. When the continental fragment Socotra was last connected to Africa is less certain, but it may

On the opposite page, the gerenuk (Litocranius walleri), a species confined mainly to the Horn of Africa, is remarkable in its ability to rise up on its hindlegs to feed at up to 2 m above ground level. In so doing, it reaches a very erect bipedal posture, facilitated by modification of the lumbar vertebrae.
© **Ferrero-Labat**/*Auscape*

have been considerably earlier. The massive limestone series covering most of the island (Beydoun and Bichan 1970) are connected with corresponding series in the escarpments of northern Somalia and the southern Arabian Peninsula.

Today, the major part of the arid Horn is covered by limestone, sandstone or gypsum, whereas Pre-Cambrian rocks form, for example, the prominent inselbergs in southern Somalia, as well as the rugged pinnacles of the mountains of Socotra. Large areas are covered by deep sand, partly derived from Quaternary coralline rocks or alluvial soils, and the fossil dune formations running along the coast of central and southern Somalia are prominent features of the landscape. Lava of more or less recent origin is found in the Rift Valley and the Afar Depression, and in parts of the southern Arabian Peninsula.

The climate of the arid Horn can generally, and not surprisingly, be described as hot and dry. It is not uncommon for temperatures to reach above 40°C during several months of the year. Characteristically, there are two rainy seasons, one in April-May and one in September-November, but there are many deviations from this. The fog oasis of eastern Yemen and Oman has summer rain during the southwest monsoon, whereas winter rain occurs along the escarpments of Eritrea and northern Somalia. Precipitation from mist plays an important role along the Arabian coast, as well as in the higher parts of Socotra and Somalia. The rocky outcrops in southern Somalia are more humid than can be expected from rainfall data alone.

The arid Horn is a kind of northeastern antipode to the other arid African hotspot, the Succulent Karoo in southwestern Africa. These two arid regions are believed to have been united by an "arid corridor" during repeatedly drier and colder periods during the Pleistocene, but most probably also earlier during the Tertiary. Some genera of flowering plants are entirely restricted to these regions, such as *Kissenia* with one species in the arid Horn and one in the Succulent Karoo, and *Wellstedia* with six species in the arid Horn and one in the Succulent Karoo. A few species of plants and animals in the Horn of Africa may also have their closest relatives in the southern United States and Central America. For example, *Chapmannia*, a genus of mostly woody legumes, has five species in the arid Horn; one in Mexico, Guatemala, and Venezuela; and one in Florida (Thulin 1999), and the scorpion genus *Heteronebo* has two species in the Socotra Archipelago and about a dozen species in the Caribbean. This pattern, which may be explained by the Tertiary "North Atlantic land bridge," is thought to be common among organisms that diversified during the Tertiary in xeric and seasonally dry vegetation (Lavin et al. 2000).

The Horn region is sparsely populated, with generally less than 20 inhabitants per km², and nomadic pastoralism is commonly practiced. Well over half the area (Somalia, eastern Ethiopia, and northeastern Kenya) is mainly inhabited by the Somali, a culturally, linguisti-

cally, and religiously homogeneous group. In southern and northeastern Ethiopia, northern Kenya, as well as in Djibouti and the lowlands of Eritrea, the situation is more complex, with many other East Cushitic groups, such as Borana and Afar, living together. In southwestern Ethiopia, there are also many groups that speak languages of the Omotic family. The native language on Socotra, Socotri, is a West Semitic language with archaic features. It is most closely related to Mahri and some other languages spoken in southeastern Yemen and Oman, along with the ubiquitous Arabic.

Biodiversity

Estimating the number of species of vascular plants in the arid Horn region is not easy. One reason is that the area falls under five different flora projects: *Flora of Tropical East Africa*, *Flora of Ethiopia and Eritrea*, *Flora of Somalia*, *Les plantes vasculaires de la République de Djibouti*, and *Flora of the Arabian Peninsula and Socotra*. Of these, only the Djibouti flora, with a relatively low number of species, has been completed (Audru et al. 1994), whilst the other projects are ongoing. According to the admittedly rough, but best possible estimate available, there are about 5 000 species of vascular plants in the region, and of these about 2 750 are endemic. In terms of plant endemism, this figure is higher than that for the Succulent Karoo (2 539 species), but then the area covered by the arid Horn is more than 16 times as large. Many of the species in the arid Horn have very restricted areas of distribution, however, with strong concentrations of endemics in northern Somalia (Thulin 1994; Friis et al., in press) and in the Socotra Archipelago (Miller and Bazara'a 1998).

There are nearly 60 endemic genera of vascular plants in the arid Horn (out of a total of about 970 genera), 13 of which are endemic to the Socotra Archipelago alone. It is also striking that the native flora of the Socotra Archipelago comprises so few armed plants. For example, the single endemic *Acacia* on Socotra, *A. pennivenia* (VU), is unarmed, whereas the thorny bushlands of the continental Horn abound in armed endemic species of *Acacia*.

Of the 170 families in the region, two are endemic. These are Barbeyaceae and Dirachmaceae, both woody, Barbeyaceae with a single species, *Barbeya oleoides*, which is relatively widespread in evergreen bushland and dry evergreen forest, and Dirachmaceae with two species, *Dirachma socotrana* (VU) on Socotra and *D. somalensis* (EN) in central Somalia. Barbeyaceae, with small unisexual flowers without petals, have usually been associated with Urticales. Dirachmaceae, with relatively large bisexual flowers with prominent petals, have been associated with Geraniales or Malvales. However, molecular evidence clearly indicates that Barbeyaceae and Dirachmaceae, despite their completely different morphology, are closely related (Thulin et al. 1998).

A total of 219 mammal species in 115 genera are

The Endangered Grevy's zebra (Equus grevyi) *has experienced one of the most dramatic declines of any large African mammal, with a 70% drop in numbers in Kenya recorded between 1977 and 1988, and a decline of around 80% in Ethiopia between 1995 and the present. It is considered already extirpated in Eritrea, Djibouti, and Somalia.*
© Joe McDonald/*DRK PHOTO*

known from the arid Horn, and of these 20 species are endemic, the most notable ones being a number of antelopes, such as the beira (*Dorcatragus megalotis*, VU), dibatag (*Ammodorcas clarkei*, VU), Speke's gazelle (*Gazella spekei*, VU), silver dikdik (*Madoqua piacentinii*, VU), and Salt's dikdik (*Madoqua saltiana*). In addition, there is an endemic subspecies of wild ass (the Somali wild ass, *Equus africanus somaliensis*, CR). There are five endemic mammal genera in the Horn, all of them monotypic, including the aforementioned beira and dibatag, and three small mammal genera represented by single species: the Somali pygmy gerbil (*Microdillus peeli*), ammodile (*Ammodillus imbellis*, VU), and Speke's pectinator (*Pectinator spekei*). Indeed, the arid Horn has been identified as an important area for rodent conservation (Amori and Gippoliti 2001). No native mammals are known from the Socotra Archipelago, except possibly some species of bats, and it has been assumed that this is because Socotra was isolated from the continental Horn too early for colonization by mammals.

There are 704 bird species regularly recorded from the arid Horn, and 25 of these are endemic. Four Endemic Bird Areas (EBAs) fall entirely within the hotspot: Socotra (with six species confined entirely to this EBA); North Somali Mountains (three species); Central Somali Coast (two species); and Jubba and Shabelle valleys (four species). There are seven species of birds found only in Somalia, including the Bulo Burti boubou (a bushshrike) (*Laniarius liberatus*, CR) —known only from a single individual and described from molecular, photographic, and vocalization data (Smith et al. 1991)— the Warsangli linnet (*Carduelis johannis*, EN), and five species of larks. Among the six species of birds restricted to Socotra is the Socotra sunbird (*Nectarinia balfouri*), a relatively abundant species regularly seen visiting the red flowers of species of *Aloe* and *Ballochia*. Another Socotra endemic, the golden-winged grosbeak (*Rhynchostruthus socotranus*), is the only representative of its genus.

There are some 284 reptile species in 94 genera recorded from the Horn, and at least 93 species are endemic. The endemic Somalian spiny-tailed lizard (*Uromastyx princeps*), for instance, is a diurnal lizard with a short, robust, spiny tail that frequents the limestone plateaus along the Indian Ocean coast in northeastern Somalia. When disturbed, these lizards quickly retreat into their holes, closing the opening using their armored tail as a lid. There are six endemic reptile genera, including *Haackgreerius*, a genus of skink represented by a single species, *H. miopus*, in Somalia; and *Aeluroglena*, comprising a single species of snake, *A. cucullata*. Three genera are endemic on Socotra, namely *Haemodracon*, with two species of geckos (*H. riebeckii* and *H. trachyrhinus*), and *Ditypophis* and *Pachycalamus*, each with a single species of snake (*D. vivax* and *P. brevis*, respectively).

Amphibians are poorly represented in the arid Horn, with only 53 species recorded, at least seven of which are endemic. Of the 20 genera represented, only *Lanzarana*, with a single species, Lanza's frog (*L. largeni*) confined to Somalia, is endemic. No amphibian species

are known from Socotra, despite the presence of suitable habitats.

It is estimated that there are around 100 species of freshwater fishes in about 48 genera in the arid Horn, of which 10 species are endemic. The endemics include three cave-dwelling species restricted to Somalia, two of which —the Somalian blind barb (*Barbopsis devecchii*, VU) and Somalian cavefish (*Phreatichthys andruzzii*, VU)— are blind. The three cave-dwelling species are each placed in their own endemic genus. No native freshwater fishes are known with certainty from Socotra, but populations of *Aphanius dispar* have been introduced to some waters as part of an anti-malaria program. However, the endemic freshwater crab *Potamon socotrensis* is common in small mountain streams, and a second endemic species, *Socotra pseudocardiosoma*, placed in its own genus, has recently been described (Cumberlidge and Wranik 2002).

Flagship Species

For thousands of years the Horn of Africa has been famous as the source of frankincense (mainly from *Boswellia sacra* in Somalia, Yemen, and Oman, and *B. frereana* in Somalia), myrrh (mainly from *Commiphora myrrha*, widespread in the Horn, and *C. guidottii* in Somalia and eastern Ethiopia), and dragon's blood or cinnabar (from *Dracaena cinnabari*, EN, on Socotra), all of which are commodities of gum-resins obtained from these trees.

In the Egyptian temple at Deir al-Bahari, near Thebes, the walls are decorated with colored relief frescoes commemorating an expedition sent out to the Land of Punt by the Queen of Egypt, Hatshepsut, about 1500 B.C. Quantities of incense were brought back by this expedition, as were living trees in tubs that apparently were then planted in the temple courtyard. The exact position and extension of Punt is uncertain, but judging from the commodities obtained from there it has to have been within the Horn of Africa in the present sense. Later, frankincense and myrrh were transported by huge caravans along the highly organized incense route from southern Arabia to ancient Greece and Rome (Groom 1981).

The production of frankincense and myrrh is still of major economic importance in Somalia, and to some extent in Ethiopia and northern Kenya. The frankincense trees in northern Somalia are owned by extended families and clans. To tap the trees, incisions are made into the inner bark of trunks and branches. The resin is left to dry and is later collected. Both *Boswellia frereana* and *B. sacra* are evergreen trees that often grow on limestone rocks, but *B. frereana* has the ability to grow even on vertical cliff faces, and the collecting of the frankincense from this species, therefore, is a particularly hard and dangerous occupation.

Dragon's blood from Socotra (then called Dioscorida) was in high demand by the ancient Greeks and Romans for its medicinal properties and as a red dye. However, it

Although Awash National Park is a stronghold for the Hamadryas or sacred baboon (Papio hamadryas), *it also has within its borders a unique hybrid zone between this species and the olive baboon* (P. anubis). *Hybrids of the two baboon species have been witnessed preying on young Salt's dikdiks* (Madoqua saltiana).
© **Patricio Robles Gil**/*Sierra Madre*

279

lost its importance long ago and, during the last centuries, dragon's blood has mainly been obtained from the related and more easily accessible dragon tree on the Canary Islands. *Dracaena cinnabari* is prominent in the vegetation of Socotra, where the gum-resin is still used as a medicine and dye. It is a spectacular tree with repeatedly ramifying branches forming a dense, umbrella-like canopy.

Another spectacular tree found only on Socotra is the cucumber tree (*Dendrosicyos socotrana*, VU), with a massive water-storing trunk. Despite being a relatively tall, free-standing tree when mature, the branches of *Dendrosicyos* have tendrils, just as in its herbaceous relatives. The daban or Bankoualé palm (*Livistona carinensis*, VU) is a slender palm reaching well over 20 m in height when mature. It is known from a few isolated localities in northeastern Somalia, Djibouti, and southern Yemen. Phytogeographically, it is of great interest, as the other 30 or so species of *Livistona* occur in Southeast Asia and Australia. The largest population is in Yemen, where regeneration is also satisfactory, but recent reports indicate that most, if not all, tall mature trees have been felled for timber. The Djibouti population is smaller, but includes both mature trees and juveniles in some sites. In Somalia, the daban, as it is called there, is highly threatened and the total population is now probably less than 40 trees in the two known localities (the author counted 11 mature trees at one locality in 1995 and 28 mature trees at the other locality in 2000). The trees have been used for house building, drainage pipes, and so on, and regeneration is prevented as the leaves of young plants are grazed or used for the production of mats or baskets.

The Yeheb nut (*Cordeauxia edulis*, VU) is a wonderful evergreen shrub or small tree with yellow flowers found in the dry bushlands of eastern Ethiopia and central Somalia, usually in areas of deep sand. The seeds are edible and nourishing and highly appreciated as food, and the foliage provides a red dye. The plant has attracted considerable interest as a potential food crop for arid areas, but is not easy to cultivate.

During fieldwork conducted for the Flora of Somalia project over the last 20 years or so, hundreds of new species have been discovered, many of them apparently narrow endemics. Without comparison, the one species among these that has attracted the most attention is the Somali cyclamen (*Cyclamen somalense*). It was first found in 1986 on one of the misty limestone escarpments in northern Somalia and is still known only from a very small area. The horticulturally important genus *Cyclamen* is otherwise distributed in the Mediterranean region, extending eastwards to Iran, and the occurrence of a species of this genus in tropical Africa was most unexpected, although there is a fairly strong Mediterranean element in the flora of this part of Somalia.

In addition to the plants and plant products that the ancient Egyptians brought back from the Land of Punt, they also brought back animals, and the most famous of these is the Hamadryas or sacred baboon (*Papio hamadryas*). This monkey is today endemic to the arid Horn,

where it lives on hillsides and escarpments bordering the southern part of the Red Sea and the Gulf of Aden. The sacred baboon is an omnivore for which desert dates (*Balanites* and *Ziziphus*) are of great seasonal importance, but it raids crops in settled areas and that often leads to conflict. The animals were held sacred in ancient Egypt and were also mummified. During the earliest Egyptian civilization, the distribution of the sacred baboon may have extended to the Egyptian border area, although they were later imported to the temples, and the relief frescoes at Deir al-Bahari show baboons swarming over the ships in Hatshepsut's expedition.

Besides the baboon, the Horn is an important region for a number of threatened antelope species, particularly the beira and dibatag antelopes (in both cases, the Somali name for the species has become the common name). The beira, with its prominent ears, is confined to dry and inhospitable hills and mountains of northern Somalia, eastern Ethiopia, and Djibouti (where its presence was only confirmed in 1993), in which it is able to survive without water. The larger, but more slender dibatag, with its characteristic erect tail and long neck, is found in the *Acacia-Commiphora* bushlands of eastern Ethiopia and adjoining lowlands of northern and central Somalia. Both the beira and the dibatag have suffered from uncontrolled hunting and habitat degradation.

Another important flagship is the desert warthog, *Phacochoerus aethiopicus*, recently confirmed to represent a distinct species from the common warthog, *P. africanus*, and distributed mainly in eastern Ethiopia, Somalia, and northern Kenya (D'Huart and Grubb 2001). In addition, species such as Speke's gazelle, Salt's and silver dik-diks, and beisa oryx (*Oryx beisa*) have their ranges entirely or almost entirely within the Horn, while Swayne's hartebeest (*Alcelaphus buselaphus swaynei*, EN), a subspecies of the common hartebeest, has its range restricted entirely to the southern Rift Valley of Ethiopia, despite once occurring throughout the Rift Valley eastwards into northwestern Somalia (East 1999).

Among the 31 endemic birds in the region, the Warsangli linnet is one of the most notables. This small bird, with colors in white, black, and various shades of grey and reddish brown, is locally common in high, steep escarpments along the Gulf of Aden in northern Somalia. Ash and Miskell (1998) reported it as resident in two sites (Daalo and Mash Caleed) in the 1980s, and the bird has been seen in both of these sites in recent years. The species is likely to occur along this whole stretch of escarpment, where access is nearly impossible. The Ethiopian bush-crow also deserves special mention as a flagship species. This small, starling-like crow is found in *Acacia* bushland in a very restricted area of southern Ethiopia. It is still locally common, but ongoing degradation of the habitat may become a threat in the near future. Finally, the Djibouti francolin (*Francolinus ochropectus*, CR) is known from only two sites in Djibouti: Forêt de Day, which is thought to be the only viable site for this imperiled species, and the nearby Mabla Mountains.

On pp. 280-281, many of the plant species in the Horn of Africa have very restricted areas of distribution, but with strong concentrations of endemics, such as in the Socotra Archipelago, which has 13 endemic genera. Croton socotranus, pictured here in the foreground, is one of a number of endemic Socotran species.
© Mats Thulin

Above, one of the larger gazelle species, the Vulnerable Soemmerring's gazelle (Nanger soemmerringii) *probably numbers fewer than 15 000 animals, with the largest protected population occurring in Awash National Park.*
© Patricio Robles Gil/*Sierra Madre*

Threats

The arid Horn is a hotspot under heavy pressure. Close to 100% of the land is used for grazing, mainly by camels, goats, and sheep, and the area, therefore, is in a seminatural state and very little can be said to be pristine nature. Overgrazing, leading to a gradual degradation of the vegetation, is a problem over large areas and is particularly severe near watering points. The stands of many unique species of trees, such as the dragon tree on Socotra and the daban palm in Somalia, are increasingly becoming overmature with little regeneration. One study has estimated that the region is represented by around 24.2% undisturbed habitats, 70.3% partially disturbed and 5.5% human-dominated habitats (Hannah et al. 1995), but this is almost certainly an underestimate of the disturbance, and perhaps only 5% can be regarded as undisturbed. However, the category "partially disturbed" would include all degrees of degradation, from almost completely destroyed to nearly pristine habitats.

Shifting cultivation, where areas of bushland and woodland are cut and burned for the cultivation of cassava over a period of a few years, is particularly destructive in parts of central and southern Somalia. However, in Somalia the worst threat to the vegetation and the biodiversity is the uncontrolled production of charcoal. Charcoal is now not only produced to cover the domestic needs within the country, but has become a major export item to the countries in the Arabian Gulf region. The tree most sought after for charcoal is *Acacia bussei*, and the woodlands formerly dominated by this tree are now rapidly dwindling. *Acacia bussei* itself is not threatened as a species, but the destruction of the big trees changes the environment completely and adversely affects numerous other species of plants and animals. Agricultural schemes in the Rift Valley and along the Wabe Shabelle and Awash rivers in Ethiopia and along the Wabe Shabelle and Jubba Rivers in Somalia also threaten the biodiversity, particularly of riparian habitats.

On Socotra, there has been considerable infrastructure development in recent years, including the building of a new port, an airport with tarmac runway, and new roads. The potential for sensitively managed ecotourism is great, but the ways in which these developments actually influence the biodiversity of the island require careful monitoring.

Despite these threats, at least among the plants we can not point to a single species that is known to be extinct. *Taverniera sericophylla*, an endemic on Socotra earlier reported as extinct (Groombridge 1994), is still thriving in parts of the island (Thulin, pers. obs.), and several other endemic species on Socotra reported as Critical (Lucas and Synge 1978), such as *Dirachma socotrana* and *Punica protopunica* (VU), also persist in viable populations. In Somalia, there are a few flowering plants that have not been seen for more than 100 years, such as the endemic Somali lupine (*Lupinus somaliensis*), but there is still hope that it survives in some inaccessible place. The situation for larger animals, in contrast, is much worse. Uncontrolled hunting, particularly of the ungulates, is a real problem in many parts of the region, with many species classified as threatened.

Conservation

Despite the vast size of this hotspot, less than 9% has some form of legal protection in 41 protected areas classified in IUCN categories I to VI, a percentage that falls to just over 3% when including only those protected areas in categories I to IV. There are several national parks and sanctuaries in the Ethiopian part of the region, such as Awash National Park (750 km²) and the Chew Bahir Wildlife Reserve (2 730 km²), mainly aimed at protecting remaining populations of desert-dwelling ungulates; the problems and challenges faced are to a large degree similar to those described for the Ethiopian Highlands. In Kenya there is the remote Malka Mari National Park (870 km²) in the northeastern corner of the country. In Somalia there are no areas with formal protection after the breakdown of the federal government in 1991, although three protected areas are officially recognized. In Djibouti, the Forêt de Day National Park (100 km²), home to the aforementioned Djibouti francolin, is the country's only reserve. The governments of Somaliland and Puntland have ministries for the environment, but their resources are totally inadequate. The Socotra Archipelago has recently been added to UNESCO's World Network of Biosphere Reserves, which should help in the implementation of conservation management and in the development of ecotourism in the area. In Oman, the massive Arabian Oryx Sanctuary (24 785 km²) is a Natural World Heritage Site famous for the successful reintroduction of Arabian oryx (*Oryx leucoryx*, EN), and Jebel Samhan is a National Nature Reserve mainly due to its population of Arabian leopard (*Panthera pardus nimr*, CR).

In general, conservation activities in the Horn of Africa hotspot are completely inadequate for the long-term preservation of its biodiversity. Today, only Socotra can be said to receive any serious international attention. Recently, for example, a major program for "Sustainable Development and Biodiversity Conservation for the People of the Socotra Islands" was signed by the United Nations Development Program (UNDP). The program, financed by UNDP, the Government of Italy, and the Yemen Government, will collectively contribute over US$5 million to continue to support the people of Socotra through conservation and sustainable use of the islands' unique biodiversity and natural resources for the next five years. Much needs to be done before the arid Horn can regain the kind of international prominence that it had 2 000 years ago.

MATS THULIN [18]

Confined entirely to northeastern Africa, Salt's dikdik is a relatively common antelope typically found in semidesert scrub, avoiding desert areas and restricted in its distribution by the mountains of the Ethiopian Massif to the west.
© **Patricio Robles Gil**/*Sierra Madre*

On pp. 284-285, Afar people with camels crossing the Awash River in Awash National Park.
© **Patricio Robles Gil**/*Sierra Madre*

IRANO-ANATOLIAN

The Irano-Anatolian Hotspot covers a topographically complex and extensive system of mountains and closed basins separating the natural communities and the indigenous cultures of the Mediterranean Basin and the dry plateaus of Western Asia. For many centuries, the historical Silk Road crossing from east to west through this area was the major route for trade and cultural exchange between the two regions, and the area is here recognized as a new hotspot because of its high endemism and rich flora and fauna.

The hotspot originally covered an area of 899 773 km², including major parts of central and eastern Turkey, Georgia (marginally), the Nahçevan Province of Azerbaijan, Armenia, northeastern Iraq, northern and western Iran, as well as the Northern Kopet Dagh Range in Turkmenistan. The region includes massive ranges of dry mountains stretching west to east in the northern part (East Anatolian Mountains, Southern Elburz Mountains, and the Kopet Dagh) and north to south in the southern part (Zagros Mountains). These highlands extend between the three major remnants of the ancient Tethys Sea: the Mediterranean, the Black Sea, and the Caspian.

In terms of its geological make-up, the hotspot has a mixture of ancient massifs, folded sedimentary rocks, and recent igneous rocks. Limestone blocks mostly from the Paleozoic Era predominate in its southern part. Between the mountain ranges, there are broken plateaus covered by alluvial soils. Several parts of the hotspot are seismically active. Here, elevations generally range from 1 000 m to 4 000 m, with some areas as low as 300 m, such as the foothills of the Kopet Dagh and western Zagros Mountains. A number of peaks exceed 5 000 m, including the dormant volcanoes of Mt. Ararat in Turkey (5 165 m) and Mt. Damavand in Iran (5 671 m). The plateaus of Anatolia, Armenia, and western Iran range between 800 and 2 000 m, and are characterized by primary plain steppes, which are climax steppes that have never been covered by any forest or shrubland (because these areas are too dry and the soils poor); the mountain areas around the plateaus are covered by dry forests or secondary steppes. Three major closed basins (Konya Closed Basin, the Van Basin and the Lake Urumiyeh Basin) lie to the north of the hotspot, including various small remnant lakes of the Tethys surrounded by primary plain steppes.

The geological history of this hotspot has triggered the evolution of its biodiversity. The mountains served both as a refuge and a corridor between the eastern Mediterranean and western Asia at the time of movements of the ancient Tethys Sea and its remnants. Roughly 10 million years ago, the Turkish and Arabian plates moving northwards crashed into Asia to create the mountains and plateaus of the Irano-Anatolian region. This cut the Tethys Sea off from the Indian Ocean, thereby creating the Mediterranean Sea. The remnants of the Tethys in the Irano-Anatolian plateaus dried up and were refilled several times. These movements have made the hotspot a site of constant dispersal and local speciation, and many endemic species, especially local plant species, originated at this time (Ekim et al. 2000). The hotspot's centers for endemism of aquatic species, the Tuz Lake Basin, Van Lake, Urumiyeh Lake, and many other small lakes in Turkey and Iran, are particularly important in representing the biodiversity of the Tethys.

During long periods of glaciation, this region was invaded by refugee species from northern Europe and Asia. Then, periods of aridity disrupted the ranges of many species and effectively isolated the Euro-Siberian forest and meadow species, such that they became restricted to the riparian forests along the mountain valleys or in alpine lakes of the hotspot.

The climate is continental, with hot summers and cold winters. Most of the region has severely cold winters, with extremes dropping to –40°C. Summers are dry, with a mean of 20°-30°C, reaching up to 48°C.

On the opposite page, the impressive Kopet-Dagh Range is the border between Turkmenistan and Iran, and the refuge of many species like the Vulnerable bezoar or wild goat (Capra aegagrus) and Vulnerable Afghan Urial (Ovis orientalis cycloceros).
© Patricio Robles Gil/*Sierra Madre*

287

Annual rainfall varies from 100 mm to over 1 000 mm, most of it falling in winter and spring. Winter rainfall occurs mainly in the form of snow, which can remain until June-July at higher altitudes. Rainfall is remarkably low in central Turkey and in the southeastern Zagros Mountains, ranging between 100 and 400 mm per year.

The Irano-Anatolian Hotspot is confined to the western part of the Irano-Turanian Floristic Region that also extends eastwards to include the arid lands bordering the Caspian Sea, the Hindu Kush, and the spurs of the western Himalaya (Takhtajan 1986). Some areas, however, express the mixed character of their biogeographic connections with Mediterranean and Irano-Turanian elements, such as the Kopet Dagh and the Zagros mountains (Davis et al. 1995). The principal habitat in the hotspot is mountainous forest steppe that supports oak-dominant (*Quercus* spp.) deciduous forests in the west and south (Anatolia and Zagros mountains), and juniper (*Juniperus* spp.) forests in the east (southern slopes of the Elburz Mountains and the Kopet Dagh). The forest steppe occurs mainly between 700 m and the timberline (1 900 to 2 200 m). Primary forests are largely degraded, and mountainous secondary steppes now dominate the landscape where the dry forest is impoverished. A relatively wide zone of subalpine and alpine vegetation covers the mountain peaks above the timberline (Zohary 1973). Thorn-cushion (tragacanthic) formations are found in the subalpine zone. The alpine zone of the Cilo and Hakkâri mountains in Turkey holds permanent glaciers (Kılıç and Eken 2004).

There is a clear separation between mountainous flora (dry forest and montane steppe) and steppes of the plateaus (primary plain steppe). In the Zagros Mountains, the lower altitudes are dominated by *Astragalus* and *Salvia* spp., while in Elburz, a number of flowering plants, such as tulips (*Tulipa* spp.), irises (*Iris* spp.) and crocuses (*Crocus* spp.) occur. The primary steppes, characterized by the presence of *Artemisia* spp., occupy the fragmented plateaus in the hotspot. The largest stand of primary steppes extends along the Konya Closed Basin in Central Turkey, which also includes a unique complex of salt steppes and halophytic marshes. The core zone of such plateaus contains a salty or brackish lake occupying the lowest part of the closed basin and fed by streams of surrounding mountains (Eken and Magnin 1999). Various types of riparian forests stretch along the river valleys, dominated by species such as *Salix* spp. and others.

The human population mainly consists of Turkish, Kurdish, Persian, and Armenian people. Some other groups include Assyrians, Azeris, Turkmens, and Yezidis. Pastoral and truly nomadic cultures still exist in a number of parts of Turkey and Iran, and traditional animal farming (goat and sheep) is the main source of income for many rural communities. Most parts of the hotspot are not accessible during long winters when high passes are closed. This makes most of the region unsuitable for large-scale industrial investments or settlement.

Grey wolf (Canis lupus) *in Badkhyz Nature Reserve, Turkmenistan.*
© Gertrud and Helmut Denzau

On the opposite page, the mountain seen in the background is the Erciyes Dagi Volcano. Sultansazligi and Yay lakes were some of the best spots for the migration of birds in the Central Anatolia. Although they were both protected by the national law, they were dried up by the General Directorate of State Hydraulic Works, which is a government department.
© Cuneyt Oguztuzun

Biodiversity

It is difficult to make an accurate estimate of vascular plant diversity in this hotspot, but there are at least 6 000 species. Of these, an estimated 2 500 are endemic. There are 332 species recorded as local endemics on the Kopet Dagh, while the Zagros Mountains have at least 500 local endemics (Davis et al. 1995). The highest level of endemism is evident in Turkey, where 1 220 species are endemic (Ekim et al. 2000). Several genera are largely confined or endemic to the hotspot, including *Astragalus*, *Centaurea*, *Acantholimon*, *Onobrychis*, *Acanthocardamum*, and *Zerdana*.

One of the most distinctive biodiversity features of this hotspot is known as the Anatolian Diagonal (Davis 1965-1985, 1971), a remarkable floristic line crossing Inner Anatolia. The Anatolian Diagonal runs from the southern foothills of the Eastern Black Sea Mountains in Turkey, through the Turkish part of the hotspot, and then splits into two branches: one reaches the Mediterranean via the Amanus Mountains and the other, via the Bolkar Mountains (Davis 1971). Approximately 390 plant species have distributions largely confined to the Anatolian Diagonal, including the monotypic genus *Neotchihatchewia* (*N. isatidea*) and *Graellsia davisiana*. Many of Turkey's other plant species occur only to the west or only to the east of this line (Ekim and Güner 1986). The origin of this diagonal is a point of discussion. Davis (1971) and Sonnenfeld (1974) emphasize paleogeographical factors, while Ekim and Güner (1986) attribute greater importance to ecological and climatic factors.

The hotspot also possesses a very diverse fauna, despite the fact that large portions are arid to semiarid. Two main factors are responsible for this richness and diversity. Firstly, the great variety of habitats ranging from alpine tundra and permanent snowfields down to semiarid plains, and from lush, humid deciduous forest in the north to sparse juniper scrub in the east and southeast. Secondly, the hotspot's position at a crossroads between three major faunal realms: the southern edge of the Palearctic realm, facing a small Afrotropical, and a strong Indo-Malayan influence in the south.

The Irano-Anatolian Hotspot is most remarkable for its avian diversity, which includes a substantial West Palearctic faunal element, including 81 species that reach the eastern extremity of their range in the hotspot, e.g., the blue tit (*Parus caeruleus*); and a smaller, but still marked, eastern Palearctic element, with 19 bird species reaching the westernmost tip of their ranges in the hotspot, e.g., the chestnut-breasted bunting (*Emberiza stewarti*). The alpine biome of the Elburz and Zagros mountains, as well as the higher peaks of mountain ranges in Iran and Turkey, support a montane fauna typical of all high mountain ranges from the Pyrenees and Alps in Western Europe to the Himalaya. Characteristic species include the lammergeier (*Gypaetus barbatus*), horned lark (*Eremophila alpestris*), yellow-billed chough (*Pyrrhocorax graculus*), alpine accentor (*Prunella*

*Steppe tortoise (*Testudo horsfieldii*) in Badkhyz Nature Reserve, Turkmenistan. The males are collected for the pet market, so females have difficulties finding mates. Listed on 2003 Red List as Vulnerable.*

© Gertrud and Helmut Denzau

collaris), wallcreeper (*Tichodroma muraria*), and white-winged snowfinch (*Montifringilla nivalis*). The unique enclave breeding population of the white-winged scoter (*Melanitta fusca*) in the montane lakes of eastern Turkey has a Euro-Siberean biogeographic history (Ekim et al. 2000; Eken et al. 2000).

In the drier and more open mixed woodlands of pistachio (*Pistacia*), maple (*Acer*), and almond (*Amygdalus*) of the eastern Zagros, only a handful of western Palearctic species occur. Characteristic birds include a mixture of Middle Eastern species, e.g., the white-throated robin (*Irania gutturalis*) and plain leaf-warbler (*Phylloscopus neglectus*); eastern Palearctic species, e.g., the rufous-tailed shrike (*Lanius isabellinus*) and Hume's whitethroat (*Sylvia althaea*); Indo-Malayan species, e.g., the bay-backed shrike (*Lanius vittatus*); and western Palearctic species at the extreme edge of their ranges, e.g., the Eurasian blackbird (*Turdus merula*). Finally, throughout the remote mountain ranges of Iran there still exist good stands of juniper (*Juniperus*) woodland, with species such as the fire-fronted serin (*Serinus pusillus*) and, in the northeast, the white-winged grosbeak (*Mycerobas carnipes*).

In total, there are at least 363 regularly occurring bird species in the hotspot, although none are endemic. However, a number of globally threatened birds have significant breeding populations in the hotspot, including the great bustard (*Otis tarda*, VU), marbled duck (*Marmaronetta angustirostris*, VU), white-headed duck (*Oxyura leucocephala*, EN), and imperial eagle (*Aquila heliaca*, VU). In addition, up to 25% of the known world population of the sociable plover (*Vanellus gregarius*, VU) stop over in the plateaus of Eastern Anatolia in autumn.

The wetlands of the spectacular Tuz, Van, and Urumiyeh basins in Turkey and Iran, centered on the very large and saline lakes, support important breeding colonies of waterfowl, notably the greater flamingo (*Phoenicopterus ruber*) (35 000-40 000 pairs; Lakes Tuz and Urumiyeh), great white pelican (*Pelecanus onocrotalus*) (1 000-1 600 pairs; Lake Urumiyeh), Eurasian spoonbill (*Platalea leucorodia*), and glossy ibis (*Plegadis falcinellus*). These wetlands are extremely important for shorebirds migrating along the African-Eurasian Flyway, such as the little stint (*Calidris minuta*) and ruff (*Philomachus pugnax*), and in mild winters can hold over 100 000 wintering ducks and geese.

The Caspian snowcock (*Tetraogallus caspius*), Armenian gull (*Larus armenicus*), and Radde's accentor (*Prunella ocularis*) are only found in the Irano-Anatolian and Caucasus hotspots. Furthermore, a large proportion of the world population of crimson-winged finch (*Rhodopechys sanguinea*), Finsch's wheatear (*Oenanthe finschii*), rufous-tailed wheatear (*O. xanthoprymna*), Upcher's warbler (*Hippolais languida*), white-throated robin, and eastern rock-nuthatch (*Sitta tephronata*) occur in the hotspot.

A total of at least 141 mammals in 77 genera are known from the hotspot. Of these, 10 are endemic, including Dalh's jird (*Meriones dahli*, EN), Anatolian vole

(*Microtus anatolicus*), Dogramaci's vole (*M. dogramacii*), Nasarov's vole (*M. nasarovi*), the recently described *M. qazvinensis* from northern Iran, Urartsk mouse-like hamster (*Calomyscus urartensis*), Brandt's hamster (*Mesocricetus brandti*), Setzer's mouse-tailed dormouse (*Myomimus setzeri*), Schaub's myotis (*Myotis schaubi*, EN), and Hakkari mole (*Talpa davidiana*). As with birds, the mammal fauna is composed of species of varied origin, including the Asian subspecies of the cheetah (*Acinonyx jubatus venaticus*, CR), jungle cat (*Felis chaus*), leopard (*Panthera pardus*), striped hyaena (*Hyaena hyaena*), Asiatic wild ass (*Equus hemionus*, VU), goitered gazelle (*Gazella subgutturosa*), and wild goat (*Capra aegagrus*, VU).

Reptiles are represented by at least 116 species, including 13 endemics, among them the Persian rat snake (*Elaphe persica*), Basoglu's racerunner (*Eremias suphani*), Van Lake lizard (*Darevskia bendimahiensis*), and Elburz lizard (*Lacerta defilippii*). There are four endemic species of the genus *Vipera*: the mountain viper (*V. albizona*, EN), restricted to the Kulmaç Dağı of central Anatolia, with a total range estimated to comprise about 20 km^2 of rocky slopes at 2 000 m altitude; Latifi's viper (*V. latifi*, VU), from the Elburz Mountains; Wagner's viper (*V. wagneri*, EN), which occurs near Lake Urumiyeh (Iran) and in Eastern Turkey; and Darevsky's viper (*V. darevskii*, CR), from the Djavakhk Mountain Range in northern Armenia.

Twenty-one amphibian species are represented in the region, four of which are endemic, all salamanders in the endemic genus *Neurergus*: *N. crocatus* (VU) from the vicinity of Beytussebap (Hakkari Province) in southeast Anatolia, the Kurdish region of northern Iraq, and also northwestern Iran; *N. kaiseri* (EN), which is endemic to Iran; *N. microspilotus* (VU), restricted to the Avroman Mountains on the Iraq-Iran-Turkey border, and *N. strauchii* (VU), which is known only from Mu, Bitlis, and Malatya provinces in Eastern Anatolia. Another interesting salamander species is the Persian mountain salamander (*Batrachuperus persicus*, VU), which is found in mountain streams on the Caspian slope of the Talesh and Alborz mountains of Iran.

There is a minimum of 90 freshwater fish species in the region, of which roughly 30 are endemic; these are mainly confined to closed-basin lakes and rivers —particularly the Konya Closed Basin, Van Lake Basin, and Urumiyeh Lake Basin. Several of these species are globally threatened, including *Salmo platycephalus* and *Capoeta pestai*.

The invertebrate fauna of this hotspot is not well known, but it is particularly rich for butterfly species, with at least 350 species estimated to occur. Information available for the Turkish part of the hotspot indicates that there are at least 240 species, of which 18 are endemic (Hesselbarth et al. 1995). Furthermore, the Kopet Dagh region has at least 20 endemic Noctuidae species (Ronkay et al. 1998). Some globally threatened species are also found in the region, including the cinquefoil skipper (*Pyrgus cirsii*, VU), the single-site endemic *Polyommatus dama* (EN), and the Apollo butterfly (*Parnassius apollo*, VU). In addition, the hotspot is known to be the richest part of the Palearctic region for scorpions, with 42 described species, of which at least 50% are thought to be endemic to the hotspot (Fet et al. 2000).

Flagship Species

The most obvious flagship species for this hotspot are the two large cats, namely the cheetah and tiger. The Caspian subspecies of the tiger (*Panthera tigris virgata*) was recently reported from the northern Zagros Mountains range in Turkey (Welch 2003). However, since the last confirmed individual of this subspecies was shot in 1970, in the same region, this latest record requires further investigation. Fortunately, this area has not developed appreciably since 1970, and the human population has dramatically decreased due to unsuitable economic and political conditions in this part of Turkey. An immediate survey is required in the region to confirm the presence of the tiger, although this appears to be extremely difficult, as large parts of the area are naturally inaccessible and the periphery of the few roads are covered by land mines.

The situation for the Asiatic cheetah is somewhat better, although only an estimated 60 Asiatic cheetahs still survive, all of them to the south of the Kopet Dagh in Iran's Great Salt Desert, the Dasht-e-Kavir. This ranks among the most arid cheetah habitat anywhere, and these animals mostly occur in the foothills and dry watercourses of desert massifs, where prey is more common than on the flats. With the calamitous decline of gazelles in Iran, the cheetahs now subsist on wild sheep, Persian wild goats, and perhaps hares. Local herders believe that cheetahs are rarely responsible for attacks on livestock, but even so cheetahs are sometimes killed when confused for leopards or other predators. This animal perhaps ranks as an odd choice for a flagship species, since the core population is outside the boundary of the hotspot, but is nonetheless considered worthy of mention here.

In historical times, the Irano-Anatolian Region between Turkey in the west and Turkmenistan in the east was inhabited by several subspecies of Asiatic wild ass. The onager or Persian wild ass (*Equus hemionus onager*) was found east of the Zagros Mountains and south of the Elburz and the Kopet Dagh. A few hundred onagers have survived in two populations in Iran, one of which, Bahram-e-Goor, falls within this hotspot. Another Critically Endangered subspecies of wild ass, known as the kulan, Transcaspian or Turkmenian wild ass (*E. h. kulan*), used to have its southwest extension along the northern foothills of the Kopet Dagh. However, the subspecies suffered a drastic decline in range and numbers due to poaching and, today, a single naturally occurring population remains in and around the Badkhyz Nature Reserve in south Turkmenistan, just marginally outside the hotspot (Feh et al. 2002).

The key flagship bird species for the large salt lakes is the greater flamingo, which in some years has extremely large breeding colonies in Iran and Turkey —between 35 000 and 40 000 pairs. The main breeding sites are Tuz Lake in Turkey and Lake Urumiyeh in Iran. Unfortunately, no breeding has occurred in Lake Urumiyeh since 2000 due to drought. On the other hand, Tuz Lake is still considered one of the most important flamingo breeding areas in the world. Since the 1970s, this lake has been regularly used by flamingos, and is home to the biggest breeding colony in Turkey. Recent surveys carried out over the area revealed that the number of chicks fluctuated between 4 000 in 1991 and 10 000 in 2000. However, there is also a negative trend (as evidenced by the decreasing numbers of chicks seen at the main crèche) in Tuz Lake that could be related to a sharp decrease in water levels. These lakes are the only major breeding site for this species in the vast area between the Camargue (France) and the Rann of Kutch (India). Archaeological evidence shows that the species has been breeding at Lake Urumiyeh for several thousand years. Ringing recoveries show that the birds of Lake Urumiyeh disperse as far west as Morocco and the Camargue, as far east as central India and Sri Lanka, and as far south as Somalia and Ethiopia.

The hotspot hosts an endemic genus of amphibians, *Neurergus*, with four species. These salamanders are extremely sensitive to environmental change because they live in marginal conditions in relation to the general dry climate of the Zagros Mountains. All four species are considered threatened, having undergone declines in abundance due to the effects of habitat destruction, pollution, and drought (Rastegar-Pouyani, in litt. 2003).

An endemic fish species, *Chalcalburnus tarichi*, has been used effectively as a flagship species by local conservation NGOs in the Van Province to trigger interest in conservation of the Van Lake Basin in Eastern Turkey. The rapid decline in the population of the species, which also has local commercial value, has directed the attention of local and national stakeholders towards the wider environmental problems of Van Lake. A number of conservation projects were initiated since then in the area to protect the basin.

Hundreds of single-locality endemic plants occur in Turkey, which are also threatened. Orchids are the most charismatic and the most threatened group, in part because they are still illegally collected in large quantities from the wild for the production of a popular traditional drink in Turkey called *sahlep*. Due to the rapid decline of orchids in Turkey, orchid collection has expanded to Iran.

The extremely localized salt plants of Anatolia and Iran are among the most outstanding plant species in the hotspot. They occur in the remaining salt steppes of the Irano-Anatolian closed basins. This vegetation type is characterized by halophytes of the families Chenopodiaceae and Plumbaginaceae. Most halophytes are C4 plants, in which the first products of photosynthesis are 4-carbon organic acids, unlike many other

The great bustard (Otis tarda) *is well distributed over Europe and Asia. Its status is Vulnerable. The Irano-Anatolian Hotspot is home to one of the most important populations in Turkey, with 4 000 birds.*
© **Chris Gomersall**/RSPB-images.com

plant species. Most of these are fast-growing species having a high photosynthesis rate. They have adapted to extreme conditions of dry, saline soils with high temperatures and radiation, as well as water deficiency. In saline soils, only these physiologically specialized species can survive. The leaves of most of these are succulent or have thick cuticles. The root cells have a high osmotic pressure value to extract water from saline soils. Excess salt is either secreted or deposited in small sacs on the leaves. The following are among the rarest of Irano-Anatolian halophytes having extremely localized distributions: *Gladiolus halophilus, Acantholimon halophilum, Ferula halophila, Asparagus lyconicus, Allium vuralii, Verbascum pyroliforme, Salvia halophila, Salsola stenoptera, Limonium iconicum, L. anatolicum, L. tamaricoides, Kalidopsis wagenitzii, Hypericum salsugineum, Onosma halophilum,* and *Taraxacum mirabile* (Vural et al. 1999).

Threats

The single most important threat to the Turkish part of the hotspot is the development of irrigation schemes for agriculture and associated infrastructure, such as dams. The excessive use of water resources for sugarbeet agriculture in the Konya Closed Basin has resulted in the loss of many large steppe areas and closed basin lakes. Elsewhere, Lake Sevan in Armenia and the Javakheti mountain wetlands in Georgia have largely been destroyed. In the Ararat Valley alone, 1 500 km² of swamps have been drained and transformed into agricultural land. Other threats that have led to extensive habitat loss across the hotspot include overgrazing, overharvesting of woody plants (shrubs and trees) for fuelwood, and mining. Several highly publicized military operations have taken place in Iraq, Iran, and Turkey during the last few decades, resulting in loss of forests and wetlands (Evans 1994). In northern Iraq, the few remaining tracts of natural forests in the more isolated northern mountains are now probably nearly depleted, largely because of intensive wood-cutting exacerbated by the political situation there.

More than 90% of natural steppes in the region have disappeared (Eken and Magnin 1999), whereas the alpine meadows covering higher parts of mountains are largely intact. In the most humid parts of the region, the mountains of Eastern Turkey, the remaining forest is around 12% of its original coverage (Özhatay et al. 2003), but this seems to be much lower in drier parts; for instance, in Iraq, only 4% of natural forests remain (Evans 1994). The only pristine parts of the forested area are found on the inaccessible mountains of southeastern Turkey and in the neighboring territories of Iran. Recent analyses, including the use of satellite imagery, indicate that the overall percentage of vegetation that remains intact in the hotspot is around 15% (Doğa Derneği Research Unit in Turkey, in litt. 2004).

The doubling of the human population since the early 1970s, coupled with increased deforestation and overgrazing, has resulted in a decline in many species present in the hotspot. This has been particularly noticeable with the bustards. Due to the expansion of agriculture and crop-improvement projects, many steppe species, such as the great bustard, appear to have declined dramatically in Turkey and Iran since the 1970s. All the main sites for this species in Iran in the 1970s occurred within this hotspot, but many may no longer have any bustards (Evans 1994). Most of the large ungulates in the hotspot suffer from illegal hunting and habitat loss.

Conservation

According to the World Database on Protected Areas, only 6.2% of this hotspot has some form of legal protection, a percentage which is more than halved (2.9%) when one considers only those protected areas in IUCN categories I to IV. The largest protected area in the hotspot is the Tuz Lake Specially Protected Area in central Turkey, covering approximately 7 000 km²; it was recently proclaimed and still requires a management plan. The 4 000-km² Alborz-e-Markazi Reserve in the central Elburz Mountains is another large protected area, which extends towards the north into the Caucasus Hotspot. In Turkey, most protected areas are small, and not very well managed. In Iran, the largest protected area within the hotspot is Urumiyeh Lake National Park (4 640 km²), although there are a number of sizable protected areas in the Zagros Mountains, including Arjan Biosphere Reserve (528 km²). In Armenia, the principal protected areas within the hotspot are Sevan National Park, as well as the Khosrov, Dilijan, and Shikahogh State Reserves. The Kopet Dagh region is reasonably well covered by a number of protected areas, of which the Meana-Chaachinskiy Sanctuary is the largest (600 km²). All countries in the hotspot are party to the Ramsar Convention (with the exception of Iraq) and World Heritage Convention. There are nine Ramsar sites in the hotspot: two in the Turkish part (the Sultansazligi Marshes and the Seyfe Lake), five in Iran (Urumiyeh Lake, Kobi Lake, Dorgeh Sangi Lakes, Parishan Lake, and Neriz Lakes) and two in Armenia (Lakes Sevan and Arpi). Turkey is currently in the process of declaring at least five new Ramsar sites in the hotspot, based on recent scientific inventories of the country's most important biodiversity sites.

An important new concept being tested in the region is that of Key Biodiversity Areas, which represent the most important sites for biodiversity conservation worldwide. Turkey is one of the few countries, and perhaps the first in the world, which has identified both Important Bird Areas and Key Biodiversity Areas. Many Key Biodiversity Areas in Turkey are not well protected (85%), although forests and wetlands are relatively bet-

On pp. 292-293, a large group of Vulnerable Afghan Urials (Ovis orientalis cycloceros) in Badkhyz Nature Reserve in Turkmenistan.
© **Gertrud and Helmut Denzau**

Above, collecting firewood is a major problem, especially along the river banks.
© **Patricio Robles Gil**/*Sierra Madre*

294

ter represented in protected areas than the more extensive and homogeneous habitats such as steppes and alpine. In Turkey, the Turkish Nature Society (Doğa Derneği) has initiated a national conservation program for all Key Biodiversity Areas in collaboration with governmental institutions and other NGOs. Although there is a large gap in legal protection, most of the key sites for conservation have been documented, paving the way for their protection in the future. Currently, Turkey has 18 different categories of protected areas under nine different laws, but these will be harmonized by the end of 2005 through the new Nature Conservation Law.

During the past five years, a strong grassroots movement for nature conservation has developed in Turkey, particularly among university students and local NGOs throughout the country. Furthermore, accession to the European Union is likely to increase enforcement of nature conservation laws, as well as help to expand the protected area network that currently has major gaps in terms of coverage and management efficiency.

The Environmental Protection and Enhancement Act (1974) is the main law dealing with nature conservation in Iran. Coverage of all the major habitat types in the four main types of protected areas recognized in Iran is considered to be good, reflecting the large amount of fieldwork that has been carried out in the last 30 years. The Commission on Environmental, Economic, and Social Policy of IUCN is based in Iran, and there are also a number of other NGOs focusing on the conservation of flagship species in the country. Since the discovery of the small population of the Persian subspecies of the fallow deer (*Dama dama mesopotamica*) in the western foothills of the Zagros Mountains in the 1950s, reintroduction and captive-breeding projects have been initiated in northwestern Iran. However, by 1988, the last wild population was on the verge of extinction, and individuals were taken to establish a semi-captive herd of 140 deer there. A captive-breeding group was also established in Germany, and individuals from there were sent to a reserve in Israel.

There is apparently no legislation to protect sites for biodiversity conservation in Iraq. There are a number of wild animal breeding stations, each of a few hundred hectares, but with little significance for *in situ* conservation of wildlife. Responsibility for the management of the natural environment in Iraq lies with the Ministry of Agriculture. In the past, that ministry has issued temporary bans on hunting, but with minimal enforcement. In Iraq, a National Forest Foundation has been established, partly to protect the remaining forests in the Zagros region. There are several nature parks in Iraq that are principally state-owned areas for public recreation, but with no wildlife management.

Turkmenistan is a relatively new, independent state and is in the process of developing its environmental laws. Although existing nature reserves are contributing significantly to the overall protection of the Kopet Dagh's diverse woodlands, they often lack effective management (Pereladova et al. 1997). The Turkmenistan Biodiversity Strategy and Action Plan was published in 2002 (Ministry of Nature Protection of Turkmenistan 2002). Relevant laws include "On Nature Protection in Turkmenistan" (adopted in 1991), "On State Specially Protected Areas" (1992), and the "Provision on Hunting and Hunting Regulations" (1995).

Lack of expertise in nature conservation is the main limiting factor throughout the hotspot, and this problem has to be addressed immediately to elevate its overall conservation status. The protected area networks in Iraq and Turkey require prompt expansion, building on sites that are known to be important for global biodiversity (e.g., Key Biodiversity Areas and Important Bird Areas). Furthermore, better management of protected areas is required throughout the hotspot. Although protected legally, several globally important sites are severely threatened and could be lost if urgent conservation action is not taken. Perhaps the most intact and endemic-rich part of the hotspot is the northern part of the Zagros Mountains —the area where Turkey, Iraq, and Iran meet. Unfortunately, this area has hosted several military operations for many years. At the same time, however, the region's globally important biodiversity might offer options for international collaboration in alleviating poverty and achieving a lasting peace. In most areas of the hotspot, there is great potential for direct participation by local people in nature conservation, as most of the region's indigenous communities maintain their traditional lifestyles and keep practicing what are perhaps the most sustainable ways of using natural resources in this part of the world. Agriculture, hydropower energy, and forestry are the key sectors that need to be tackled on a landscape level and harmonized with the principles of biodiversity conservation.

Given that it is situated in such a politically sensitive area, the Irano-Anatolian Hotspot is perhaps among the least surveyed hotspots. Yet, even the existing scarce information indicates the importance of this region for global biodiversity conservation. If the status of this hotspot's biodiversity is to be improved, strong international cooperation will be essential.

GÜVEN EKEN [19]
MIKE EVANS [19]
AHMET KARATAŞ [20]
ÖZGE BALKIZ [22]
EVRIM KARAÇETIN [21]
TUBA KILIÇ [22]
NURI ÖZBAĞDATLI [22]
GERTRUD NEUMANN-DENZAU [23]
ENGIN GEM [22]
AYŞEGÜL KARATAŞ [20]

The hunting of wild game by local people for food is another situation that is wiping out many species throughout the region.
© **Patricio Robles Gil**/*Sierra Madre*

MOUNTAINS
OF CENTRAL ASIA

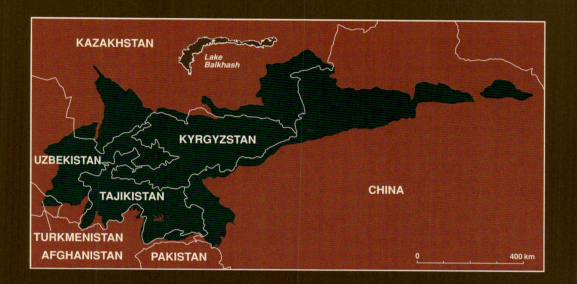

The Mountains of Central Asia Hotspot consists of two of Asia's major mountain ranges, the Pamir (including the Pamir-Alai) and the Tien Shan. These are situated within Kazakhstan, Kyrgyzstan, Tajikistan, Uzbekistan, western China, extreme northeastern Afghanistan, and a small part of Turkmenistan. The total area covered is about 863 362 km^2. The highest peak, Kongur, in the Chinese Pamir, rises to 7 719 m; four others are above 7 000 m and many more exceed 6 500 m. Glaciers number well over 20 000 and their total extent covers around 18 000 km^2. The mountains were mainly formed by folding due to tectonic movements during the Caledonian, Hercynian, and Alpine orogenic (or mountain-building) periods. Some features also result from faulting and from volcanic activity. The hotspot includes major desert basins, the largest of which is the Fergana Valley.

The elevated massif of the Pamir was known to early Persian geographers as *Bam-i-Dunya*, or "roof of the world" and is situated at the center of several great ranges. The Tien Shan lie adjacent to the north, the Hindu Kush to the southwest, the Karakoram to the southeast, and the Kun Lun to the east. The Pamir extend east to the isolated Muztagh Ata Massif in western China and south to the Wakhan Valley of northeastern Afghanistan. The northern rim of the Pamir is formed by the Trans-Alai Range that drops steeply to the Alai Valley, a deep fault trench carrying the waters of a major tributary of the Amu Darya, and dividing the Pamir from the Gissar-Alai mountain system.

The Eastern Pamir have a mean elevation of over 4 000 m and are plateau-like in character, with limited elevational variation and even relief. The surface is crossed by broad, shallow, valleys or *pamir*, that give the name to the whole range. The Western Pamir, by contrast, are characterized by sharp ridges and steep slopes cut by deep valleys and gorges. They have great elevational variation and typical alpine relief. The Western Pamir are heavily glaciated, and include the Fedchenko Glacier, which is over 75 km in length and one of the two longest glaciers in the world outside the polar regions. The highest peaks in the

Pamir are also situated in this part of the range: Garmo, formerly Peak Communism (7 498 m), and Peak Lenin (7 165 m). To the west and southwest, a series of ridges radiates out into the desert and these extend across the Pyanj River into Badakhshan Province of northern Afghanistan.

The Pamir-Alai Mountains, including the Gissaro-Alai system, lie between the Pamir and the Fergana Valley, a deeply downfaulted desert basin, about 300 km long and 150 km wide. The Gissaro-Alai system extends roughly northeastwards to join the Tien Shan. Its ridges are generally around 5 000 m.

To the north of the Fergana Valley, the Tien Shan —Chinese for "heaven" or "sky"— Mountains extend for 2 500 km from west to east. The Tien Shan are made up of a complex series of ranges and are around 300 km wide in the center, narrowing at the eastern and western ends. The highest peaks are located in a central cluster on the borders of China, Kyrgyzstan, and Kazakhstan, and include Peak Pobeda or Tuomuer Feng (7 439 m) and Han Tengri (6 995 m). The Inylchek Glacier, over 50 km long and the largest in the Tien Shan, is also located in this part of the range. Across the fertile Ili Valley, the Borohoro Shan links the Dzungarian Alatau (4 464 m) Range to the Tien Shan. Glaciers occupy more than 10 000 km^2 and occur along most of the range, east to the Bogda Shan in the Chinese Tien Shan. The central Tien Shan, with a mean altitude of over 3 000 m, contains a high,

On the opposite page,
the spectacular Tien Shan
Mountain range of Kyrgyzstan.
© Patricio Robles Gil/Sierra Madre

have resulted in high endemism, and evolution of mutants, polyploids, and ecotypes among several taxa.

The Himalaya are home to many unique and diverse human groups. Culturally diverse ethnic groups living in the river valleys and mountain slopes of the Himalaya differ from each other in terms of language, culture, tradition, religion, and patterns of resource use. Over 27 ethnic groups are found in Nepal, either of Tibetan-Burmese or Indo-Aryan descent, while Bhutan has three main ethnic groups: the Ngalongs, Sharchogpas, and Lhotsampas, all three of which are dominant, with many smaller groups with their own unique cultural practices. The northeast part of India, however, has over 500 distinct ethnic groups (Stirn and Van Ham 2001). The people belong to numerous tribal groups with ancient cultures and traditions, although there is also a sizeable population of non-tribal groups as well.

Biodiversity

Of the estimated 10 000 species of vascular plants in the Himalayan region, approximately 3 160 are endemic. Angiosperms are divided into 192 families and 2 100 genera. The largest families of flowering plants are Orchidaceae (750 species), Compositae (734 species), Gramineae (520 species), and Fabaceae (507 species). The Eastern Himalaya is also a center of diversity for several widely distributed plant taxa, such as *Rhododendron*, *Primula*, and *Pedicularis* (Sahni 1979).

The endemic flora are represented by 71 endemic genera, of which about 40 are confined to the Eastern Himalaya and about 15 to the Western Himalaya. The endemic genera include *Jaeschkea, Parajaeschkea, Drimycarpus, Parrotiopsis, Listrobanthes, Megacodon, Pseudaechmanthera, Pseudostachyum, Pteracanthus, Sympagis, Catamixis, Physolena, Pottingeria, Roylea, Trachycarpus,* and *Triaenanthus*. *Drimycarpus* and *Parrotiopsis* are monotypic genera that represent arborescent taxa, while *Listrobanthes, Megacodon, Pseudaechmanthera, Pseudostachyum, Pteracanthus, Sympagis,* and *Triaenanthus* are shrubs. Five families are endemic to the region, namely Tetracentraceae, Hamamelidaceae, Circaeasteraceae, Butomaceae, and Stachyuraceae, while over 90% of the species in Berberidaceae and Saxifragaceae are endemic to the Himalaya (Singh et al. 2000).

A large number of orchids, many representing neoendemic taxa, have been recently reported from Sikkim and Arunachal Pradesh, which probably indicates that further exploration in the Himalaya will reveal a higher degree of plant endemism. Although many of the other non-vascular taxonomic groups have yet to be adequately documented, nearly 13 000 species of fungi and around 1 100 species of lichens have been described.

Overall, the fauna of the Himalaya is not well known; most of the information available for this region pertains to larger vertebrates, especially large mammals and birds that are easily observed. Smaller mammals, reptiles, amphibians, and fishes have been undersampled, while the insects have been largely ignored, with the exception of a few studies of the Himalayan Lepidoptera (e.g., Mani 1986; Haribal 1992).

Around 300 mammal species have been recorded across the Himalayan Range, of which 12 are endemic to the Himalaya. The endemics include the golden langur (*Trachypithecus geei*, EN), which has a very restricted range in the Eastern Himalaya; the Himalayan tahr (*Hemitragus jemlahicus*, VU); and the pygmy hog (*Sus salvanius*, CR), a species restricted to grasslands in the Terai-Duar savannah and grasslands, with its stronghold in the Manas National Park. The Namdapha flying squirrel (*Biswamoyopterus biswasi*, CR) also represents the only endemic genus in the Himalaya, but is a poorly known species described on the basis of a single specimen taken from Namdapha National Park. The mammalian fauna in the lowlands is typically Indo-Malayan, consisting of langurs (*Semnopithecus* spp.), Asiatic wild dogs (*Cuon alpinus*, VU), sloth bears (*Melursus ursinus*, VU), gaurs (*Bos gaurus*, VU), and several species of deer, such as muntjac (*Muntiacus muntjak*) and sambar (*Cervus unicolor*). In the mountains, the fauna transitions into Palearctic species, consisting of snow leopard (*Uncia uncia*, EN), black bear (*Ursus thibetanus*, VU), and a diverse ungulate assemblage that includes blue sheep (*Pseudois nayaur*), takin (*Budorcas taxicolor*, VU), and argali (*Ovis ammon*, VU).

Around 979 bird species are recorded from across the region, with 15 endemics, including one species, the Himalayan quail (*Ophrysia superciliosa*, CR), which represents an endemic genus. However, it has not been recorded with any certainty since 1876 (although there were reports of possible sightings around Nainital in 2003). Four Endemic Bird Areas (EBAs), as defined by BirdLife International (Stattersfield et al. 1998), overlap entirely or partly with the Himalaya Hotspot. The Western Himalaya EBA, which is almost entirely contained within the hotspot, has 11 bird species restricted entirely to it, including the aforementioned Himalayan quail, the cheer pheasant (*Catreus wallichii*, VU), and the western tragopan (*Tragopan melanocephalus*, VU), which is also endemic to the hotspot. The Central Himalaya EBA has two bird species confined entirely to within its boundaries, the spiny babbler (*Turdoides nipalensis*) and the Nepal wren babbler (*Pnoepyga immaculata*), and both are also endemic to the hotspot. The Eastern Himalaya EBA, which encompasses part of the Chin Hills (here considered part of the Indo-Burma Hotspot), has 19 bird species endemic to it, including the rusty-throated wren babbler (*Spelaeornis badeigularis*, VU), chestnut-breasted partridge (*Arborophila mandellii*, VU), white-throated tit (*Aegithalos niveogularis*), and orange bullfinch (*Pyrrhula aurantiaca*), all four of which are also endemic to the Himalaya Hotspot. Finally, the Assam Plains EBA is shared with the Indo-Burma Hotspot. The black-necked crane (*Grus nigricollis*, VU), a large bird of cultural and religious significance to the people in the Himalaya, spends the winters in the Himalayan region, but migrates into the wetlands of the Tibetan Plateau across the Himalayan Crest.

Systematic surveys of reptiles and amphibians are lack-

On the opposite page, Rhododendron arboreum, *from the Pulmuthang Valley Forest above Chintang, Nepal. Rhododendrons reach a high level of diversity in the Himalaya.*
© **Gerald Cubitt**

Above, Pleione praecox, *from southern Sikkim, one of many orchid species occurring in the Himalaya, and among the first to flower. The Orchidaceae is the largest family of flowering plants in the hotspot.*
© **Gerald Cubitt**

ing for this hotspot, but it is known that at least 177 species of reptiles have been recorded, of which 49 are endemic. The lizard *Mictopholis austeniana* is the only representative of the sole endemic genus, but is known only from the holotype. Other genera are well represented, and have many endemic species. These include *Oligodon* (nine species, six endemic), *Cyrtodactylus* (10 species, seven endemic), and *Japalura* (seven species, all endemic). In terms of amphibians, 124 species are known to occur, and 41 species of these are endemic. The amphibian fauna is dominated by anurans, although two species of caecilians occur. One of these (*Ichthyophis sikkimensis*) is endemic and occurs in northern India (in the States of Sikkim and West Bengal) and extreme eastern Nepal (in Dabugaun in the Ilam District) at elevations of 1 000 to 1 550 m.

The Himalaya Hotspot has fish species from three major drainage systems, the Indus, Ganges, and Brahmaputra. However, the cold, steep high-altitude drainages have fewer fishes than the lowland rivers, and many species ranges only just reach into this hotspot; as a result, few species (33 out of 269) are endemic. The three most diverse of the 30 different families represented here are minnows and carps (Cyprinidae; 93 species and 11 endemics), river loaches (Balitoridae; 47 species and 14 endemics), and sisorid catfishes (Sisoridae; 34 species and four endemics). The genus *Schizothorax* is represented by at least six endemic species in the high mountain lakes and streams, while two other genera of these "snow-trout," the genus *Ptychobarbus* and the Ladakh snowtrout (*Gymnocypris biswasi*) —a monotypic genus now thought to be extinct— are also unique to the Himalaya.

Flagship Species

The Himalaya support globally significant populations of several large mammals, including the tiger (*Panthera tigris*), Asian elephant (*Elephas maximus*), and greater one-horned rhinoceros (*Rhinoceros unicornis*, EN), in the foothill grasslands and forests. The range of the Asian elephant in the Himalayan Region is marginal; however, the populations along the north bank of the Brahmaputra River in Assam are one of India's largest and most important (Sukumar 1992). The alluvial grasslands support some of the highest densities of tigers in the world (Karanth and Nichols 1998), while the greater one-horned rhinoceros is restricted to several small, isolated populations within protected areas. The Eastern Himalayan Region is the last bastion for this charismatic megaherbivore with its armor-plated and prehistoric appearance. The Brahmaputra and Ganges rivers that flow along the Himalayan foothills also support globally important populations of the Gangetic dolphin (*Platanista gangetica*), a freshwater dolphin with two Endangered subspecies. It is endemic to the river system that flows along the foothills of the Himalayan Mountain Range. Dolphin populations are threatened by various human activities, including fishing, dams, and pollution, which affect both the animals themselves and their prey base.

Other flagships are wild water buffalo (*Bubalus arnee*) and swamp deer (*Cervus duvaucelii*), which are restricted to protected areas in southern Nepal and northeastern India, and represent some of the last remaining populations of these species in the world. The snow leopard has a wide distribution across the Himalaya, extending into the high mountains of the Trans-Himalaya, but the populations in the Himalayan Mountains are important because of the low density of this high-altitude predator.

Some of Asia's largest birds live in the Himalaya, and are represented by globally significant populations. Most are threatened by various anthropogenic causes, such as the vultures (*Gyps* spp.), which have undergone dramatic declines after feeding on carcasses of cattle that have been treated with Diclofenac (Risebrough 2004). This is a classic example illustrating the effect of drugs and pesticides along the food chain. The greater and lesser adjutants (*Leptoptilos* spp.) in the foothill grasslands and broadleaf forests, as well as the hornbills in the broadleaf forests, are threatened by loss of nesting trees and lack of food sources. Other large birds include the sarus crane (*Grus antigone*), which inhabits the wetlands along the foothills; the black-necked crane, which spends winters in montane wetland sites; and the lammergeier (*Gypaetus barbatus*), which soars among the high mountains.

There are also several smaller mammals and birds that carry flagship status. The golden langur is a beautiful, golden-yellow primate that lives in the broadleaf forests between the Sankosh and Manas rivers in the Eastern Himalaya in both Assam and Bhutan, while the red panda inhabits the old-growth mixed conifer forests. The white-winged duck (*Cairina scutulata*, EN), the endemic white-bellied heron (*Ardea insignis*, EN), and the Bengal florican (*Houbaropsis bengalensis*, EN) are just a few of the other avian flagships in the region.

Threats

Despite their apparent remoteness and inaccessibility, the Himalaya have not been spared human-induced biodiversity loss. People have lived in the mountains and eked out a livelihood there for thousands of years. However, with better access to global market economies, both dependence on natural resources and the economic expectations and aspirations of the people have increased in recent years. Access has also encouraged immigration into montane areas from outside in some regions, such as Arunachal Pradesh, as well as movements within the Himalayan Mountains, such as in Nepal, where people have migrated from the mountains to the lowland terai. The consequences of the latter movements have been to concentrate people in the more productive ecosystems that are also the richest in biodiversity, whereas the former have resulted in a breakdown of cultural and social traditions and ties to conservation of natural resources among the tribal people in the mountains. Moreover, better health care and disease control have resulted in a net increase of human

On pp. 314-315, the Bengal tiger (Panthera tigris tigris) of India, Nepal, Sikkim, Bhutan, and Bangladesh, was the first recognized tiger subspecies. Kaziranga National Park in northeastern India, an alluvial plain grassland, is known to hold the highest adult tiger density —almost 17 tigers per 100 km²—, evidence that tiger densities can still be high in optimal habitats.
© Patricio Robles Gil/*Sierra Madre*

Above, the Vulnerable musk deer (Moschus moschiferus) do not have antlers, and only the bucks grow greatly elongated, tusklike upper canines. There are musk glands in the male, and their secretion always is in great demand as medicine.
© Gerald Cubitt

On the opposite page, the golden langur (Trachypithecus geei), is an Endangered primate with a very restricted range on the Bhutan-Assam border. These animals were photographed in Manas National Park.
© Gerald Cubitt

populations, placing a greater burden on the sensitive montane ecosystems.

Today, the distribution of remaining habitat in the Himalaya is patchy. The steadily increasing human population has been responsible for extensive clearing of forests and grasslands for cultivation, and widespread logging. Cultivation has a soft, upper-elevation limit of around 2 100 m on slopes exposed to the monsoon, but many people farm crops like barley, potato, and buckwheat at higher elevations in the inner valleys and transmontane regions, and in some areas, such as Jumla, Kashmir, Lahoul, and Ladakh, there are major agriculturally based population centers well above this elevation. The land is also often cleared by pastoralists for their livestock during the summer months. The conversion of forests and grasslands for agriculture and settlements has led to large-scale deforestation and habitat fragmentation in Nepal, and in the Indian States of Sikkim, Darjeeling, and Assam. In the northeast Indian states, loss of dense forests is estimated to be as high as 317 km² every year. The impact of forest clearing is less intense in Bhutan compared to the neighboring countries because of the low density of human population and the government's policy of a cautious approach to development and a commitment to the conservation of natural resources.

Large areas of remaining habitat are highly degraded. Overgrazing by domestic livestock in the resilient lowlands as well as in the sensitive alpine ecosystems is widespread. In the former, huge numbers of free-ranging, unproductive cattle graze the forests and grasslands, destroying all undergrowth and preventing regeneration; in the alpine ecosystems, virtually all areas are grazed by increasingly larger herds of domestic yak (Miller 2002). The fragile meadows are also subject to overexploitation of their flora for the traditional medicine trade. Because the medicinal plant collectors invariably uproot entire plants, regeneration is retarded. Wood extraction for fuel and fodder also contribute to loss of undergrowth and regeneration, and changes in species composition. Fuelwood is collected for domestic consumption as well as for export. These activities have inflicted severe and sometimes irreversible damage, and in many areas forests are no longer able to support natural ecosystems and their associated biodiversity.

It is possible to make an estimate of natural vegetation remaining intact by considering the state of natural habitat of the various ecoregions that make up this hotspot (Wikramanayake et al. 1998). The Himalayan subtropical broadleaf forests ecoregion has lost more than 70% of its natural habitat (although most of the hill forests above 1 000 m still remain uncut because the shallow, erosion-prone soils are unsuitable for cultivation), with the remaining forests in scattered fragments. Over 90% of the adjacent Terai-Duar savanna and grassland ecoregion has been converted to agriculture and settlements, and most of the remaining habitat is now within protected areas. The temperate broadleaf forests in the western extent of the Himalayan range have lost over 70% of their natural vegetation, although several large patches remain in the extreme western part. The eastern temperate broadleaf forests have fared better, with almost 70% of the natural habitat still remaining in large patches (particularly in northeastern India and Bhutan), but shifting agriculture has resulted in extensive habitat degradation. Likewise, the adjacent Brahmaputra Valley, a region characterized by remarkable productivity, and hence a long history of cultivation, is three-quarters cleared, with the largest forest blocks confined to protected areas in central Assam.

As with the temperate broadleaf forests, habitat loss in the Western Himalayan Sub-Alpine Conifer Forests is severe, with over 70% of the natural vegetation being lost. Notwithstanding, this region contains some of the least-disturbed forests in the Western Himalaya. In the Eastern Himalaya, the reverse is true, although on gentler slopes within the northeastern hill states of India most of the broadleaf forests (over 80%) have been affected due to slash-and-burn (jhum) agriculture. Most of the Alpine Shrub and Meadows is remote and inaccessible and, consequently, largely intact thanks to high elevation and harsh climate. However, all the gentle and accessible meadows have undergone extensive habitat degradation due to overgrazing, trampling, and commercial harvest for medicinal plants. In total, then, nearly 50% of the alpine vegetation in the region can be said to be intact, although in Sikkim, Bhutan, and Arunachal, over 60% of the alpine vegetation is still intact. Since this degradation can not be estimated from remote-sensed data sources, it is difficult to assess its extent, as grazing is prevalent all throughout the alpine regions. In total, we estimate that around 25% of the original vegetation of this hotspot, including alpine areas, remains in intact condition.

Besides habitat loss and degradation, poaching is rife across the Himalayan Mountains: tigers and rhinoceros are hunted for their body parts, which are much prized in traditional Chinese medicines, while the snow leopard and red panda are taken for their beautiful pelts. The remoteness of the Himalayan Region and the open borders have facilitated this illegal trade.

Political unrest, usually in the form of insurgencies, plague certain sites in the Himalayan region. Protected areas and forests that harbor wildlife also serve as refuges for insurgents, who indulge in indiscriminate poaching and felling of trees to obtain funds. In Nepal, the Maoist insurgency has severely constrained conservation activities on the ground since 1996. Similar insurgencies occur in Assam and Nagaland in India, while the dispute between India and Pakistan over the Kashmir border has had implications for wildlife conservation in these areas.

Conservation

Approximately 15% of the Himalaya Hotspot has some form of legal protection, although this percentage drops to 10% when one considers only those in IUCN categories I to IV. Protected areas have a mixed history in the Himalaya. In Assam, Manas and Sonai Rupai were first

On the opposite page, the Endangered greater one-horned rhinoceros (Rhinoceros unicornis) disappeared from much of its range in northwestern India and Pakistan due to the loss of alluvial plain grasslands to agricultural development, which destroyed the species' prime habitat and also led to increased conflict with humans. In addition, many were hunted, and countless slaughtered as a result of a government bounty established to protect tea plantations. By the early 1900s, the species was near extinction.
© **Patricio Robles Gil**/*Sierra Madre*

Above, the Endangered red panda (Ailurus fulgens) is a characteristic flagship species of the Himalaya. Despite its name, the species is not considered closely related to the Endangered giant panda (Ailuropoda melanoleuca), a flagship of the Mountains of Southwest China Hotspot.
© **Gerald Cubitt**

established as wildlife sanctuaries in 1928 and 1934, respectively, and are among the earliest contemporary protected areas in Asia (IUCN 1990). Most other protected areas are relatively recent, having been established within the past three to four decades. However, many hill-tribe communities have traditionally recognized and protected sacred groves, which have been effective refuges for biodiversity for centuries (Gadgil, 1985). Today, several protected areas —Corbett National Park, Manas National Park, Kaziranga National Park, Chitwan National Park, and Sagarmatha National Park— have been distinguished as World Heritage Sites for their contribution to global biodiversity.

In the 1970s and 1980s, several protected areas were established or extended in the northeastern Himalayan states of India, creating a network that showcased the biodiversity in the area. The protected areas in the northwestern Indian states include some of the world's most renowned, such as Corbett and Rajaji national parks, which harbor important populations of flagship species like elephants and tigers.

In Nepal, at least 26 666 km² of land has been designated as protected areas, including eight national parks, four wildlife reserves, one hunting reserve, three conservation areas, and five buffer zones (WWF-Nepal 2004). Chitwan, the country's first national park, was established in 1973. Previously a hunting preserve for the royal family, the park is well known for its tiger and greater one-horned rhinoceros populations. Of particular significance are the Annapurna Conservation Area, the Kanchenjunga Conservation Area, and the Makalu-Barun National Park, which have become models for community-based biodiversity management.

The protected area system of Bhutan includes five national parks, three wildlife sanctuaries, and one strict nature reserve, as well as 12 corridors covering almost 16 000 km² (Biodiversity Action Plan 2002). The current system was bequeathed as a "Gift to the Earth from the People of Bhutan" in 1999. Although a protected area system was established in Bhutan as early as the 1960s, this system was dominated by the Jigme Dorji Wangchuck National Park. The park was mostly confined to the north of the country, and did little to contribute towards biodiversity conservation because most of the park protected vast areas of permanent rock and ice. In 1995, the protected area system was revised to include all nine of the current protected areas accounting for almost 26% of the total land area in Bhutan. In 1999, another 9% was added to the system in the form of biological corridors, which linked the protected areas to create a conservation landscape extending across the country. The landscape is known as the Bhutan Biological Conservation Complex (Sherpa et al. 2003).

The many protected areas that lie adjacent to each other across national borders present promising opportunities for transboundary conservation activities. The Manas National Park in Bhutan and Manas Tiger Reserve in Assam, India is one such complex. Biological corridors also provide opportunities to link the protected areas across international boundaries and create habitat linkages, such as between Bardia in Nepal and Katerniaghat in India. Another important transboundary initiative is Kanchanjunga Conservation Area (KCA) in the Taplejung District in Nepal, an area covering some 1 650 km² named for Mt. Kanchanjunga (8 586 m) —the third highest mountain in the world— and planned as a tri-national peace park with the Tibet Autonomous Region of China to the north, and Sikkim in India to the east. The Kanchanjunga Conservation Area adjoins the Kanchendzoga National Park in Sikkim, and extension of the Qomolungma Nature Reserve in the Tibet Autonomous Region is under way to include the area bordering Kanchanjunga. The new strategy for creating conservation landscapes in the Himalaya will not only help to conserve the region's species and ecological processes that sustain biodiversity, but also contribute towards building regional cooperation through transboundary conservation efforts, thereby paving the way for a secure future for Himalayan biodiversity.

Despite the efforts to revise the protected area system across the Himalayan Mountains, about 17% of it, or over 40 000 km², still consists of permanent rock and ice (Alnutt et al. 2002). The protected areas of the alpine regions, in particular, are over-represented by these biologically depauperate habitats. Across the range, 15 protected areas consist of more than 50% rock and ice. Further expansion of the protected area network should consider minimizing representation of these areas.

Investment in biodiversity conservation in the Himalayan Region comes primarily from national governments, bilateral and multilateral agencies, and international and regional NGOs. The national governments, backed by international agencies such as the Global Environmental Facility (GEF), United Nations Development Program (UNDP), the World Bank, the European Union (EU), the Danish International Development Agency (DANIDA), WWF, and the MacArthur Foundation, are supporting projects to improve protected area management, sustainable natural resources, and livelihoods. All countries in the Himalaya Hotspot have ratified the Convention on Biological Diversity, and have prepared National Biodiversity Conservation Strategies and Biodiversity Action Plans.

While there have been many successes in establishing protected areas and more experimental, multiple land-use conservation areas, much remains to be done to safeguard the biological wealth of the Himalayan Region currently lying outside formally protected reserves. The protected areas of the Himalaya, particularly in the lowlands along south-facing slopes, are too small to maintain viable populations of threatened species. Successful long-term conservation requires that efforts be made to expand the conservation benefits beyond existing protected areas to adjacent habitats, as many species are dependent upon the seasonal use of habitats distributed along elevational gradients and across national boundaries.

MINGMA SHERPA[64]
ERIC WIKRAMANAYAKE[91]
GOPAL RAWAT[92]

The Vulnerable takin (Budorcas taxicolor) *is found in the mountainous regions of the Himalaya and western China, at altitudes of up to 4 500 m. Weighing as much as 400 kg, the flesh of the species is highly prized, and the takin is heavily hunted using snares and deadfall traps.*
© **Pete Oxford**/naturepl.com

On the opposite page, much of Nepal's original native habitat has been converted for agriculture and settlement.
© **Gavriel Jecan**/Art Wolfe Inc.

INDO-BURMA

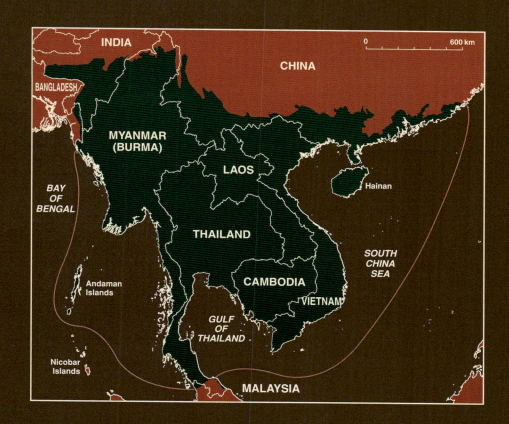

The redefined Indo-Burma Hotspot has emerged as a result of the exclusion of the Himalayan chain and associated foothills in Nepal, Bhutan, and India (now included in a new Himalaya Hotspot, the addition of southern and western Yunnan, and an expansion of the area of southern subtropical China (southern Guangxi and Guangdong). The area covered by this redefined hotspot is at times referred to as the Indo-Chinese Subregion and can be described as Tropical Asia east of the Ganges-Brahmaputra Lowlands, excluding the Malesian region. The Indo-Burma Hotspot begins at the evergreen forests in the foothills of Chittagong in Bangladesh and extends through the Garo and Khasi Hills of Meghalaya, India, then eastwards through the States of Manipur, Mizoram, and Nagaland to encompass most of Myanmar (except the extreme northern alpine areas), a part of southern and western Yunnan, China, all of the Lao People's Democratic Republic (P.D.R.), Vietnam, and Cambodia, the coastal lowlands of southern China, Hainan Island, the vast majority of Thailand, a small fraction of Peninsular Malaysia, and the Andaman Islands of India. As redefined here, the original extent of the hotspot is 2 373 000 km^2.

The transition to the Sundaland Hotspot occurs on the Thai-Malay Peninsula. The boundary between the two hotspots is here taken to be the Kangar-Pattani Line, which cuts across the Thailand-Malaysia border, marking the transition between the Indochinese and Sundaic floras (Van Steenis 1950; Whitmore 1984). However, other analyses indicate that the phytogeographical and zoogeographical transition between the Sundaland and Indo-Burma biotas may lie just to the north of the Isthmus of Kra, associated with a gradual change from wet seasonal evergreen dipterocarp rainforest to mixed moist deciduous forest (Woodruff 2003). For example, more than half of the 544 forest bird species present on the Thai-Malay Peninsula have their species limits north of the Isthmus at 11°-13°N (Hughes et al. 2003).

Indo-Burma has a complex geological and evolutionary history. The Indian intrusion into the Asian continental landmass has been responsible for the formation of most of the hotspot's topography, including the general north-south orientation of the mountains and main rivers. The wide variation in land form, climate, and latitude within the hotspot has led to the development of diverse natural habitats that support a high diversity of plant and animal species. This diversity is enhanced by a significant endemic element, which may largely derive from habitat isolation caused by periods of high sea level and vegetation changes during the glacial episodes of the Pleistocene. Consequently, the hotspot contains many localized centers of endemism, particularly montane isolates, but also areas of lowland wet evergreen forest that were isolated at some stage, and river basins.

At present, much of Indo-Burma is characterized by distinct seasonal weather patterns. During the northern winter months, dry, cool winds blow from the stable continental Asian high-pressure system, resulting in a dry, cool period under clear skies across much of the south, center, and west of the hotspot (the dry, northeast monsoon). As the continental system weakens in summer, the wind direction reverses and air masses forming the southwest monsoon pick up moisture from the seas to the southwest and bring abundant rains as they rise over the hills and mountains. In northern Vietnam and southern coastal China, the dominant weather pattern is the north or northeasterly monsoon during the northern winter and east or southeasterly monsoon in the summer.

On the opposite page,
the white-headed black langur
(Trachypithecus poliocephalus
leucocephalus) occurs in the
limestone hills in southwest
Guangxi, China. Critically
Endangered, they are among the
world's most threatened primates.
© Patricio Robles Gil/*Sierra Madre*

Originally, nearly all of Indo-Burma would have been dominated by broadleaf forests. The complex composition and distribution of the hotspot's principal vegetation formations are determined by the seasonality of rainfall, soil characteristics, temperature, and history. The richest forests —in terms of tree diversity and overall plant species numbers— are the lowland mixed wet evergreen forests, which occur in climates with one to four dry months. The southern mixed wet evergreen formations comprise the *Parashorea stellata* association, characteristic of zonal yellow-red clay loams, and the *Dipterocarpus costatus* association on yellow sandy soils, with low nutrient levels and high sensitivity to erosion, which occurs locally as islands within the widespread clay loams. The former were once widespread in Tenasserim south of Tavoy, Peninsular Thailand from Chumphon to northwestern Malaysia, and on the lower slopes of granite outcrops in southeastern Thailand, as well as south of Da Nang and in the hills north of Hue in Vietnam, but now survive only as a few fragments. The forests of *D. costatus* have been severely degraded, although significant stands remain on the southern slopes of the Cardamom and Kamchay ranges, and isolated patches in the Thai-Malay Peninsula. The northern mixed wet evergreen forest association is at present fragmented by mountain ranges and habitat conversion, and remnant patches are restricted to the northern part of the hotspot (northern Myanmar; southern China, including southern Yunnan and also Hainan; the Lao P.D.R.; and northern Vietnam).

In lowland areas where rainfall is more limited and the dry season lasts for five to seven months, the *Dipterocarpus turbinatus* dry evergreen forest formation is the natural climax stage in many lowland and hill regions. In the driest areas, it is confined to galleries in stream and river valleys, in areas otherwise dominated by deciduous forest types. This dry evergreen forest type is still widespread across substantial areas of Indo-Burma.

Deciduous forests occur in areas with five to nine dry months. The *Dalbergia-Lagerstroemia* mixed deciduous forest formation is widespread on yellow clay soils throughout the hotspot. Teak (*Tectona grandis*) may be a major component where soil and climatic conditions are right. On sandy and shallow lateritic soils, mixed deciduous forest is replaced by deciduous dipterocarp forest, which generally forms a low, broken canopy. Several factors contribute to the formation and maintenance of this forest type, including high frequency of fire (probably anthropogenic). In the dry, central Ayeyarwady Plain of Myanmar, a variety of semidesert thorn communities occur (Stamp 1925), which support fewer species than most other deciduous forest types but have relatively high levels of endemism. Some deciduous forests contain highly valuable timber species (e.g., teak, rosewood). Their leafless period and often broken canopy permit enough light to reach the ground

and stimulate a dense undergrowth of grasses and herbs, making these forests excellent feeding areas for large herbivorous mammals. Historically, these forests supported some of the most diverse and abundant mammal and bird megafaunas in Asia.

Throughout the hotspot, montane forests extend on humus-rich soils from about 800 masl. These forests are lower in stature with fewer emergents; oaks (Fagaceae) dominate, while laurels (Lauraceae) and magnolias (Magnoliaceae) become notable constituents. Montane tree species composition is generally less diverse than that of lowland forests, but it contains proportionally more endemic species. Diverse edaphic, topographic, and microclimatic conditions at higher elevations give rise to a range of mixed coniferous and broadleaf evergreen forest formations. On dry hills and plateaus subject to fire, conifer-dominated savanna forests occur (typically dominated by *Pinus merkusii* or *P. kesiya*). At the highest elevations, on ridgelines and ridge crests, stunted, xerophytic formations, characterized by the presence of *Rhododendron* spp., occur. In general, the diversity and richness of shrubs, herbs, epiphytes, and acid-loving species increase at higher altitudes, as tree diversity declines. Among them are many endemic species.

Heath forest occurs on some raised beaches in coastal areas. This evergreen forest type is less species-rich, but probably contains the highest proportion of endemics of any regional evergreen forest type. A related forest occurs on similar soils above 800 masl in association with sandstone mountains. Limestone karst outcrops support distinctive shrub and woodlands on their summits, as well as rich, mostly herbaceous floras on sheltered cliffs. Limestone karst formations can support relatively high levels of endemism, particularly in groups such as orchids (Orchidaceae). In addition, a wide variety of distinctive, localized vegetation formations occur in Indo-Burma, including lowland floodplain swamps, mangroves, seasonally inundated grasslands, and successional assemblages, as well as croplands and plantations.

The hotspot is home to a wide diversity of ethnic groups, cultures, and languages. Several language groups, including Mon-Khmer, Austroasiatic, and Tai-Kadai, originated and developed in the hotspot, and were later joined by the Hmong-Mien and Sino-Tibetan language groups. Agriculture developed very early in the hotspot, and gave rise to different land-use forms, including both semi-nomadic and rotational swidden cultivation, and irrigated floodplain rice cultivation. Among the human population of the hotspot, there is a broad spectrum in terms of the degree of integration with the global economy, from the Paleolithic life-styles of certain ethnic groups in the Thai-Malay Peninsula and the Jarawa, Onge, Sentinelese, and Andamanese tribes of the Andaman Archipelago, to the urban life-styles of the residents of Bangkok, Hong Kong, and other major cities.

The grey peacock-pheasant (Polyplectron bicalcaratum), also known as the chinquis, *is the national bird of Myanmar (Burma). It is one of a number of pheasant species that occur in the Indo-Burma Hotspot.*
© **Gerald Cubitt**

Biodiversity

Attempts to estimate species diversity and endemism for Indo-Burma are hampered by uneven knowledge of taxonomy and distribution of species and groups. New, locally endemic species are regularly discovered, while advances in taxonomy continue to reveal that single widespread "species" actually comprise complexes of separate species, many of which are local or regional endemics. Socio-political divisions have also complicated biodiversity assessments because populations in neighboring countries may be independently described as locally endemic species, although an independent revision would consider such pairs to represent just a single species. Nevertheless, reasonable estimates of species diversity and endemism can be made for some groups in the hotspot.

The total plant diversity of the former Indo-Burma Hotspot was estimated at about 13 500 species of flowering and gymnosperm plants, of which about 7 000 were estimated to be endemic to the hotspot (Dijk et al. 1999). A reassessment of the revised Indo-Burma Hotspot results in similar estimates for numbers of hotspot species and endemics: the modest losses of species restricted to the Himalayan chain and associated foothills being compensated for by the species gained in southern China. These estimates are, however, quite conservative: Davis et al. (1995) estimated that there are 12 000-15 000 species of vascular plants (i.e., including ferns) in Cambodia, Laos, and Vietnam combined. This flora includes a profusion of orchid (Orchidaceae) and ginger (Zingiberaceae) species (for example, there are more than 1 000 orchid species in Thailand alone), as well as the variety of fine tropical hardwoods.

The vertebrate fauna of the hotspot is quite diverse. Mammals number 430 species in 171 genera and 37 families, of which 71 species and seven genera (six monotypic) are endemic to the hotspot. In addition, there is a single endemic family, the Craseonycteridae, which is represented by one species, Kitti's hog-nosed bat (*Craseonycteris thonglongyai*), which is no larger than a bumblebee, and among the world's smallest mammals.

Over the last 12 years, the hotspot has witnessed the discovery of six large mammal species. Five of these were discovered in the Annamite Mountains: the saola (*Pseudoryx nghetinhensis*, EN), large-antlered muntjac (*Muntiacus vuquangensis*), Annamite muntjac (*M. truongsonensis*), grey-shanked douc (*Pygathrix cinerea*), and Annamite striped rabbit (*Nesolagus timminsi*) (Do Tuoc et al. 1994; Vu Van Dung et al. 1994; Nadler 1997; Giao et al. 1998; Timmins et al. 1998; Averianov et al. 2000). The sixth species, which was discovered in the mountains of northern Myanmar, is the leaf deer (*Muntiacus putaoensis*) (Amato et al. 1999).

The bird fauna is also very diverse, with some 1 277 species, of which 74 are endemic. There are also three endemic genera, all represented by single species: the golden-crested myna (*Ampeliceps coronatus*), short-tailed scimitar-babbler (*Jabouilleia danjoui*), and wedge-billed wren-babbler (*Sphenocichla humei*). Six Endemic Bird Areas (EBAs), as identified by BirdLife International (Stattersfield et al. 1998), are found within the hotspot, namely the Andaman Islands, the Irrawaddy Plains, Hainan Island, the Annamese Lowlands, the South Vietnamese Lowlands, and the Da Lat Plateau. The Eastern Himalayas and the Assam Plains EBAs are shared with the Himalaya Hotspot.

The non-marine reptiles number at least 519 species in 151 genera, of which 189 species and 12 genera are endemic. Nine of the endemic genera are represented by single species, among them a recently described form of pit viper from Vietnam (*Triceratolepidophis sieversorum*) (Ziegler et al. 2000). The rich amphibian fauna contains some 139 endemics among a total of around 323 species; yet, of the 57 genera represented, three (*Ophryophryne*, *Bufoides*, and *Glyphoglossus*) are endemic to the hotspot. *Bufoides* and *Glyphoglossus* comprise single species: the Khasi Hills toad (*B. meghalayanus*, EN) is known from only a few sites in northeastern India, while the last-mentioned (*G. molossus*) is more widespread in the hotspot.

The hotspot's inland fish fauna is remarkably diverse, with 1 262 documented species or 10% of the world's fishes that enter fresh water. The total may ultimately approach 2 000 species. The 566 fishes that are restricted to the region amount to more than half of the hotspot's endemic vertebrates, and constitute an obvious priority for conservation efforts. Endemism is also considerable at higher phyletic levels, with 30 endemic genera and an endemic family, the Indostomidae, or armored sticklebacks. This family of strange fishes is an extraordinary element to be found in tropical fresh waters, and may be remotely related to the marine seamoths. Diversity of freshwater fishes is particularly high on the lower to middle flanks of mountain ranges, where riffle and pool habitats in small streams have been the sites for extraordinary diversification, particularly in the loach families, Cobitidae and Balitoridae.

Flagship Species

First on the list of flagship mammal species is the saola. The known distribution of the saola is restricted to the Annamite Mountains, along the border between Vietnam and the Lao P.D.R., and outlying hills to the east. Although the ecology of the species is little known, it is believed to be largely restricted to wet evergreen forests at elevations below approximately 1 000 masl. This habitat has been extensively degraded, fragmented, and converted throughout the species' known range, and most remaining areas are subject to high levels of human use. While the saola is not a species in particular demand in the wildlife trade, it is

The Siamese fireback (Lophura diardi), *found in Thailand, Laos, Cambodia, and Vietnam, is considered Near Threatened due to hunting and habitat loss across the Indo-Burma Hotspot, to which it is endemic.*
© Gerald Cubitt

susceptible to indiscriminate snaring, which may be expected to increase in some parts of its range with the ongoing construction of the Ho Chi Minh National Highway and associated road network. Despite the global attention that was focused on the species following its discovery, none of its populations has been placed under effective conservation management, and the very real possibility exists that this enigmatic species may become extinct within a decade.

Other flagships include the Vietnamese population of Javan rhinoceros (*Rhinoceros sondaicus*, CR), estimated to number only a handful of individuals at Cat Tien National Park, and the kouprey (*Bos sauveli*, CR), a large bovid formerly found in forest areas of northern and eastern Cambodia and adjacent countries, but which may now be extinct. Also of special significance are the endemic primates, a number of which are included on a list of the world's top 25 most threatened primates prepared by Conservation International and advisors: the eastern black-crested gibbon (*Nomascus nasutus*, CR), Tonkin snub-nosed monkey (*Rhinopithecus avunculus*, CR), grey-shanked douc, white-rumped black leaf monkey (*Trachypithecus delacouri*, CR), white-headed black langur (*T. poliocephalus leucocephalus*, CR), and Tonkin hooded black langur (*T. p. poliocephalus*, CR) (Mittermeier et al. 2002).

Flagship bird species include Gurney's pitta (*Pitta gurneyi*, CR), a lowland evergreen forest specialist endemic to Peninsular Thailand and adjacent parts of southern Myanmar. During the twentieth century, the species underwent a dramatic decline due to extensive clearance of its habitat to the point that, by the end of the century, it was known to persist only at a single locality: Khao Nor Chuchi in Thailand. However, it has recently been rediscovered in the Tanintharyi division in Myanmar, which potentially supports a very significant population (BirdLife International 2004). Although not endemic, the majority of the world population of green peafowl (*Pavo muticus*, VU) is found within the hotspot. This species has undergone a dramatic decline over the last century as a result of hunting and expansion of human populations into natural landscapes, particularly the spread of human settlements along permanent water sources. Edwards' pheasant (*Lophura edwardsi*, EN), a species endemic to the lowlands of central Vietnam, is, like the saola, a flagship for the lowland wet evergreen forests of the Annamite Mountains and foothills. The Bengal florican (*Houbaropsis bengalensis*, EN) is a flagship for the threatened grassland ecosystems in Cambodia and Vietnam.

Tortoises and freshwater turtles collectively form a flagship group. The hotspot's non-marine turtle fauna is probably the most diverse in the world, with at least 40 (and, depending on taxonomic opinions, up to 52) species in 31 genera. This represents one-sixth of the world's turtle species and over one-quarter of the genera; about two-thirds of the species are endemic to the hotspot. Noteworthy also are the endemic Siamese

crocodile (*Crocodylus siamensis*, CR), now greatly reduced in the wild with a severely fragmented population; and the Chinese crocodile lizard (*Shinisaurus crocodilurus*). Although the latter is not quite endemic (occurring in northeastern Vietnam and southern China), it deserves mention for being the sole member of the family Shinisauridae, which has its closest relatives in the lizards of the genus *Xenosaurus* in southern Mexico and Guatemala.

Flagship amphibians are considered as groups rather than individual species. Numerous remarkable and endemic frog species occur, but several groups such as the *Rhacophorus* gliding frogs, the megophryid litter toads, and various ranid groups stand out for their local evolutionary radiations, conservation concern, and eye-catching appearance. Salamander diversity is not very high in the hotspot, but the salamanders contain a high proportion of species with very restricted ranges and of high conservation concern, including four endemic species in the genus *Paramesotriton*, two of which are globally threatened: the Vietnamese salamander (*P. deloustali*, VU) from Vietnam and the Guangxi warty newt (*P. guangxiensis*, VU) from Guangxi Autonomous Region, China, and northern Vietnam.

Indo-Burma's streams and rivers are inhabited by fish species that are not only of global conservation significance, but also include some of the extremes of size among freshwater fishes. The Tonle Sap Lake and deep pools of the Mekong River, up to 60 m deep, are critical habitats for some of the world's largest freshwater fishes: the Mekong giant catfish (*Pangasianodon gigas*, CR), giant carp (*Catlocarpio siamensis*), and giant freshwater stingray (*Himantura chaophraya*, proposed CR). Other flagship fishes include the dragonfish (*Scleropages formosus*, EN), a relict of a Gondwanan group that is rapidly being depleted by illegal collecting of its juveniles for the aquarium trade.

Threats

Indo-Burma may have been one of the first places on the globe where agriculture developed (Solheim 1972; Diamond 1997), creating a long history of forest burning and clearance for shifting or permanent small-scale cultivation. In recent centuries, steadily increasing trade in agricultural commodities and timber, combined with population growth, have led to widespread forest destruction. Very little, if any, natural vegetation has been unaffected by human actions. In particular, lowland evergreen forests have been extensively cleared, having been reduced to well under 30% in Thailand, less than 20% in Vietnam, and only 7% on Hainan Island by the early 1990s (BirdLife International 2003). Shifting cultivation and logging have also degraded large tracts of hill and montane forest, particularly in Chin State in Myanmar (which, during the 1980s, had one of the highest deforestation rates in

The green magpie (Cissa chinensis) *is a forest bird species found in the Indo-Burma Hotspot and also in southern China.*
© Gerald Cubitt

On the opposite page, Thi Lan Su Waterfall in the Umphung Wildlife Sanctuary, Thailand.
© Gerald Cubitt

326

train, the *Shinkansen*, in less than three hours from Tokyo. Many more vacationers travel to those once remote and sparsely populated areas. With the increase in tourists has come a greater demand for services and recreational facilities, which in turn has put more pressure on undeveloped areas.

Since World War II, the country's high-elevation conifer forests have been under the administration of the Forestry Agency of Japan. In response to demands for timber and pulp following World War II, the agency promoted clear-cutting of these forests and the replanting of deforested areas with *Larix leptolepis*. Today, plantations are widespread throughout Japan, with about 90% of them made up of *Cryptomeria japonica* (*Sugi*), *Chamaecyparis obtusa* (*Hinoki*), and *Larix leptolepis* (*Kara-matsu*), all native Japanese species. *Fagus* was traditionally not used for construction until after about 1900. From then on, *Fagus* was used in increasing amounts for furniture, pulp, and construction, and during World War II for building light aircraft. Clear-cut areas that supported *Fagus* have been replaced with *Cryptomeria* or *Larix* plantations, or by pure stands of *Sasa* where it has been impossible to establish *Cryptomeria* or *Larix*. Natural *Fagus crenata* vegetation still occurs in the central mountainous areas of Honshu, but is replaced by evergreen broadleaf forests in the southern parts of the island.

As a result of the National Survey on the Natural Environment, Japan maintains vegetation maps (scale 1:50 000) covering the entire national landmass, with 766 plant-community categories. The plant communities are classified into ten types: natural vegetation of grasslands; natural vegetation of moorlands; natural vegetation of forests; secondary forests approximating the natural vegetation; substitute vegetation of secondary forests; planted forests; substitute vegetation of high-profile grasslands; substitute vegetation of low-profile orchards; substitute vegetation of low-profile paddies and fields; and urban land. When considering the percentage of each vegetation type occupying the overall national land area, forests (natural forests, secondary forests approximating natural forest, secondary forests, and planted forests) comprise 67.5% of the national land. Natural forest vegetation constitutes 18.2%. Adding the natural vegetation of grasslands and moorlands provides a total natural vegetation of 19.3%. Secondary forests (including secondary forests approximating natural forest) comprise 24.6% of the national land, while planted forests occupy 24.7%, secondary grassland 3.2%, paddies and fields 22.7%, and urban land 4.0%. The natural forests and natural grasslands referred to here indicate forests or grasslands that are climax or are regarded as climax. The most heavily forested region is the island of Hokkaido, of which 50% is covered with natural vegetation. Shikoku, however, has the highest percentage of forest cover in Japan, while Kyushu has the highest percentage of land in cultivated forests, paddy fields, and croplands in the coun-

try. Overall, deforestation has now ceased to a large degree in the lowlands, and there are still extensive tracts of forest cover in the higher-lying regions.

Besides forested areas, coastal regions and wetlands have also been subject to disturbance. On Hokkaido, the wetlands favored by nesting red-crowned cranes continue to be lost to development, mainly agricultural expansion, river channelization, and road building. For instance, one-third of almost 300 km² of marshland in Kushiro has been converted to agricultural, industrial or residential use since the 1970s (BirdLife International 2003).

Unfortunately, as a result of past habitat loss and also the effects of hunting and pesticide use, several species have undergone precipitous declines in their populations, including the oriental stork (*Ciconia boyciana*, VU), which no longer breeds in Japan, and the crested ibis (*Nipponia nippon*, EN), which is now known to survive only in the You Prefecture in Shaanxi Province in central China, where it is a localized breeder. In both cases, efforts are under way to reintroduce these species to Japan, with several captive-bred crested ibises from China having been sent to Japan, and similar plans to reintroduce captive-bred oriental storks. The population of short-tailed albatross (*Phoebastria albatrus*, VU) crashed to near extinction during the twentieth century following massive exploitation for its feathers, although protection since the 1960s has helped the population to recover; today, it breeds only on Torishima and the Senkaku Islands (BirdLife International 2003).

Like much of the rest of Japan, the Ryukyus and Ogasawaras have suffered from habitat loss due to the planting of timber plantations and urban development (and volcanic eruptions in 2000 resulted in serious damage to forests on Miyake-jima in the Izu Islands). Almost all the original subtropical forest on the Ogasawaras has been cleared, likely one of the factors that led to the extinction of three avian endemics during the nineteenth century (Bonin wood-pigeon, *Columba versicolor*; Bonin thrush, *Zoothera terrestris*; and Bonin grosbeak, *Chaunoproctus ferreorostris*). In the Ryukyus, only small areas of forest remain on Amami and Okinawa, mainly in protected areas, and mature forest now only covers less than 5% of Amami (BirdLife International 2003).

As with other subtropical parts of the world, one of the greatest threats to the native fauna and flora of Japan is from alien plants and animals, some of which were introduced for the purposes of snake control, including the Indian grey mongoose (*Herpestes edwardsi*), Javan mongoose (*H. javanicus*), and Siberian weasel (*Mustela sibirica*). For example, the introduction of the Siberian weasel to Miyake-jima in the 1970s and 1980s caused significant declines of Japanese night-herons (*Gorsachius goisagi*, EN) and Izu thrushes (*Turdus celaenops*, VU). On Amami, the Javan mongoose is thought to be responsible for declines in the Amami woodcock (*Scolopax mira*, VU) and Amami rabbit. Other introduced species in Japan include the fish *Tilapia zillii* and the

On the opposite page, ayu fish (Plecoglossus altivelis) are a troutlike species with an interesting shuttlecock-like dorsal fin. They are an esteemed food item in Japan.
© **Ryu Uchiyama**/*Nature Production*

Above, the Iriomote cat (Prionailurus iriomotensis) is found only on Iriomote-jima, and may number no more than 100 individuals.
© **Makoto Yokotsuka**/*Nature Production*

toad *Bufo gargarizans miyakonis*, while introduced goats are a problem on some islands. Largemouth bass (*Micropterus salmoides*), too, pose a serious threat to native fishes throughout Japan.

Conservation

Although Japan's 28 national parks have been designated to preserve "areas of the greatest natural scenic beauty," they also protect some of the richest areas of biodiversity. Together, they cover about 5.5% of Japan's land area. In addition to the national parks, there are numerous quasi-national parks, prefectural natural parks, and prefectural wildlife protection areas. Taking into account all protected areas in IUCN categories I to IV, just under 6% of this hotspot can be considered to have a high level of protection, although as much as 16% of the hotspot has at least some form of legal protection when one also includes those protected areas not classified in these categories. There are also two Natural World Heritage Sites in Japan, both established in 1993, namely Shirakami-sanchi, in northern Honshu, and Yaku-shima in the Satsunan-shoto, which contains ancient trees of sugi or Japanese cedar. Many of the parks, or parts of the parks, may not be completely preserved areas, and often there are private agricultural lands or other commercial development activities within the park. Furthermore, there are weaknesses in reserve management in some areas, such as in the Izu-shoto, which although declared a national park, continues to suffer habitat loss.

The main obvious gaps in the protected area system are in the Ryukyus; small, protected areas exist in northern Okinawa and on Amami, but most forested areas are not properly protected. One example is Yanbaru, which supports important populations of six of the 32 Critically Endangered and Endangered species in Japan, including the entire global populations of Okinawa rail and Okinawa woodpecker. Around 25% of Yanbaru on the eastern slope of the central montane area is located in the U.S. Marine Corps Training Area, while the rest of the forest is threatened by clear-cutting and removal of forest undergrowth: during a 13-year period, from 1979 to 1991, some 24 km² of forests were cut down, more than 60% of which was in the central part of the forests, while it has been estimated that the undergrowth has been removed from half of the natural forests (Ito et al. 2000). It is also worth noting that 19% of Okinawa-honto's land area is under exclusive use by U.S. military bases.

The policy until now regarding protected areas has been to try to establish the parks with the least negative impact on the local economy, while at the same time preserving landscape areas of great national importance. Wildlife within the parks is strictly protected, and the destruction and collecting of plants and animals is prohibited. The parks, however, are used for such activities as hiking, skiing, mountain climbing, camping, boating, swimming, bird watching and general sightseeing. On the Ogasawaras, more preserves have been established and tourism has become regulated.

Although pressures on once-remote parts of the country have increased, in recent years the people of Japan have returned to embracing the concept of a green, sustainable world where humans value and care for their natural resources, and again recognize themselves as one part of the environment, just as their ancestors did. A significant indication of the value being placed on renewable resources and green technology is the Cosmos Prize, one of the world's top environmental awards, established by the Expo'90 Committee and presented annually by the Expo'90 Foundation of Japan. Expo'90 was an event dedicated to the theme "The Harmonious Coexistence of Nature and Mankind: How we as human beings can truly respect and live in harmony with nature." The purpose of the prize is to honor those who have, through their work, applied and realized the ideals promoted at the Expo, but it has also focused the attention of the public on the need for conservation and the preservation of nature. Nature and greenery are now constantly being mentioned in advertising, by the news media, and in government policy announcements.

Finally, it is worth mentioning that Japan in recent years has become an important player in international biodiversity conservation and an advocate for the hotspots. Indeed, the Japanese Government is one of five partners (along with the World Bank, the Global Environment Facility, the MacArthur Foundation, and Conservation International) in the Critical Ecosystem Partnership Fund (CEPF), which is providing $125 million over five years to hotspot conservation. Now that Japan itself has entered the hotspot list, we hope that the country's commitment to these critically important regions of our planet will increase even more.

DAVID E. BOUFFORD [94]
YASUSHI HIBI [93]
HIROMI TADA [93]

The Bonin flying fox (Pteropus pselaphon) is a Critically Endangered bat species known only from a handful of islands in the Ogasawara-gunto (also known as the Bonin Islands).
© **Takashi Uzu**/*Nature Production*

On the opposite page, deforestation and forest road network in Shirakami-sanchi World Heritage Site in the northern part of Honshu, Japan.
© **Kazuma Anezaki**/*Nature Production*

EAST MELANESIAN ISLANDS

Although it was not previously identified as a biodiversity hotspot, this region's accelerating habitat loss and additional research done there have led to the identification of the group of East Melanesian islands northeast and east of New Guinea as requiring hotspot status. This assemblage of great tropical oceanic islands is without parallel in its combination of insular biodiversity, unique environment, and amazingly rich diversity of traditional cultures.

The East Melanesian Islands Hotspot encompasses the islands of the Bismarck Archipelago, the Solomon chain, the Santa Cruz Islands (Temotu), and the islands of Vanuatu. Politically, this includes the northeastern insular portion of Papua New Guinea (including the large islands of New Britain, New Ireland, and Manus); Buka and Bougainville, which are at the northern end of the Solomon chain, but politically part of Papua New Guinea; and the entirety of the nations of the Solomon Islands and Vanuatu. These islands are little known because of their inaccessibility and because they lie within the considerable shadow cast by the subcontinental island of New Guinea —the great biodiversity generator of the tropical Pacific. Being truly oceanic, the islands of the East Melanesian Islands Hotspot are relatively species-poor when compared to the biotic riches of New Guinea. However, when compared to other tropical Pacific island groups or any other islands of comparable size, they are the most diverse physiographically, biotically, and ethnically.

Lying directly on the Pacific "Ring of Fire" strings of active volcanoes erupt periodically, shaking the earth and sending plumes of ash over the surrounding landscape. Rabaul City, capital of East New Britain Province, was destroyed by the eruption of Tavurvur in August, 1994. The island of Tanna in Vanuatu also has an active volcano, which is famed for being the world's most accessible. Rough and rocky coastlines are found along many shore areas, while in other parts, mangroves or fringing coral reefs are more typical. This inaccessibility has hindered development and commerce. The region's reef ecosystem diversity is high, containing some of the

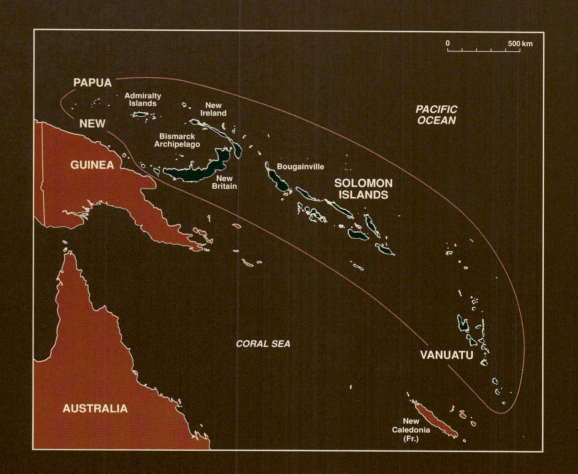

most pristine reefs on Earth. The region's rainforests look much like those found on New Guinea, and many of New Guinea's common forest trees are also found dominating the forests of this hotspot.

The oceanic island arcs of this hotspot are a mixture of young volcanics and very old basement rocks that date back to the Cretaceous, the same geological period in which New Zealand and New Caledonia were drifting away from the disintegrating Gondwanaland. Thus, while the hotspot contains classic examples of relatively recent adaptive radiation typical of oceanic islands, such as the white-eyes (family Zosteropidae) and monarch flycatchers (family Monarchidae), it also carries some odd colonizers from times past such as the giant monkey-tailed skink of the genus *Corucia*, whose closest living relatives are the blue-tongued skinks (genus *Tiliqua*) of Australia, New Guinea, and Indonesia; and the giant *Placostylus* land snails shared with the Gondwanaland fragments of Australia, New Caledonia, New

On the opposite page, aerial view of rainforest-covered islands and coral reefs in the New Georgia group of the Solomon Islands. The Solomons have been heavily impacted by logging and conversion to coconut plantations over the last decade.
© Michael Pitts/naturepl.com

Zealand, and also with Fiji. The East Melanesian Islands Hotspot has affinities with Fiji (included as part of the Polynesia-Micronesia Hotspot, but which probably sits better culturally within Melanesia), such as *Platymantis* frogs, ancient "monkey-faced" fruit bats of the genus *Pteralopex*, and *Nesoclopeus* rails —all of which trace back to colonization in a distant archipelagic past shared with Fiji.

The East Melanesian Islands Hotspot is one of the most geographically complex areas on Earth. Intricate tectonic plate movements have produced a mix of colliding and subducting plates, which, in turn, have generated deep oceanic trenches and affiliated strings of islands of varying age and development. At the top of the hotspot, at 2°S latitude, lies the Bismarck Archipelago's Admiralty group, dominated by Manus Island (1 834 km^2), which is surrounded by a constellation of small islands, the largest of which are Rambutyo and Lou. Northeast of the Admiralties lies the Saint Matthias Group; the largest, Mussau (or St. Matthias; 414 km^2) stands as the head of a chain of small island groups (Tabar, Lihir, Tanga, Feni, and Nissan) that lead southeastward to Buka and Bougainville, in the Solomon chain.

The two main islands of the Bismarck Archipelago —New Ireland (7 174 km^2) and New Britain (35 742 km^2)— lie south and southwest of the Tabar-Nissan islands string. Both islands are complex and mountainous, with peaks exceeding 2 000 m. Just west of the northern tip of New Ireland lies New Hanover (1 186 km^2), while north and west of New Britain one finds several island outliers —the Witu Islands, Siassi Islands (including Umboi), and Long and Crown in the extreme west, just north of the coast of mainland Papua New Guinea. The island chain that includes Long and Umboi arcs northwestward off the coast of New Guinea and comprises a series of recent volcanoes, some still active.

Mountainous Bougainville, the largest in the Solomon chain, covers 8 591 km^2 and supports several high massifs (some volcanic), the highest of which, Mount Balbi, stands 2 685 m above sea level, the high point of the hotspot. Together with Buka (611 km^2), the northernmost of the Solomon group, these two islands were part of the German New Guinea colonial administration, and are today part of Papua New Guinea. The remainder of the Solomons constitutes the independent nation of the Solomon Islands (a former British protectorate). Together they comprise two parallel chains of large islands. The northern chain includes (from west to east): Choiseul, Santa Isabel, and Malaita, while the southern chain comprises Vella Lavella, Kolombangara, New Georgia and Rendova, the Russell Islands, Guadalcanal, and Makira. Isolated Rennell Island (684 km^2), one of the most remarkable and unique islands in the region, lies some 175 km to the south of Guadalcanal; this island is home to the largest freshwater lake in the insular

The Solomons prehensile-tailed skink (Corucia zebrata) is a large, arboreal skink genus that is endemic to the Solomon Islands. Although usually considered a single species, it is likely that further research will indicate that a number of species exist on the different islands in this country.

© **Joe McDonald**/*Auscape*

Pacific (Lake Tegano). Most isolated of all in this island nation are the Santa Cruz Islands, 375 km east of Makira and dominated by Nendo, Tinakula, Utupua, and Vanikoro. These lie at the top of the hotspot's easternmost island chain that leads south to Vanuatu (another legacy of nineteenth-century colonialism, the Solomons being a British protectorate and Vanuatu being a French-British Condominium of the New Hebrides, referred to in history texts as the "Pandemonium").

The diverse islands of Vanuatu (formerly the New Hebrides) lie almost 300 km south-southeast from the Temotu group. Geographically, Vanuatu resembles the Solomons, but has smaller, lower, younger islands. To the north lie the Banks and Torres Islands, followed by a double chain of large islands (Espiritu Santo and Malakula to the west; Maewo, Pentecost, Ambrym, and Efate to the east). Below Efate, a single chain of smaller islands appears: Erromango, Tanna, and Anatom.

Thus, this insular hotspot supports in excess of 1 600 islands, encompassing a land area of around 99 384 km^2. Although a tiny area in global terms, the East Melanesian Islands Hotspot has more land than all of the remaining islands in the tropical Pacific, being a little more than double the land area encompassed in the Polynesia-Micronesia Hotspot (*ca.* 47 000 km^2).

The geological history of these island groups is very complex and poorly known. Most of their history seems to be recent, these groups being of Late Tertiary emergence from the sea. The major formative events, however, relate to the break-up of Gondwana, the rafting of the Indo-Australian Plate northward, and its long contact and interaction with the Pacific Plate and several smaller plates (South Bismarck Plate, Solomon Sea Plate). The Indo-Australian and Pacific plates are currently converging at a rate of 12 cm/yr (Honza et al. 1987). One finds the development of island arcs in association with a single long and sinuous subduction zone that has created a series of 7 000-m deep-sea trenches.

In essence, there has been a substantial tectonic interaction between what has been characterized as the West Melanesia Arc and the New Guinea/Australia craton, and it is this interaction that has apparently produced all of the island chains and groups mentioned above. A close examination of a bathymetric map shows a series of trenches and deeps that arc from the southern verge of New Britain east and southeastward along the southern verge of the Solomons and southeastward along the western verge of the islands of Vanuatu. In addition, an examination of island patterns displayed in relation to this deep water is that two or even three chains of islands are arrayed in parallel along this Melanesian arc. It perhaps shows up most clearly in the vicinity of New Ireland and Bougainville, where one can find a line of high, massive islands, a smaller set of rugged islands (e.g., Feni, Lihir), and finally a low set of atolls (e.g., Lyra Reef, Nuguria Islands, Carteret Islands); one can also see this in the Solomons (especially the New Georgia Group, Choiseul, Ontong Java Atoll). The pattern is only broken by the oddball positioning of New Britain and its affiliated islands to the west —a product of little-understood actions of the two Bismarck microplates in contact with the Indo-Australian Plate.

The islands of this hotspot have never been in land contact with New Guinea, and the current 100-km-long Vitiaz Strait separating New Guinea from New Britain was formerly a much broader ocean channel. As a result, the biotas of these islands are a mix of long-distance immigrants and older indigenous lineages derived from ancient Pacific-Gondwanan stock. Given the uncertain above-sea histories of these islands, one might presume that the more ancient lineages survived by hopping from island group to island group as they periodically arose, submerged, and arose anew.

In terms of climate, the East Melanesian Islands Hotspot is composed of small and large, low and high islands that are uniformly tropical and humid. All receive in excess of 1 500 mm of rain per year, and the wetter sites receive in excess of 5 000 mm per year. The Weather Coast of the main Solomon Islands (especially on Makira and Guadalcanal) receives huge amounts of rain, as do regions in southern New Britain (Gasmata receives 6 m; Pomio, 6.5 m). The entire hotspot lies south of the Equator, from 2ºS to 20ºS and, therefore, is located wholly within the tropics. In addition, southernmost Vanuatu exhibits a cool and dry season from May to October. One major climatic feature that varies from west to east is susceptibility to cyclones during the December to March season. The eastern Solomons and all of Vanuatu lie on the cyclone track, and those forests most exposed have suffered the repeated devastation of high winds. In the Solomon Islands, there are tall gallery forests in Western Province, while on Makira Island to the east, which suffers regular cyclone damage, the forest is more like a natural mosaic of secondary successions.

This hotspot is culturally and linguistically very rich. Vanuatu, with 109 living traditional languages, has more languages per unit area than any nation on Earth. The Solomon Islands, with 74 languages, is only slightly less diverse. With such a large number of languages over a small population, it is not surprising that there are many languages with only a few hundred speakers. Languages are dying or mixing into "Pijin-Austronesian Creoles" in the Melanesian Islands. The disappearance of linguistic diversity results in a rapid loss of traditional knowledge and traditional practice. Typically, this leads to erosion of traditional links between communities and the forests that have long served as their pri-

mary source of wealth and subsistence. However, a shift to the modern cash economy is the underlying force behind the rise in destructive exploitation of the region's natural environments.

Biodiversity

Mueller-Dombois and Fosberg (1998) delineated a series of natural vegetation types in the Solomon Islands, and these typify the region as a whole: coastal strand vegetation; mangrove forest; freshwater swamp forest; lowland rainforest; seasonally dry forest and grassland; and montane rainforest. Most are species-poor, with several tree species dominating (the dominants varying from site to site and island to island). In certain sites, single tree species dominate, as with the monodominant stands of *Campnosperma brevipetiolata* and *Terminalia brassi* in swamps (Johns 1993). Recent studies by Bayliss-Smith et al. (2003) indicate that many "old-growth" forests in the Solomons are secondary and show the impacts of past human disturbance. This fact probably applies to most or all of the lowland and hill forests of the hotspot.

Based on the analysis of Mueller-Dombois and Fosberg (1998), Wikramanayake et al. (2002) summarized the floristics of forest habitats in the various ecoregions of the East Melanesian Islands Hotspot. The Bismarck Archipelago is characterized by a range of typical species and genera of forest trees that are well known in New Guinea, and mentioned above, but certain taxa are conspicuously absent. The genus *Araucaria*, an emergent conifer of ancient Gondwanic origins, does not occur in the hotspot, though its relative *Agathis* occurs throughout. *Nothofagus*, another Gondwanan relict so important in montane New Guinea, is found at relatively low altitudes in the mountains of New Britain, but absent on New Ireland and the Solomons, where the highlands are locally dominated by *Metrosideros salmomonis*. The Dipterocarpaceae, which dominate in Southeast Asia and are rather common in New Guinea, are essentially absent from the hotspot. Overall, the region's forest flora is poor compared to that of New Guinea, with dominant trees being *Pometia*, *Dillenia*, *Elaeocarpus*, *Endospermum*, *Campnosperma*, *Calophyllum*, *Terminalia*, *Canarium*, *Agathis*, *Metrosideros*, and *Sararanga*. All of these genera are found on mainland New Guinea.

In total, the vascular plant flora of the region is estimated to be 8 000 species, and of these some 3 500-4 000 species are thought to be endemic to the region (D. Frodin, pers. comm.). The fauna of the East Melanesian Islands Hotspot is an attenuated sample of that from New Guinea, plus a minor but distinctive oceanic element. Certain groups (for example, birds of paradise, bowerbirds, scrub-wrens, tree-kangaroos, echidnas, gliders) that are prominent on mainland New

The small Pacific boas (Candoia spp.) are found on a number of islands in the East Melanesian Islands Hotspot.
© **Patricio Robles Gil**/*Sierra Madre*

On pp. 350-351, aerial view of undisturbed rainforest on the island of New Britain, a rare sight on an island increasingly impacted by logging and clearance of forest for oil palm plantations.
© **Patricio Robles Gil**/*Sierra Madre*

Guinea are absent from this insular hotspot. Other taxa (honeyeaters, white-eyes, monarchs, fantails, flying foxes and allies, and murid rodents) abound on the islands. Finally, certain sylviine warbler lineages, and certain gecko and frog lineages are more prominent on these islands, but rare or absent on mainland New Guinea. Because of different regimes of oceanic isolation and local adaptive radiation, endemism is very high on the islands, with some species endemic to the hotspot, others endemic to subsets of the hotspot, and yet others confined to single islands. The insular and fragmented nature of species ranges also leads to high levels of endangerment.

The hotspot supports 365 regularly occurring bird species, 154 of which are endemic. Compositionally, the avifauna is distinct from that of New Guinea, and has seven endemic genera (*Microgoura*, *Nesasio*, *Woodfordia*, *Guadalcanaria*, *Stresemannia*, *Mayrornis*, and *Neolalage*). The hotspot also includes six Endemic Bird Areas (EBAs), as defined by BirdLife International (Stattersfield et al. 1998): the Admiralty Islands, with six species confined entirely to this EBA; St. Matthias Island (two species); New Britain and New Ireland (35 species); the Solomon group, with a staggering 61 species endemic; Rennell and Bellona (five species); and Vanuatu and Temotu (15 species).

The region holds a varied mammal fauna, but can be characterized as poor in nonvolant species and rich in volant species (bats). Flying foxes and allies (Pteropodidae) and Microchiroptera occur in almost equal diversity, with 36 and 33 species, respectively. In total, of the 86 mammal species native to the hotspot, 39 are endemic. There are three endemic genera: *Anthops*, with a single species, the flower-faced bat (*A. ornatus*, VU); *Melonycteris* (three species); and *Solomys* (three species).

A total of 114 species of reptiles (54 endemic) and 44 species of amphibians (38 endemic) are known to occur in this hotspot. The region is home to six endemic genera of reptiles, five of which are represented by single species, including four species of snake —*Bothrochilus boa*, *Loveridgelaps elapoides*, *Parapistocalamus hedigeri*, and *Salomonelaps par*— and a lizard, *Corucia zebrata*. The sixth endemic genus, *Geomyersia*, consists of two species of lizards. There are also four endemic genera of amphibians; two of the amphibian genera are monotypic, namely *Palmatorappia solomonis* (VU), a species from the Solomon Islands that may actually represent two species, and *Ceratobatrachus guentheri*, found on the Solomon Islands and Bougainville and Buka islands. It is perhaps not surprising that the herpetofauna of this hotspot is rather impoverished, given its physical isolation. However, there is interesting within-region variation in this pattern. For example, there are 40 species of lizards from Bougainville (many endemic), but only 26 and 30 species recorded from New Ireland

and New Britain, respectively (Allison 2001). New Ireland is indicative of the herpetofauna of a large island in the region. Allison's catalog for New Ireland includes the following families (with species numbers in parentheses): Amphibia: Hylidae (2), Ranidae (5); Reptilia: Crocodylidae (1), Agamidae (2), Gekkonidae (6), Scincidae (19), Varanidae (2), Boidae (2), Pythonidae (2), Colubridae (4), Elapidae (1), Laticaudidae (1), Typhlopidae (3). Thus, it is a hotspot typified by skinks and geckos. It is also notable that both the boas and the pythons co-occur in this hotspot.

The hotspot supports a small but highly unique freshwater ichthyofauna, and includes families such as Eleotridae, Gobiidae, and Mugilidae. Until recently, there has not been a concerted effort to catalogue the freshwater ichthyofauna inhabiting the South Pacific. However, conservation groups like the Wildlife Conservation Society, Wetlands International, and Conservation International, as well as several academic institutions, are now beginning to document the region's freshwater biota.

It is estimated that there are approximately 52 species of freshwater fishes throughout the hotspot and, of those, three species are considered endemic: *Stenogobius alleni*, found on New Britain Island in Papua New Guinea; *S. hoesei*, found throughout the Admiralty and Solomon Islands and the Bismarck Archipelago; and *Stiphodon astilbos*, found in Vanuatu. The number of taxa decreases further inland from the ocean and as altitude increases, with gobioid fishes likely being the only native taxonomic group observed once a precipitous obstruction has broken the continuity of a stream. Because the fishes inhabiting the hotspot are of marine origin, diadromous behavior is not uncommon and all the freshwater fishes are capable of tolerating a wide range of saltwater concentrations. These factors have helped create the distinct fish faunal assemblage for this region.

The invertebrate fauna is poorly known. As with the other life-forms, the invertebrate faunas of each more distant island group are ever more attenuated subsets of that from the source island of New Guinea. Butterflies are relatively well known among arthropods. The *Ornithoptera* (birdwing) butterflies find their center of species richness in New Guinea. The genus ranges eastward through the Bismarcks to the Solomons, where three species are found (*O. allotae*, *O. urvillianus*, and *O. victoriae*). By contrast, the papilionid genus *Troides* (*sensu stricto*) is widespread in the Moluccas and New Guinea, but absent from the East Melanesian Islands Hotspot. The blue emperor swallowtail (*Papilio ulysses*), so well known in tropical Queensland, ranges westward to the Moluccas, northward into New Guinea, and is also widespread in the Bismarcks and Solomons, but does not reach Vanuatu (D'Abrera 1990).

On the opposite page, impressive tree buttresses on a rainforest giant on the island of Espíritu Santo, Vanuatu, part of the East Melanesian Islands Hotspot.
© **Patricio Robles Gil**/*Sierra Madre*

Above, the Solomons leaf frog (Ceratobatrachus guentheri) is the only representative of a genus endemic to the Solomon Islands.
© **Mike Tinsley**/*Auscape*

Flagship Species

While not necessarily a center for typical flagship species, the East Melanesian Islands Hotspot has its share of unusual creatures and plants, all of which merit attention and conservation. The Kauri pine (*Agathis* spp.) is perhaps the most logical selection as a plant flagship. This ancient Gondwanan conifer is the largest tree in the islands, and is an important timber species. It grows to a huge girth, and makes for a remarkable forest where it is common. Foresters, of course, lust after it, and it tends to be high-graded out of forests wherever it is found.

Besides bird species such as the superb pitta (*Pitta superba*, VU) of Manus Island, perhaps the most beautiful species in the hotspot (although one that is very difficult to see), and the fearful owl (*Nesasio solomonensis*, VU), a Solomon Islands endemic and the hotspot's largest nightbird, the most majestic avian flagship is the Solomons sea-eagle (*Haliaeetus sanfordi*, VU), another Solomons endemic. This species favors coastal forests, but pairs also hunt further inland and, at least on the eastern islands, they appear to have entirely inland ranges where they prey largely on northern common cuscus (*Phalanger orientalis*) and fruit bats. Among flagship mammals, the most remarkable are the flying foxes, which are known to play an important role in pollination and seed dispersal of plants. Of the 13 threatened species of pteropid bats recorded from the hotspot, three are Critically Endangered and poorly known, but highlighted here to draw attention to their plight: the Bougainville monkey-faced bat (*Pteralopex anceps*) was known mainly from specimens collected in the 1920s, until six bats were observed during a 1995 survey (and apparently no sign of this bat was found during fieldwork on Choiseul in 1992 or on Buka in 1997); the montane monkey-faced bat (*P. pulchra*) is known from only a single specimen collected on Mt. Makarakomburu on Guadalcanal; and the Guadalcanal monkey-faced bat (*P. atrata*) was last recorded in 1991, although there has been limited survey work in its likely range. Besides the flying foxes, the Admiralty cuscus (*Spilocuscus kraemeri*) is the only endemic cuscus in the hotspot, being confined to the Admiralty Islands; this beautifully patterned brown, black, and white species is a popular game animal on Manus.

Other flagship species in the East Melanesian Islands Hotspot include the Solomons prehensile-tailed skink (*Corucia zebrata*), a very large, arboreal skink that feeds primarily on the leaves of epiphytes (McCoy 1980), and the two birdwing butterflies, *Ornithoptera allotae* and *O. victoriae*. The latter two species are large, prominent, and spectacular, and depend upon specialized food plants for their reproduction. In addition, the marvelous green tree snail of Manus Island, *Papustyla pulcherrima*, is another good flagship. It is collected and widely appreciated throughout the region and globally.

Threats

Until the 1970s, the region supported relatively intact lowland forests in abundance. The clearance and degradation of these over the past three decades is a prime reason why the region is now being classified as a hotspot. Today, less than 25% of the region's lowland forests remain as "old growth," primarily in the least accessible areas, especially in places where local communities have resisted the siren's song of the foreign logging companies. Upland humid forests remain in better condition, but with population growth even these are being reduced, primarily by clearance for subsistence gardens.

Given the insular environment and absence of large expanses of contiguous habitat, oceanic island biodiversity is vulnerable to threats in many ways. The islands of the East Melanesian Islands Hotspot have remained pristine longer than more accessible island groups, but over the last decade virtually all of the negative impacts that we know for those other island groups have come to the region. Industrial-scale logging, conversion of forest for monoculture plantations, exotic invasive species, and clearance of habitat by expanding human populations have all taken their toll on this region. In addition, it is common for village inhabitants to engage in habitual burning of vegetation. These burning practices cause gradual erosion of the forest frontier and lead to soil erosion, which consequently intensifies sedimentation in streambeds.

By comparing remote sensing analyses with a finer resolution analysis of logging concessions and oil palm plantations on New Britain and New Ireland, we calculate that the percentage of remaining habitat for the entire East Melanesian Islands is around 39%. We believe this figure is perhaps a generous estimate, though probably close to 2003 conditions, and further it is likely that it includes a considerable amount of secondary forest. In light of this, and given the rapid rate of deforestation in this region, we feel that a reasonable estimate of the extent of remaining primary habitat in the region is around 30%.

The Bismarck Islands have been most heavily impacted by extensive logging of lowland and hill forests and also subsequent clearance of forests for copra and oil palm monocultures near the coast. The plantation impacts are mainly confined to New Britain, whereas logging has taken place widely in the hotspot, wherever there is accessible forest. By contrast, the Admiralties have been most affected by rural agricultural expansion, though logging has had an impact as well.

The Solomon Islands are much like the Bismarcks, but even more vulnerable because of the smaller size of the islands. Logging has had a devastating effect on lowland forests, and copra plantations are also wide-

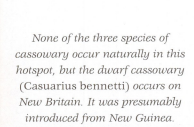

None of the three species of cassowary occur naturally in this hotspot, but the dwarf cassowary (Casuarius bennetti) occurs on New Britain. It was presumably introduced from New Guinea.
© **Patricio Robles Gil**/*Sierra Madre*

On the opposite page, the coconut crab (Birgus latro), the largest terrestrial invertebrate, is widespread in the Pacific, its distribution coinciding with that of coconut palms. It is thought that the post-larval stage of these crabs rafted from island to island on coconuts.
© **Patricio Robles Gil**/*Sierra Madre*

spread. Forest conversion is expected to be particularly important on Makira and New Georgia, and perhaps elsewhere in the Solomons. The extent of impact of exotic invasive species, especially pigs, cats, rats, and little red fire ants, is serious, but poorly studied. Flannery (1995) noted the apparent extirpation of several species of giant rodents from Guadalcanal, apparently caused by cat predation. It is unknown what sort of impact invasives have had in the Bismarcks, but it has probably been serious there as well. An expedition to New Ireland in 1992 found invasives (cane toads and feral cats) in old-growth forest. The invasive fire ant *Wasmannia* sp. invaded the Solomon Islands in the 1980s and has reached plague levels on many islands today. It has most recently arrived in Vanuatu. In the Solomons, the area under cultivation doubled between 1972 and 1992 (Thistlethwait and Votaw 1992).

The situation in Vanuatu is similar. About 35% of the land of Vanuatu supports some sort of forest cover and logging remains an important economic activity, mainly on Espiritu Santo. Additionally, clearance for plantations and subsistence agriculture is removing the last remnant lowland forests of the nation. Grave pressures on Vanuatu's natural resources are undoubtedly being exacerbated by human population growth. Introduced species, uncontrolled habitual burning of the island's native vegetation, and deteriorating social structures are other threats to biodiversity.

In all of the larger islands of the East Melanesian Islands Hotspot, the rugged highland forests are largely still intact and in good condition, but it remains unclear whether the original native faunas of these montane forests are comparably intact, especially given the threat from invasive species such as pigs, cats, and rats. Mining is a minor threat on the terrestrial side, quite localized to catchment areas where a particular mine is operating (as in Bougainville and Lihir), but offshore impacts from tailing runoff are a major concern.

Another broad-scale and diffuse threat is poor governance and government instability. This leads to inadequate management of resources, poor deals (and poorly managed deals) with international resource development companies (mining and logging in particular), and social and cultural disruption. The Solomon Islands have been the most heavily affected, suffering a constitutional crisis in 2000. Governance troubles that plague Papua New Guinea also impact the Bismarck Islands. A nearly decade-long war on Bougainville was tied to poor management of the large Panguna Copper Mine —especially the Bougainvillean people's perception that they were inflicted with the ill effects of the mine, while reaping too few of the profits. The implications of this little-known war will be felt in Bougainville for decades, and its long-term negative impact on Bougainville's environment should not be underestimated. With poor governance there is a typical tendency to overexploit resources as a quick solution to budgetary shortfalls, which compromises the health and stability of forests, fisheries, and watersheds.

Conservation

There is little formal protection of land and sea resources in the East Melanesian Islands Hotspot, mainly because the three island nations respect local customary tenure and have had minimal alienation of land or coastal marine territory for creation of government-managed parks and protected areas.

Overall, protected areas coverage in the hotspot is poor. According to the World Database on Protected Areas, there are 24 protected areas covering some 6% of the hotspot, none of which are classified in IUCN categories I to IV, and only eight are included in categories V and VI (these eight protected areas cover only 1% of the hotspot).

What national parks are in place tend to be leftovers from colonial times. The Queen Elizabeth II National Park near the capital Honiara in Solomon Islands, the nation's only National Park, has been completely degraded in the 50 years since it was established in 1954 from primary forest to secondary forest and grassland. In Vanuatu, many natural areas are protected under custom law, but these are rarely of sufficient size for species and habitat protection.

The fundamental constraint on any conservation initiative in the hotspot, particularly one involving the establishment of protected areas, is the customary land tenure system. Unlike the neighboring Melanesian nation of Fiji, where customary title is formally codified, the nations of the East Melanesian Islands Hotspot recognize customary tenure in broad terms, and it is generally left up to a system of land dispute hearings to settle conflicting claims to ownership or usage rights over land. The first basic step in undertaking any conservation initiative, be it protected-area establishment or species-specific actions, is in knowing at that point in time who or where the land-owning community is.

The Human Poverty Index for the islands in this hotspot is the lowest in the Pacific region, and among the lowest in the world (UNDP 1999). Given the lack of clearly defined legal title over land and widespread rural poverty, community-managed protection associated with community development activities is the most common strategy followed for establishing conservation areas, but the results are mixed and highly dependent on the standard of village-level engagement and the level of community cohesiveness and collective decision-making capacity. Sustainable incentives and locally meaningful motivations for rural Melanesian

On the opposite page, collection of the eggs of the Melanesian scrubfowl (Megapodius eremita), a megapode endemic to the island of New Britain. These amazing birds lay enormous eggs in volcanic soils, and the eggs are regularly harvested by local people.
© **Patricio Robles Gil**/*Sierra Madre*

Above, man from Rabaul with newborn chick of the dusky scrubfowl (Megapodius freycinet).
© **Patricio Robles Gil**/*Sierra Madre*

communities to accept a conservation regime over their communally owned resources are necessary, as is objective selection of project sites based on national and global conservation value.

International and local NGOs have been, and continue to be, major players in conservation in the East Melanesian Islands Hotspot, either in formal or informal partnerships with the respective government's conservation offices. The regional conservation and environmental body, SPREP (South Pacific Regional Environment Programme) is a multi-governmental organization which works closely with member governments, including the nations of the East Melanesian Islands Hotspot.

Conservation International and a number of partner institutions have been active in parts of the region for over a decade. CI fieldwork was initiated in partnership with the East New Britain Social Action Committee (ENBSEK) in 1993, focusing on coastal communities in the Wide Bay region of East New Britain, and has resulted in the designation of the Klampun Wildlife Management Area (WMA) in 2003, with the neighboring Tiemtop WMA due for designation in 2004. CI has also been working in the Bauro Highlands of Makira in the Solomons since 1994, in partnership with the Maruia Trust of New Zealand and the Solomon Islands Development Trust (and most recently the Makira Community Conservation Foundation), with a goal to establish a formally recognized conservation area in the Bauro Highlands (60 000 ha).

The Nature Conservancy (TNC) has been active in the Kimbe region of New Britain since 1994 developing a network of locally managed marine protected areas, promoting sustainable development, and encouraging community-based conservation and resource management. In 1996, a cooperative venture between TNC, the European Union, and Walindi Plantation Resort culminated in the establishment of the Mahonia Na Dari Research and Conservation Center —a locally managed non-governmental organization—, which has focused primarily on marine environmental education and awareness related to logging and fishing practices, oil palm plantation development, and human population growth.

Since 1996, the Worldwide Fund for Nature (WWF), in partnership with the Tetepare Descendants' Association, has been developing the Tetepare Island Community Resource Conservation and Development project in Western Province, Solomon Islands. This initiative is located on the largest uninhabited island in the South Pacific, touted for its natural inheritance and archaeological values.

Finally, SPREP has developed a community-based conservation project in Koromandi, on Guadalcanal in the Solomon Islands and at Vatthe on Espiritu Santo, Vanuatu. The Koromandi project has led to the creation of a local conservation area of lowland and montane rainforest, while the Vatthe project has focused on conservation of the largest tract of remaining lowland rainforest on Espiritu Santo by means of a community-based project (Read 2002). Unfortunately, the project was terminated in 2000 due to unrest and ethnic tension in the region.

In general, there is very little large-scale conservation action currently under way in the hotspot, and the region is in urgent need of increased attention and investment from the conservation community.

The habitat protection initiatives to date have just begun to wrestle with the difficulties of conservation on uncodified customary land in the Melanesian cultural and social context. There is still no area that could be called a secure protected area. The greatest successes have come where relationships are built between communities and conservation agencies over time and collaboration is mutually beneficial. Without conservation agencies valuing community needs and aspirations, or the land-owning communities valuing their biodiversity heritage, such collaboration is not possible. The future of the East Melanesian Island Hotspot's biodiversity lies in developing these successful partnerships.

BRUCE M. BEEHLER [1]
ROGER JAMES [30]
TODD STEVENSON [1]
GUY DUTSON [31]
FRANÇOIS MARTEL [32]

Young girl from Yakel village, Tanna Island, Vanuatu.
© **Patricio Robles Gil**/*Sierra Madre*

On the opposite page, wood harvest on Espíritu Santo Island, Vanuatu. This small country, part of the East Melanesian Islands Hotspot, is one of the culturally richest corners of our planet, with some 109 languages still spoken.
© **Patricio Robles Gil**/*Sierra Madre*

TAIWAN

Taiwan is situated at the western edge of the Asian continental shelf. It lies south of Japan via the Ryukyu Island chain, and is separated from the Asian mainland by a narrow strait (130 km at the narrowest point). The Tropic of Cancer cuts across the middle of Taiwan, and the warm Kuroshiwa Current passes along its eastern shore. As defined here, Taiwan includes 72 small islands, most of them with limited forest cover, except for Turtle Island (2.85 km²) and Lanyu Island (45 km²), which have substantial remaining tracts of natural forest, and has a total land area of 36 210 km². Although Taiwan, happily, has not lost so much of its natural habitat to meet the threshold for consideration as a hotspot, and also does not quite meet the hotspots threshold for plant endemism, detailed assessment of the island was necessary to demonstrate this. This chapter is, therefore, included here for the sake of documentation, and to make sure that this important island is incorporated into global conservation strategy.

Mountains and geographical location have combined to make Taiwan a beautiful place, giving rise to the well-known sixteenth-century Portuguese name, Ilha Formosa. More than two-thirds of Taiwan's surface is mountainous, with over 200 mountain peaks above 3 000 m in elevation, and the highest, Mt. Yushan or Jade Mountain, reaching 3 952 m. Taiwan is longer than it is wide, running 377 km north to south, and 142 km west to east. The eastern side of the island has steep slopes, narrow valleys, and small plains, while the western side has gentler slopes and broader plains.

Taiwan was formed around 4 million years ago, when a small piece of the Eurasian Plate was subducted under the Philippines Plate, resulting in the dramatic uplift of Luzon and Taiwan (Teng 1990). Indeed, the Taiwan Strait is only 60 m at its shallowest part at the current sea level (Yue-Gau Chen, pers. comm.), and when sea level was 60 m below its present level, it was connected with Fukien Province of mainland China. A landbridge has existed at four different stages over the course of the last 240 000 years (Chappell and Shackleton 1986), which has enabled faunal exchange to take place. However, the rising of the sea level at the end of the glacial periods rapidly reestablished the isolation of Taiwan from the mainland (Ferguson 1993).

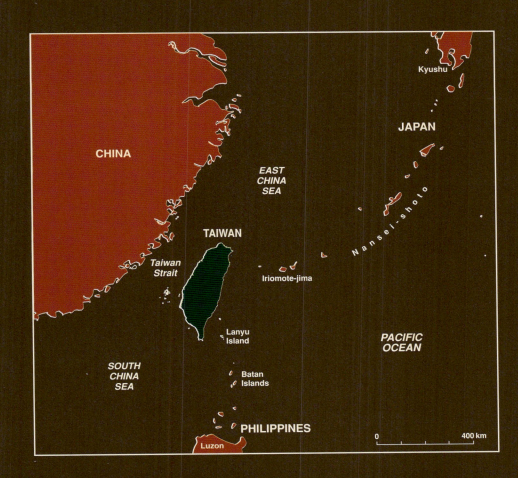

The climate on the main island Taiwan is subtropical in the north and tropical in the south. Mean monthly temperature ranges from 34.1°C in July for Taipei to –5°C in January on the highest mountain. The distribution of rainfall on Taiwan is uneven; mean annual rainfall over the last 30 years has varied between 951 mm and 4 892 mm. In winter, northeastern winds bring persistent drizzle to northern and eastern Taiwan. Typhoons that come mostly in July to September usually cause abundant rainfall in eastern and southeastern Taiwan. Weather fronts that stall above Taiwan every May and June bring light rain interspersed with heavy downpours to northern Taiwan. Due to the topography, annual rainfall on Taiwan is higher in the north, the east, and in the mountains than on the southwestern plains. Because rivers on Taiwan are short and steep, the storage capacity of all watersheds is limited. Rivers typically swell up soon after heavy rain, but are then reduced to a narrow, shallow flow in a few days. Rainstorms and frequent earthquakes exert strong impact on the steep and unstable mountain slopes. Small-scale natural landslides are common.

On the opposite page, Dabajiashan Mountain. Nearly 70% of Taiwan is mountainous, with more than 200 mountain peaks above 3 000 m in elevation.
© Jen-Shiu Hsu

361

Typhoons often cause blow-downs, create gaps within forests, and influence the height of forests.

There are five life zones on the island: tropical rainforest in southern Taiwan and Lanyu, evergreen broad-leaved forest, mixed forest, coniferous forest, and alpine grassland. The richest and least disturbed lowland evergreen broad-leaved forests are found in Hengchun Peninsula at the southern tip of Taiwan, and on Lanyu. Roughly 52.9% of the 820 species from Lanyu and 42.3% of the 912 species from Hengchun Peninsula have tropical affinities, while eastern Asian elements are relatively poorly represented. Hengchun Peninsula (280 km² in area) supports 49 endemic species, whereas 36 species are confined to Lanyu. In the global floristic system, these forests belong to the Philippinean Province of the Paleotropical Kingdom (Takhtajan 1986; Hsieh 2002), but are included here with the rest of Taiwan for geographic proximity and political convenience.

Less than 2% of the population on Taiwan can be considered indigenous people; the rest are Han Chinese who immigrated to Taiwan within the last four hundred years. Taiwan's indigenous people belong to 10 tribes, nine of which traditionally resided on Taiwan, while the Yami tribe lived on Lanyu. Each of these tribes has its own language and culture. The tribes on Taiwan have a hunting and slash-and-burn agricultural tradition, and their folklores contain rich stories of wildlife, hunting, and harvest. The Yami tradition is tied to fish, sheep, and yam and taro roots. All the indigenous people are now heavily influenced by Chinese culture, after several hundred years of contact, interracial marriages, and Chinese education. The lowland plain (Pingpu) tribes have been entirely assimilated into Chinese society. Excellent hunters with traditional knowledge of wildlife and nature were still common among Taiwan's tribes 30 years ago, but modernization and economic incentives have further diluted these traditional cultures. Only the Yami people still commonly practice their traditional knowledge of the sea, although there is a widespread movement for all the indigenous peoples to re-identify with their own traditions.

Biodiversity

Taiwan has high levels of endemism in both plants and animals. About 26% of vascular plants, 25% of mammals, 10% of resident birds, 25% of non-marine reptiles, and 33% of amphibians are endemic. In addition, a number of Taiwan's plants, amphibians, and freshwater fishes are relict species, meaning that Taiwan has served as a refugium for ancestors of these species during glacial periods. Upon the retreat of the ice sheets, the distribution of their relatives shifted north or up into the Himalayan Mountains, leaving them isolated on Taiwan. These populations survived in the mountains of Taiwan, and eventually diverged from their ancestors, becoming unique endemic species.

Taiwan has 4 101 species of native vascular plants belonging to 1 331 genera and 232 families. Around 1 071 species are known only from Taiwan, and for this reason it has been considered a Center of Plant Diversity (Davis et al. 1995). Two plant genera are endemic (*Sinopanax* and *Kudoacanthus*), and endemic species exist in 57.5% of the families. The ferns (at least 645 species) and orchids (337 species) are especially species-rich.

Plant diversity is higher in the more heavily impacted lowlands (below 500 m in elevation) than at upper elevations, although the proportion of endemism increases with elevation: 17.4% in the lowlands to 59.9% above 3 000 m. Evergreen broad-leaved forests between 500 and 1 500 m, which for the most part are subject to frequent human disturbance, contain at least 1 688 species of plants, including 419 species endemic to Taiwan. Between 1 500 and 2 500 m, there is mixed forest in which broad-leaved trees gradually give way to conifers. These forests boast an abundance of mosses, epiphytes, lichens, and tree climbers. Conspicuous emergent conifers tower above the largely evergreen broad-leaved canopy. Of the 1 324 species of vascular plants in these forests, 34.6% are endemic. Coniferous forests occur above 2 500 m and are relatively well protected, with more than 80% still pristine; of the 539 species of vascular plants occurring in these forests, 277 are endemic to Taiwan. The other species are the typical boreal-alpine species of Eurasia, distributed discontinuously in the Arctic north and the alpine zone in the south. Alpine grassland appears above 3 500 m. The dominant species in this habitat is the dwarf bamboo (*Yushania niitakayamensis*), which is often less than one meter tall on exposed areas. This species has a broad elevation range (*ca*. 1 400-3 600 m), but attains maximum development along high mountain ridges and slopes. This habitat is an important center of endemism, with 124 endemic plant species.

Currently, 79 species of mammals in 53 genera are known to occur in Taiwan (Liang-kung Lin, pers. comm.). Although no family or genus is endemic to Taiwan, around 20 species are, including seven bats and one carnivore, the Taiwan weasel (*Mustela formosana*). In addition, the Formosan macaque (*Macaca cyclopis*, VU) is endemic, although it has since been introduced to Japan, where it hybridizes with the Japanese macaque (*M. fuscata*). Most endemic mammals can be seen in more than one life zone, with the exception of five species of bats (two restricted to evergreen broad-leaved forest, two in mixed forest, and one in coniferous forest), one rodent, Coxing's white-bellied rat (*Niviventer coxinga*) in the mixed forest, and the Taiwan vole (*Volemys kikuchii*, VU) in the evergreen broad-leaved forest. The mixed forest contains the highest number of endemic mammals (14 species), whereas the coniferous forest and the evergreen broad-leaved forest each support nine endemics. The alpine grassland has six endemic mammals, while the only one found in the lowlands is the

The Taiwan japalure (Japalura swinhonis) is a common lizard in Taiwan's low-elevation forests. This species begins hibernating in November.
© Jen-Shiu Hsu

On the opposite page, the Vulnerable Taiwan or Formosan macaque (Macaca cyclopis) is a gregarious and diurnal species, spending its time either in trees or on the ground.
© Jen-Shiu Hsu

The Endangered Asian yellow pond turtle (Mauremys mutica) *is widespread in southern China, Vietnam, Taiwan, Hainan, and parts of Japan's Ryukyu Islands. This Endangered species is thought to be in decline throughout much of its range, mainly as a result of habitat loss and collection for the food trade.*
© **Jen-Shiu Hsu**

Formosan or Taiwan macaque, which is distributed widely on Taiwan.

Taiwan's native avifauna is characterized by 147 resident species, 15 summer breeders, and five suspected or occasional summer breeders. Fifteen species are endemic and, as such, BirdLife International has designated the island of Taiwan as an Endemic Bird Area (Stattersfield et al. 1998). Most species are found widely within their preferred altitudinal ranges, although above the tree line (3 500 m) only five species are found. The evergreen broad-leaved forests and mixed forests are of crucial importance to the maintenance of avian biodiversity in Taiwan, with the former supporting 58 species, and some 50 species of birds inhabiting the mixed forests between 1 500 and 2 500 m. Besides being exceptionally important for endemic birds, Taiwan lies on the main flyway for birds migrating between Japan and the Philippines, and is, therefore, of great importance for migrants from Japan, mainland China, and areas further north. Hence, in addition to the species already noted, there are 169 non-breeding migrants, 105 vagrants, and five species with unclear status, making a total of 446 species of birds that have been recorded from Taiwan.

Taiwan's reptile fauna includes 33 lizards, 45 snakes, and five turtles, of which 20 species (13 lizards and seven snakes) are endemic. Most snakes and lizards are found below 1 500 m, with only seven species of snakes and three species of lizards above 2 000 m. As regards amphibians, Taiwan is also home to 30 species of frogs and three salamander species, of which 13 frog species and all three salamander species are confined entirely to Taiwan. The family Ranidae is represented by 13 species, and four species are endemic; in contrast, seven out of 10 species in the family Rhacophoridae are endemic. More than 80% of the frogs and toads have an upper distributional limit of 1 500 m, and only four species reach 2 500 m; a single species of frog and three species of salamander are found at 3 000 m or higher. All the endemic species are at least locally abundant.

In terms of other animals, Taiwan's freshwater fish fauna is characterized by 227 species in 150 genera, of which 37 species are endemic. The landlocked salmon (*Oncorhynchus masou*) in central Taiwan is another relict species and has the southernmost distribution of the world's salmon species. Taiwan is also very rich in invertebrates. Butterflies are represented by 384 species, of which 12.5% are endemic (Yu-feng Hsu, pers. comm.), and there are 275 species of land snails on Taiwan, of which about 70% are endemic (Wen-lung Wu, pers. comm.).

Flagship Species

Taiwan's two endemic cypress species (*Chamaecyparis* spp.) are very important flagship species. The seven species of cypress that form ancient forest types now grow only on the west and east coasts of North America and in the mountainous regions of Japan and Taiwan. The two Taiwanese species found between 1 800 and 2 400 m are the only ones in the subtropical region. On the best sites, they can reach 50 m in height and more than 5 m in diameter, and live 3 000 years or more. Logging between 1900 and 1980 greatly reduced the virgin stands of these forests. Currently, about 48 500 ha of these forests remain. Taiwan cypress trees often form mixed stands with other conifers and broad-leaved species.

Another important plant flagship is Taiwania (*Taiwania cryptomerioides*, VU), like *Metasequoia* and *Sequoiadendron*, one of the world's classic Tertiary relict gymnosperms. Recently, what is probably the world's largest population of Taiwania was discovered in southern Taiwan (Yang and Wang 2002). In an area of about 1 300 ha, at least 10 000 mature trees stand shoulder to shoulder, some of them measuring 60 to 70 m in height, with trunks more than four meters in diameter. The Taiwan beech (*Fagus hayatae*, VU) has a relict distribution in northern Taiwan and forms one of the rare deciduous forests in Taiwan. It is found in a nearly pure stand of at least 1 300 ha, located between 1 300 and 2 000 m along the northern ridge of Hsuehshan Range, with evergreen oak forest below and mixed coniferous forest above. Strong northeasterly winds in winter stunt these trees to less than five meters on the summit, although they grow to over 10 m on the adjacent leeward slopes.

The clouded leopard (*Neofelis nebulosa*, VU) used to be found in eastern and southern Taiwan in forests above 1 000 m, but the last confirmed sighting of this species was in 1983. Given its extremely secretive habits and the rugged topography of Taiwan, conservationists had hoped that some individuals might survive in deep forests. Unfortunately, recent intensive efforts aided by automatic infrared photography turned up no sign of this species and it probably no longer occurs on Taiwan. The Asiatic black bear (*Ursus thibetanus*, VU) is the largest mammal on Taiwan. It lives in the mountains between 1 500 and 3 500 m, foraging mostly on plant matter mixed with wasp nests and animal carcasses. The current population is estimated to be between 200 and 1 000 individuals.

The two endemic pheasants are also obvious flagship species. The Mikado pheasant (*Syrmaticus mikado*) was first discovered when two male tail feathers were found on an aboriginal headdress. These feathers were so unique as to form the basis of a description of a new species named in 1906. The plumage of the Mikado pheasant is elegant and understated, whereas Swinhoe's pheasant (*Lophura swinhoii*) is flashy in its color pattern. The Mikado pheasant lives in forests above 2 000 m on steep slopes, while Swinhoe's pheasant occurs in lowland forests up to 2 200 m on gentler slopes. They are both secretive, producing almost no vocalization, and are extremely wary of people. They only come into the open at dawn or dusk or when it is foggy or raining. Once the sun is out, they withdraw into the shade of deep forests.

The Taiwan flamecrest (*Regulus goodfellowi*) is another endemic bird that was characterized by W.R. Ogilvie-Grant in 1907 as being more colorful than others in its genus. In fact, this flamecrest is a relict species once classified as a subspecies of the European flamecrest (*R. ignicapillus*). Given that the genus has not yet been recorded between Asia Minor and Taiwan, it has been cited as an excellent example of disjunct species distribution in birds (Hachisuka and Udagawa 1951).

A few migratory bird species are also important flagships. Indeed, one such species, the black-faced spoonbill (*Platalea minor*, EN), is the best-known bird in Taiwan. The species is found only in eastern Asia, and totals a little more than 1 000 individuals. Two-thirds of the world population of this species winter in one concentrated flock at the Tsengwen Estuary in southern Taiwan. Since 1995, international and local conservation efforts have put this species in newspaper headlines numerous times. Hundreds of tourists go to watch them rest or bathe in shallow water each day during the time they are present on Taiwan. A conservation action plan was formulated for the black-faced spoonbill in 1995, to be updated in 2003 (Severinghaus et al. 1995).

The grey-faced buzzard eagle (*Butastur indicus*) is another important migratory species. This bird breeds in the temperate region and goes south to winter. The southern tip of Taiwan is a point of concentration for migratory raptors, and the peak of this species' southward migration often falls around October 10; consequently, the grey-faced buzzard eagle has been nicknamed the National Day bird. Each year during the National Day holiday, huge crowds arrive to observe the National Day bird as it gathers in flocks of thousands. Every time a flock is seen coming to roost at dusk or departing at dawn, it draws excitement from the enthusiastic crowd. Many people become bird watchers subsequent to such an experience.

Among the invertebrates, a beautiful birdwing butterfly (*Troides magellanus*) is an important flagship. Found only on Lanyu, it has been reduced by overtrapping for the butterfly trade. Its larvae feed on only one species of plant (*Aristolochia kankaoensis*), and grazing by cattle and other human activities have reduced the abundance of this key food plant. Now with cattle mostly removed from Lanyu, planting of *A. kankaoensis* seedlings and releasing captive-raised butterflies into the wild appear to have increased the butterfly population, but future monitoring is needed before success can be claimed.

Threats

Habitat loss is the greatest threat to biodiversity on Taiwan. Being a small island with a high population density (622 persons per km^2 in 2002; Population Reference Bureau 2003), Taiwan is under intense development pressure. Most of the natural habitat below 500 m has been converted to human use, and increasing development pressure and economic aspirations have already begun to alter habitat at higher elevations. Improper land-use practices have led to habitat loss upstream and habitat degradation downstream, and have accelerated water and soil erosion. Channelization of rivers or the construction of check dams as measures to control flooding has destroyed riparian habitat, and often substituted natural river conditions with cemented river banks or even stream beds which are foreign and hostile environments for aquatic organisms. Nevertheless, even under high population and development pressure, 59% of Taiwan is still forested, and 73% of the forests are natural forests (more than 35% are mature forests), suggesting that some 43% of Taiwan's original forests remain intact. However, much of the remaining intact vegetation is at higher altitudes and, in fact, less than 1% of the original lowland vegetation is estimated to remain on Taiwan (Editorial Committee of the Flora of Taiwan 1993-2002).

There was a long history of traditional hunting, trapping, logging, and collecting of forest products on Taiwan, but the government began regulating the harvesting of wildlife in the late 1970s. Although illegal hunting still occurs, public education efforts have reduced the general demand for wildlife. Logging of primary forest and other ecologically important forests was stopped in 1991. However, certain plants continue to be harvested without sufficient control, especially those that are rare, have showy flowers or foliage, or have supposed medicinal qualities.

Invasive species are an issue in Taiwan, with several having entered through the pet trade, for agricultural purposes, for private collections or by accident. Not enough data exists about Taiwan's natural conditions prior to the arrival of most of these species, or about their point of entry and subsequent expansion, and in most cases they were not noticed until ecological or commercial damage was already serious. Examples include the freshwater apple snail (*Pomacea canaliculata*), armored catfish (*Hypostomus* spp.), bullfrog (*Rana catesbeiana*), red-eared slider turtle (*Trachemys scripta*), a crawling plant (*Mikania micrantha*), and water hyacinth (*Eichhornia crassipes*). Among the few well-documented examples of the impact of an invasive are hybridizations between the endemic Taiwan bulbul (*Pycnonotus taivanus*, VU) and the Chinese bulbuls (*P. sinensis*) or between the Taiwan hwamei (*Garrulax canorus taewanus*) and the Chinese hwamei (*G. c. canorus*), both of which are reducing the genetic distinctiveness of the Taiwan endemics such that genetically pure populations remain in only a few isolated parts of their former range (Severinghaus and Chi 1999; BirdLife International 2003; Liu 2003).

The Nantou flying frog (Rhacophorus moltrechti) is a widely distributed and common species occurring in hilly areas below 2 500 m. It lives in forests, orchards, and tea plantations, and breeds in still-water habitats such as ponds, pools, cisterns, and blocked roadside ditches.
© **Jen-Shiu Hsu**

365

Conservation

Many laws provide the legal basis for nature and biodiversity protection in Taiwan. The Cultural Property Protection Act covers natural heritage such as important endemic species or special landscapes (1982). The National Park Law (1983), the Wildlife Conservation Act (1989), the Forestry Law (1985), and other laws together regulate land use, human behavior, and the use of biodiversity. In 1994, Taiwan passed the Environmental Impact Assessment Act, which requires major development projects to carry out environmental impact evaluations before development permits are granted.

About 15% of Taiwan has some level of protection, a figure that drops just slightly when one considers only protected areas classed in IUCN categories I to IV. Taiwan's protected areas include five national parks, 15 nature preserves, 19 wildlife refuges, 29 important wildlife habitats, and nine national forest protected areas. These areas are set aside to protect relatively large tracts of natural habitat and the wildlife within them or to preserve special landscapes. Nevertheless, an increased level of protection is required for the lower-altitude forests.

Nature education programs are numerous in the cities. These are either sponsored by government agencies, schools or other institutions, or organized by environmental NGOs with funding from government agencies or the private sector. Researchers are often invited to give public lectures to introduce their new findings. Media exposure helps to draw public attention to charismatic species or special habitats such as mangroves with viviparous plants (*Kandelia obovata*). The story of the landlocked salmon has been included in high school textbooks. Satellite tracking of the green sea turtle (*Chelonia mydas*, EN), which comes on shore to lay eggs, has greatly increased its prominence with the general public. News of the recovery of migratory Taiwan butterflies (*Parantica sita niphonica*) in Japan catapulted the already popular sport of butterfly watching into organized public monitoring activities. With the exception of the highly popular bird-watching and butterfly-watching activities, most existing education programs focus on flagship species. Future education needs to increase people's understanding of ecological functioning and the significance of all species, including the large number of non-charismatic ones.

Biodiversity inventories have been established by government agencies and academic institutions. The usefulness and quality of these inventories can only be strengthened with continued monitoring of species distribution, population sizes, and ecological interactions, as well as an increased understanding of their genetic diversity. The critical nature of this task is reflected by the fact that a large proportion of Taiwan's terrestrial vertebrates have never been studied and their natural history remains largely unknown. Government agencies have implemented various conservation actions, including artificial propagation of the landlocked salmon and the birdwing butterfly. After 20 years, salmon restoration work remains far from complete. Inappropriate land use along streams has proven very difficult to change. More research is needed to identify the exact water and river conditions required by the species.

Many communities have organized and implemented biodiversity conservation programs for their own areas, including issuing community-based fishing permits to earn income, patrolling streams to prevent overfishing, and establishing fishing bans to allow stocks to recover. These programs have proven highly successful for a number of streams. However, although the benefits of such actions are enormous, the question of whether or not privatization of biodiversity resources is consistent with social justice, and to what extent natural resources (e.g., water in the river) should be privatized, requires further analysis.

Finally, given that a large amount of habitat on Taiwan was damaged in the past, it is now important to look into restoration, to carry out research to bring back critical areas, and to develop plans to return degraded areas to ecologically healthy conditions.

LUCIA LIU SEVERINGHAUS [62]
CHANG-FU HSIEH [63]

The retiring Swinhoe's pheasant (Lophura swinhoii) is confined to the mountains of central Taiwan. Hunting pressure is no longer serious, and this species is now considered only Near Threatened.
© **Rod Williams**/naturepl.com

On the opposite page, the Formosan sambar (Cervus unicolor swinhoei) is the largest native herbivore in Taiwan and is an endemic subspecies to Taiwan that is usually found in virgin forests at elevations of 300-1 500 m.
© **Sz-Yi Liu**

366

QUEENSLAND WET TROPICS

At the base of Cape York Peninsula in northeastern Australia, guarded by the coral ramparts of the Great Barrier Reef, is an outpost of equatorial splendor in an otherwise vast, brown land. As its name implies, the Queensland Wet Tropics is located in the State of Queensland, abutting the coastline for over 400 km, between south latitudes 15°40' and 19°15', and varying in width from 20 to 80 km. This region of extraordinary diversity also includes a number of mountainous offshore islands, the largest of which is Hinchinbrook Island (399 km^2). Altogether, the rainforests and associated forests and woodlands of the Queensland Wet Tropics form an assemblage of ecological communities spanning 18 487 km^2.

Today, the rainforests of Australia represent almost an alien presence in a land dominated by eucalypts and acacias. Occupying less than 0.2% of the land area of the continent, and about 1% of Queensland, rainforests are indeed a rarity, but this was not always the case. When flowering plants first appeared on Earth, Australia was part of the supercontinent of Gondwana. At the final breakup of this continent, about 50 million years ago, Australia took with it a significant component of the original flora of Gondwana. However, despite the fact that broadleaf rainforest originally covered much of the continent, from that time until the present —with many short-term fluctuations—, Australia has become increasingly drier and today is a largely arid continent.

Out of the ancestral Gondwanan stock arose sclerophyllous (thick-leaved) plants adapted to drier climates, increasingly impoverished soils, and a landscape in which fire became a prominent evolutionary force. It is believed by some that these plants arose from rainforest progenitors under selection pressure from harsh new environments. It is more likely, however, that sclerophyllous and rainforest species co-existed from the earliest days of angiosperm history, their proportions being modified as the environment changed (White 1986). As the Australian Continent drifted northwards into warmer latitudes, compensating for a general global cooling, the tropical flora of Gondwana was preserved in Australia to a greater extent than anywhere else. Its long isolation as the island continent finally ended about 15 million years ago, when the Australian continental plate

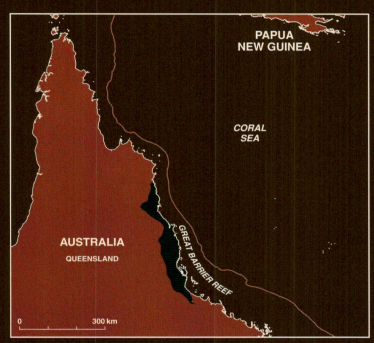

collided with that of Asia, and some interchange of flora and fauna that had been evolving separately for over 80 million years occurred.

Today, the Queensland Wet Tropics retains a unique record of these major events. Within its deep gorges and on its mountain tops survives an unparalleled collection of flowering plants with primitive characters unchanged since the beginnings of angiosperm evolution. As a result of this unique geological and climatic history, combined with a present-day environment of great physical diversity, the Queensland Wet Tropics harbors a vastly disproportionate share of the biodiversity of Australia, which itself is recognized as a megadiversity country (Mittermeier et al. 1997).

The Queensland Wet Tropics, as defined here, conforms to the Wet Tropics Bioregion (Goosem et al. 1999) and is part of a larger area identified by WWF as the Queensland Tropical Forests Ecoregion, which extends south of the Wet Tropics to incorporate the Central Queensland rainforests. However, the Central Queensland rainforests are separated by a gap of 200 km from the Wet Tropics and enjoy a significantly drier climate (a maximum of 2 000 mm per annum against a maximum of 4 000 mm per annum in the Wet Tropics). Accordingly, we have not included the Central Queensland rainforests in the Wet Tropics for the purposes of this analysis.

The features that set the Wet Tropics apart as a unique region in the Australian context are related to its physiography and high rainfall, and also its

On the opposite page, fan palm (Licuala ramsayi) from Tam O'Shanter State Forest. This beautiful palm occurs along river banks and swamps of the northeast Queensland rainforest.
© Patricio Robles Gil/Sierra Madre

situation well within tropical climes. The physiography of the area is dominated by a north-south spine of high mountains cut by eight major water courses which have incised gorges or deep valleys. From north to south these include the rivers of Daintree, Mossman, Barron, Mulgrave, Russell, Johnstone, Tully, and Herbert. While other parts of eastern tropical Australia have a rainfall high enough to support well-developed rainforest, the potential of mountains to strip moisture from the onshore stream by orographic uplift reaches its maximum in the Wet Tropics. This process is one of the four rain-generating mechanisms that influence tropical regions, including convergence, convection, and cyclonic phenomena, and which here function synergistically as they do in few, if any other rainforested regions of the world. Its rainfall regime, therefore, can not be directly compared to any of them, occupying the extreme wet end of the spectrum (Bonell et al. 1991). Unlike that of equatorial regions, however, it is strongly seasonal, with a marked concentration of rainfall in the summer months, over 60% of annual rainfall falling between December and March. The region is noted for reporting some of the world's most intense rainfall events, as well as the heaviest individual events. Rainfalls of up to 1 140 mm in a 24-hour period have been reported.

The Wet Tropics Bioregion was originally defined "as the limits of rainforest in the wet tropics, the western boundary approximating the 1 500 mm rainfall isohyet" (Stanton and Morgan 1976). In spite of the emphasis on rainforest in the definition, only 8 816 km^2 of its 18 487 km^2 is actual rainforest (Wilson et al. 2002) and it is estimated that the total area of rainforest never exceeded 10 885 km^2. The relationship between the rainforest and the vegetation communities surrounding it is a dramatic one. Rainforest expands under suitable climatic and soil conditions into adjacent communities if its scattered invaders can consolidate to change the microclimate and ground cover before they are destroyed by fire. In the presence of regular fire its boundaries are sharp, and there are few more striking contrasts in the Australian environment than the change along a straight-line boundary from eucalypt forest to rainforest.

Apart from the frequency of fire, limits to the expansion of rainforest within the bioregion are largely set by the depth and drainage of the soil, as well as exposure on steep slopes. The biodiversity of the region resides in its complex interweaving of habitats as diverse as rainforest, sclerophyll shrubland, sclerophyll woodland, tall sclerophyll forest, and melaleuca-dominated woodlands and swamp forests. Indeed, and particularly on the coastal plain, where vegetation type is determined by small changes in soil depth down to a permanent water table, the long-term survival of a wide range of communities is dependent on preservation of the landscape and vegetation complexes in which they occur.

A traveler on the highway north from the dry tropics city of Townsville may see the southern margins of the

Wet Tropics as a line of mountains to the west of the road, their flanks covered by eucalypt woodland, with pockets of rainforest in "fire shadows" created by rocky valleys. However, it is easy to overlook the low woodlands of melaleuca and eucalyptus that stand at the portals of one of the most biologically rich and scenically splendid parts of the continent.

Past this point, one enters the wide valley of the Herbert River. The ranges now sweep inland to a far-distant blue scarp rimming the floodplain. Woodlands that once filled the valley have been replaced by an endless sea of sugarcane. Gone, too, are most of the picturesque grassy woodlands, lily-covered lagoons and swamps, and riverine rainforest which, 120 years ago, graced this widest and most complex floodplain of all the region's rivers. Beyond the floodplain, the glory of the river remains, however, as it cuts a wide gorge through the region. Tributary streams that have cut their headwater course from the Herbert River now provide, at their knick points, some of the highest waterfalls in Australia.

The Herbert River works a 10-km-wide gap in the north-south distribution of continuous rainforest within the Wet Tropics. North of the river, rainforest continues unbroken to the northern end of the region, although shrinking to a tenuous, narrow band just north of the city of Cairns. South of the river, rainforest is confined to two distinct blocks separated by a gap of 30 km in which it retains only a foothold as scattered patches on steep slopes and in deep valleys protected from fire.

Between the Herbert River and the Tully River, the next major river as one heads north, is the largest surviving remnant of the sclerophyll communities of the coastal sand plain. It is a complex mix of paperbark (*Melaleuca* spp.) swamp forests and woodlands, eucalypt forests on dunes, and patches of rainforest dominated by the fan palm *Licuala ramsayi*. As one approaches the ancestral and current floodplain of the Tully River, rainfall doubles within a few kilometers and the "super-wet" belt, with annual average rainfalls of 4 000 mm or more, is reached. This "super-wet" belt continues to within 30 km of the city of Cairns, coinciding with an extremely sharp drop in annual rainfall. Until the 1960s, when massive clearing for a pastoral development scheme took place, the plains on either side of the lower Tully River supported a complex vegetation mosaic of grassland, sedge swamps, swamp forests of melaleuca and palm, and eucalypt forests and woodlands. These are now almost entirely gone and survive, elsewhere on the coastal plain, largely as dismembered fragments of the original mosaic.

The most complex and best-developed rainforests clothe the deeper soils of the coastal plain footslopes from the Tully River to the Mulgrave River and occupy basalt slopes and plateaus in a wide transect of the region following the catchment of the Johnstone River. More than half of these forests on basalts have been cleared, and the largest part of what remains has been selectively logged. However, an outstanding example of

The tooth-billed catbird (Ailuroedus dentirostris) *is endemic to higher-elevation rainforest of the Atherton region in northeast Queensland.*
© **Patricio Robles Gil**/*Sierra Madre*

On the opposite page, the southern cassowary (Casuarius casuarius) *is a Vulnerable species which is being severely impacted by development in Australia, and often suffers from road fatalities.*
© **Patricio Robles Gil**/*Sierra Madre*

virgin complex mesophyll vine forest survives in the valley of the Russell River, while the rarest type of rainforest on basalt survives only as small, scattered remnants on the western side of Atherton Tablelands. Some of the most extensive remaining tall wet sclerophyll forests in the Wet Tropics, dominated by *Eucalyptus grandis* and *E. resinifera*, cover the slopes of the Great Dividing Range west of Atherton, and to the northeast of it in the Tinaroo Range.

To the east of Cairns, there are communities developed on wind-formed dunes that are unique to the Wet Tropics. These are covered with closed sclerophyll shrublands in which the myrtaceous plant *Thryptomene oligandra* is a common canopy species. In depressions amongst the dunes, extensive open sedge and melaleuca-dominated swamp communities are formed. The insectivorous pitcher plant (*Nepenthes mirabilis*) is common in some of these swamps, which along with Wyvuri Swamp and adjacent areas to the south, are the only localities within the region from which it is known.

To the north of Cairns, rainforest shrinks to a narrow band at the Black Mountain corridor before expanding northwards into the great wilderness of the mountains of the Mossman and Daintree river catchments. The headwaters of the Daintree River are lightly impacted by human activity. North of the river, Thornton Peak (1 374 m) dominates the scenery and forms, with the headwaters of the Bloomfield River, another area of rugged wilderness almost entirely dominated by rainforest. This northern wilderness outpost of the Wet Tropics provides refuge for many habitat types that elsewhere have been drastically impacted by humans. These include complex mesophyll vine forests and tall wet sclerophyll forests in the headwaters of the Daintree River. This is the only area left where mosaics of intact lowland forest habitats still have direct connection with communities of the high mountain peaks.

The area between Cooktown and Cardwell contains the only existing Australian Aboriginal rainforest culture. The oral prehistory of the surviving Aboriginal rainforest culture is the oldest known for any indigenous people without a written language (Bottoms 2000). Aboriginal occupation of the Wet Tropics of Queensland is thought to date back at least 40 000 years (Sluiter and Kershaw 1982), and the tribes of the area are considered to be among the oldest rainforest cultures in the world (Dasett 1987). Rainforest culture differs markedly from that of most other Australian Aboriginal tribes, with a heavy dependence on arboreal skills, everyday use of toxic plants, and unique weapons (Horsfall 1984).

Biodiversity

The Queensland Wet Tropics contains 3 181 vascular plant species in 224 families representing approximately 18% of Australia's vascular flora. Of this total, 576 species and 44 genera are endemic. There are also two endemic plant families (Austrobaileyaceae and Idio-

spermaceae), the former containing species with pollen features consistent with primitive flowering plants; both plant families are represented by single species, *Austrobaileya scandens* and *Idiospermum australe*. Of a total of 19 of these primitive rainforest angiosperm families in the world, 13 are found in the Wet Tropics.

Vertebrate diversity and endemism are also very high, with 107 mammal species found in the Wet Tropics, including 11 endemic species and two monotypic endemic genera, the musky rat-kangaroo (*Hypsiprymnodon moschatus*) and the lemuroid possum (*Hemibelideus lemuroides*). The mammal endemics include four ringtail possums, confined to altitudes above 300 m, along with a native rodent, the Thornton Peak melomys (*Melomys hadrourus*). Two endemic tree-kangaroo species, Bennett's (*Dendrolagus bennettianus*) and Lumholtz's (*D. lumholtzi*), are found at all altitudes, although the latter is rarely encountered in the lowlands. Several mammal species that extend into New Guinea reach their southern limits in the Wet Tropics, including the attractive striped possum (*Dactylopsila trivirgata*) and long-tailed pygmy possum (*Cercartetus caudatus*). At the same time, other species reach their northern limit in the Wet Tropics, especially in the open forests and woodlands. Two species of mammals, the arboreal yellow-bellied glider (*Petaurus australis*) and swamp rat (*Rattus lutreolus*), are confined in the Wet Tropics to the tall open forests adjoining the western edge of the rainforests.

In terms of avifauna, there are 368 bird species, of which 11 species are endemic. The golden bowerbird (*Prionodura newtoniana*) is a monotypic endemic genus restricted to the higher-altitude rainforest. The Queensland Wet Tropics as we have defined it overlaps to a large degree with the Endemic Bird Area of the same name identified by BirdLife International.

Australia is renowned for its reptile diversity and this is evident in the Wet Tropics, which contains 113 reptile species of which 24 species are endemic. The small, brown, leaf litter skinks of the genera *Saproscincus* and *Lampropholis* and the slightly larger *Glaphyromorphus* are particularly well represented, with four, two, and two endemic species, respectively. There are three endemic reptile genera, and all are represented by single species: the chameleon gecko (*Carphodactylus laevis*) and prickly rainforest skink (*Gnypetoscincus queenslandiae*) are located in moist rainforest, mostly above 300 m, while the Mount Bartle Frere skink (*Bartleia jigurru*) is found only in boulders and wind-swept vegetation of the highest peak in the region, Mt. Bartle Frere.

The diversity of amphibians (51 species, including 22 endemic species) is also significant, with all Australian families represented. However, there are no genera restricted to the area. The family Microhylidae and the rainforest stream frogs of the family Hylidae such as the Australian lace-lid (*Nyctimystes dayi*, EN) and the waterfall frogs and mistfrogs (*Litoria nannotis*, EN), although having their greatest Australian diversity in the Wet Tropics, exhibit higher species diversity in New Guinea.

The freshwater fish fauna is characterized by 51 native species including seven endemics. Furthermore, there are two endemic genera, both monotypic, and restricted to clear, fast-flowing, perennial streams. The Cairns rainbowfish (*Cairnsichthys rhombosomoides*) has a narrow distribution from Cairns to Tully. There are no records of the species on the coastal plains, which have been developed for sugarcane. The recently discovered Bloomfield River cod (*Guyu wujalwujalensis*) has a limited distribution on the Bloomfield River.

Flagship Species

The southern cassowary (*Casuarius casuarius*, VU) is usually regarded as the region's flagship species, although it also ranges into northern Cape York and southern New Guinea. With an average weight of 60 kg, the southern cassowary is one of the world's largest birds and Australia's largest land animal; its eggs are the third largest of any bird species. The southern cassowary can live to 50 years of age, and is an important seed disperser, helping to spread the seeds of as many as 150 species of trees and shrubs. The southern cassowary is still regularly encountered throughout the Wet Tropics, although populations are only estimated to number between 1 200 and 1 500 individuals. Perhaps the most striking bird of the rainforests is the golden bowerbird, which is confined to altitudes above 800 m. This species engages in elaborate courtship displays, including the construction of bowers —dens of twigs and other plant matter that are sometimes decorated with material such as egg shells— which may be up to three meters high.

Of particular scientific interest is the musky rat-kangaroo. Standing only about 25 cm high, and the only member of its genus, this species is considered to represent an early stage of evolution of the kangaroos from an arboreal, possum-like stock. It is one of the few Australian mammals that is completely diurnal. Another curious creature is the mahogany glider (*Petaurus gracilis*, EN), which was believed extinct until its rediscovery in 1989. It now clings to a precarious existence in the lowland eucalyptus forests and woodlands of the Wet Tropics. Over 80% of its habitat has been cleared, mainly for sugarcane, and additional measures are urgently needed to ensure its survival (Maxwell et al. 1996). The northern bettong (*Bettongia tropica*, EN), one of Australia's rarest kangaroos, survives only in three small populations in the drier eucalyptus woodlands and open forests. Habitat change in these sclerophyll communities poses some urgent problems for its conservation.

Among carnivorous mammals, only the Atherton antechinus (*Antechinus godmani*) and rusty antechinus (*A. adustus*) are considered endemic to the region. The Atherton antechinus, weighing less than 100 g, feeds on a variety of insects, arachnids, frogs, and lizards. One notable feature of the biology of this species, and indeed of all members of the genus that have been studied, is that males die soon after the mating season, when they are probably only 11-12 months old (Strahan 1995).

The microhylid frog genus *Cophixalus* is a distinctive element of the Wet Tropics amphibian fauna, with most species confined to mountain tops and tablelands at altitudes greater than 300 m or in special habitats. The Black Mountain boulder frog (*Cophixalus saxatilis*, VU) is found only between 100 and 300 m altitude in 580 ha of the granite boulderfields of the Black Trevethan Range south of Cooktown. Females at night are recognized by their spectacular canary-yellow coloration. Two mountain-top nursery frogs, the Bellenden Ker nursery frog (*C. neglectus*, VU) and the Mt. Elliot nursery frog (*C. mcdonaldi*, VU), are restricted to the cloud forest at high altitudes of mountain tops, where they occur in leaf litter and lay their eggs on the ground where the young develop, hatching as fully developed froglets.

The chameleon gecko is an endemic encountered on the rainforest floor or facing head-down on small twigs and shrubs. It will readily cast its distinctive black-and-white banded tail, which can be regenerated. The cast tail produces a squeaking sound —an attribute that has not been noted in any other Australian gecko. The other endemic gecko of the rainforest, the leaf-tailed gecko (*Saltuarius cornutus*), has a lichen-colored body with a spiny-edged, leaf-like tail and lime-green and brown eyes. The flattened tail and body results in the animal's having a very low profile as it clings to the lichen-covered tree trunks. It has the ability to remain active at ambient temperatures at which other reptile species become inactive.

Threats

The European settlement of northeastern Australia has been a very recent event. One hundred and thirty years of development have resulted in a thriving and prosperous region that has been carved out of a wilderness, and this has led to the almost total annihilation of an indigenous way of life that had survived for tens of thousands of years.

In those 130 years, 23% of all the vegetation of the area has been totally cleared, mostly in the lowlands and on the tablelands to the west of the main coastal range, for the growing of sugarcane and for pastures. Of the 14 242 km² remaining uncleared, an estimated 3 000 km² has been subject to selective logging activity and, although its essential features remain, can not be considered pristine. Some areas of woodland have also been subject to light grazing activity, although these ecosystems remain essentially intact. Looking at the region as a whole, we estimate that 58% of the Queensland Wet Tropics remains in pristine condition.

Although much of the region is officially protected as part of a World Heritage Site, clearing of forest for agriculture, pastoral activities, and urban infrastructure development continue outside the World Heritage Area;

On the opposite page, Boyd's rainforest dragon (Hypsilurus boydii) is an arboreal agamid species, usually observed perching on small trees at a height of approximately one to two meters.
© **Patricio Robles Gil**/*Sierra Madre*

Above, the spectacled flying fox (Pteropus conspicillatus) occurs in primary and secondary rainforest from Halmahera in Indonesia eastwards through New Guinea to the Queensland Wet Tropics. This species plays an important role as a disperser of the fruits of many rainforest species, particularly those drab-colored fruits not dispersed by birds.
© **Patricia Rojo**

however, it is increasingly being regulated by legislation. The greatest threats to the area now arise from altered fire regimes, introduced weeds, feral animals, water extraction from streams and aquifers, and drainage of lowland areas.

Global warming poses serious threats to the region, which have yet to be clearly defined (Williams et al., 2003). A number of high-altitude species may find that they are unable to survive and reproduce in a warmer climate. A one-degree increase in temperature, considered a certainty, is predicted to decrease the range of endemic species to an average 63% of their current range size. A temperature variation of 3.5°C, considered a strong possibility within the next century by the Intergovernmental Panel on Climate Change, will reduce range sizes to an average of 11% of their current area (Williams et al. 2003).

In recent years, the appearance of chytrid fungus has devastated frog populations (Berger et al. 1998), while tree deaths in widely scattered patches of rainforest have been caused by the soil-borne disease *Phytophthora cinnamomi* (Gadek and Worboys 2003), such that there is now a growing awareness of the destructive potential of introduced diseases.

Relatively few invasive plant or animal species are able to survive in intact rainforest. The most harmful of these is the feral pig, which has occupied —at various population levels— all habitat types. Their impact on the ground cover can look severe, but has not been quantified. The cane toad (*Bufo marinus*) can invade more successfully along roads and trails of disturbed rainforests, and the toxic venom they exude is potentially lethal for mammalian and reptilian predators. In recent years, rusa deer (*Cervus timorensis*), escaped from deer farms, have begun spreading into disturbed and open forest habitats. A wide range of plant species has been recorded invading disturbed rainforest habitats and sclerophyll habitats. The most serious of these, which has the capacity to prevent the regeneration of many of the communities it invades, is the pond apple (*Annona glabra*), a small tree from southern parts of the United States which favors wetland environments.

With the removal of regular fire from many areas of sclerophyll forests and woodlands, particularly within the last 50 years, changes in the understory have created conditions due to which canopy species no longer regenerate. In particular, the removal of fire has allowed rainforest species to invade sclerophyll habitats, particularly those dominated by tall eucalypts. These habitats can not regenerate without the periodic exposure of the soil surface following the removal of ground cover and understory species by fire. In the absence of fire, the understory and canopy are progressively replaced by rainforest species, and the sclerophyll community is replaced by a rainforest one. Anywhere in the wet tropics where soils are fertile enough to support rainforest growth, the interface between sclerophyll and rainforest communities is maintained by fire. The loss of any sclerophyll habitat as a result of this process represents a significant loss of biodiversity and raises particularly serious questions for the future of species such as the yellow-bellied glider.

Conservation

A critical moment in the conservation of the Wet Tropics was the inscription in 1988 of 8 944 km² of the Wet Tropics, including most of the state-owned lands in the area, as the Wet Tropics World Heritage Area. Around that time, most of the selective logging of rainforest, which had proceeded at varying levels of intensity for more than 80 years, was halted by federal legislation. The cessation of logging activity created enormous controversy in north Queensland. The Wet Tropics became a major national political issue, with relevant environmental laws being unsuccessfully challenged in Australia's High Court.

Since World Heritage listing, the area of the Wet Tropics with national park status has increased to 3 762 km². Major national parks in the region include Barron Gorge (28 km²), Cedar Bay (56 km²), Daintree (760 km²), Edmund Kennedy (69 km²), Ella Bay (37 km²), Hinchinbrook Island (399 km²), Lumholtz (1 400 km²), Paluma Range (106 km²), and Wooroonooran (798 km²). A further 4 694 km² is in the process of transfer to national park tenure. Recent state and federal legislation provides additional protection, with groundbreaking new federal legislation (the Environment Protection and Biodiversity Conservation Act of 1999) stipulating fines of over $5 million for any actions adversely affecting World Heritage Site values. Notwithstanding, there are still areas of rainforest outside the Wet Tropics World Heritage Area and not under protection that are at risk of being cleared in the future.

An emerging strategy for conservation in the Wet Tropics, as it is in other parts of Australia, is the development and implementation of private sector (non-government) initiatives to protect habitat. The largest non-government conservation area in the Wet Tropics, the Mount Zero-Taravale Wildlife Sanctuary, is owned by the non-profit Australian Wildlife Conservancy (AWC). In addition to protecting critical habitat for several threatened species, AWC is working with government agencies to conduct management-focused research on key issues such as the ecological role of fire in maintaining wet sclerophyll communities. The role of NGOs and other "off-reserve" measures will become increasingly important in delivering landscape-scale conservation in the Wet Tropics.

JAMES PETER STANTON [111, 112]
PETER D. BOSTOCK [113]
KEITH R. MCDONALD [114]
GARRY L. WERREN [115]
ATTICUS FLEMING [116]

Although much of the Queensland Wet Tropics is protected as part of a World Heritage Site, clearing of forest for agriculture, pastoral activities, and urban infrastructure development continue outside the World Heritage Area, and it is not uncommon to see tracts of rainforest land for sale.
© **Patricio Robles Gil**/*Sierra Madre*

On the opposite page, the Daintree Rainforest, in Tropical Far North Queensland, Australia, is between 100 and 135 million years old —the oldest in the world. Approximately 430 species of birds live among the trees, including 13 species that are found nowhere else in the world.
© **Patricio Robles Gil**/*Sierra Madre*